Okinawa: The Rise of an Island Kingdom
Archaeological and cultural perspectives

Proceedings of a Symposium, Kingdom of the Coral Seas, November 17, 2007, at the School of Oriental and African Studies, University of London

Papers by
Shijun Asato, Hiroto Takamiya, Naoko Kinoshita, Akito Shinzato, Susumu Asato, Meitoku Kamei, Takashi Uezato, and Arne Rokkum

Edited by

Richard Pearson

BAR International Series 1898
2009

Published in 2016 by
BAR Publishing, Oxford

BAR International Series 1898

Okinawa: The Rise of an Island Kingdom

ISBN 978 1 4073 0380 2

© The editors and contributors severally and the Publisher 2009

COVER IMAGE
Sarcophagus No. 1, Urasoe Yodore, Okinawa Island, 15th century. Courtesy of Urasoe City Board of Education

The authors' moral rights under the 1988 UK Copyright,
Designs and Patents Act are hereby expressly asserted.

All rights reserved. No part of this work may be copied, reproduced, stored,
sold, distributed, scanned, saved in any form of digital format or transmitted
in any form digitally, without the written permission of the Publisher.

BAR Publishing is the trading name of British Archaeological Reports (Oxford) Ltd.
British Archaeological Reports was first incorporated in 1974 to publish the BAR
Series, International and British. In 1992 Hadrian Books Ltd became part of the BAR
group. This volume was originally published by Archaeopress in conjunction with
British Archaeological Reports (Oxford) Ltd / Hadrian Books Ltd, the Series principal
publisher, in 2009. This present volume is published by BAR Publishing, 2016.

Printed in England

BAR titles are available from:

        BAR Publishing
        122 Banbury Rd, Oxford, OX2 7BP, UK
EMAIL   info@barpublishing.com
PHONE +44 (0)1865 310431
  FAX   +44 (0)1865 316916
        www.barpublishing.com

BRITISH ARCHAEOLOGICAL REPORTS

Okinawa; the Rise of an Island Kingdom. Archaeological and Cultural Perspectives

List of Contributors Addresses (in order of contribution)

Shijun ASATO	asato-s@wine.plala.or.jp
Hiroto TAKAMIYA	tkm@phoenix-c.or.jp
Naoko KINOSHITA	kinon@gpo.kumamoto-u.ac.jp
Akito SHINZATO	aktsz@hotmail.com
Susumu ASATO	asato@okigei.ac.jp
Meitoku KAMEI	kamei@isc.senshu-u.ac.jp
Takashi UEZATO	tuezato@nifty.com
Arne ROKKUM	arne.rokkum@khm.uio.no
Richard PEARSON	pearsonrj@shaw.ca

Foreword *Simon Kaner*	ii
Preface *Richard Pearson*	v
Archaeology of the Ryukyu Islands: Major Themes. *Shijun Asato*	1
Okinawa's Earliest Inhabitants and Life on the Coral Islands. *Hiroto Takamiya*	5
Shell Exchange in the Ryukyu Islands and in East Asia. *Naoko Kinoshita*	13
Kamuiyaki and Early Trade in the Ryukyu Islands. *Akito Shinzato*	41
The Emergence of Ryukyu Royal Authority and Urasoe. *Susumu Asato*	57
The Significance of Chinese Trade Ceramics from Ryukyu: Focusing on Yuan Dynasty Blue and White Porcelain. *Meitoku Kamei*	63
The Architectural Landscape of the Kingdom of Ko Ryukyu. *Takashi Uezato*	71
The Kingdom of Ryukyu: Culture, Politics, Mentality. *Arne Rokkum*	81
Appendix 1. Recent Discoveries on Kikai Island. *Richard Pearson*	95
Appendix 2. Archaeology of Sakishima. *Richard Pearson*	97
Appendix 3. Useful Reference Materials for Ryukyu Archaeology. *Richard Pearson*	101
Appendix 4. The Successive Rulers of Chuzan (Ryukyu). *Richard Pearson*	102

Foreword

Recognition of the diversity of cultural forms that are encountered across the Japanese archipelago is central to the mission of the Sainsbury Institute for the Study of Japanese Arts and Cultures. Perhaps nowhere is this diversity more apparent than in the rich material and written record of the occupation of the Ryukyu Islands. The oldest known human remains from the Japanese archipelago are from Okinawa, and yet the Ryukyus only became part of the nation state of Japan in the late 19th century. Occupied in a different form by the Americans from the end of the Second World War until 1972, Okinawa is now a fully integrated part of twenty-first century Japan.

Richard Pearson has done more than most to bring the rich heritage of the Ryukyus to the attention of the rest of the world. His 1969 monograph *The Archaeology of the Ryukyus* (University of Hawai'i Press) set out the cultural framework for the early inhabitation of the islands, followed by a series of publications in books and academic journals. The Sainsbury Institute was delighted when he agreed to give our 2007 *Toshiba Lectures in Japanese Arts*, a series of three talks given at the British Museum, SOAS, and in Norwich, which will be published as a separate monograph in due course. The symposium from which the current volume arises, complementing the 2007 Toshiba Lectures, for the first time brought the major figures in the field to the United Kingdom, creating an unprecedented opportunity for debate and raising awareness of the significance Okinawan archaeology.

As the papers in this volume demonstrate, the prehistory and history of the Ryukyus took a somewhat different trajectory to the Japanese main islands. The development of the Chuzan Kingdom in the medieval period gave Okinawa a very special position in relation to the connections between Japan and China. The leading specialists who gathered in London truly brought the Ryukyu story to life on the day of the symposium. What the papers cannot convey are the animated discussions around the papers and at the dinners, or the excitement generated through visits to the Okinawan holdings of the Victoria and Albert Museum and the British Museum. The day concluded with an exuberant performance of Okinawan music by Sanshinkai, the Okinawan music group at SOAS led by David Hughes and Gina Barnes.

The symposium and lectures brought Okinawan archaeology to a wide audience, including many students, professionals and those with an interest in this fascinating part of the Japanese archipelago from across Europe and elsewhere. The Okinawan theme was subsequently taken up in a special section of the journal *Current World Archaeology*, brought together by Richard Pearson, and the current volume represents a full record of the proceedings of the symposium, hopefully bringing the Ryukyus to an even broader readership.

The Sainsbury Institute is grateful to all those who made this remarkable symposium possible, and offers special thanks to our sponsors, the Toshiba International Foundation and the Daiwa Anglo-Japanese Foundation, and to Sotheby's, who so generously supported Professor Pearson's involvement with the Sainsbury Institute.

Nicole Rousmaniere, *Director*
Simon Kaner, *Assistant Director*

*Sainsbury Institute for the
Study of Japanese Arts and Cultures*

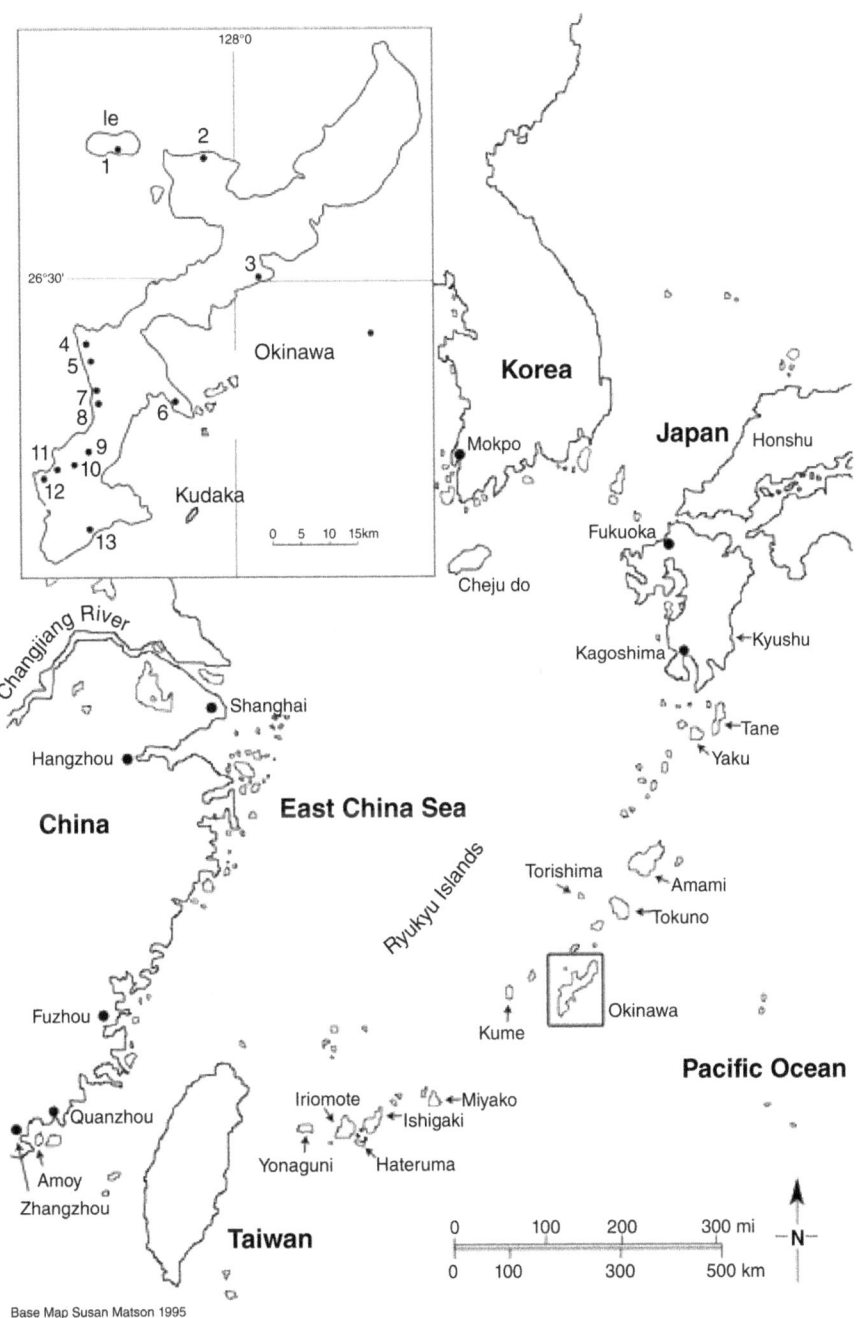

Okinawa in the East China Sea region and major sites on Okinawa mentioned in the text (See also maps in individual papers). 1. Nagarabaru Higashi 2. Nakijin 3. Meebaru 4. Takachikuchibaru 5. Toguchi Agaribaru 6. Katsuren 7. Ireibaru 8. Aragusuku Shichabaru No.2, 9. Urasoe 10. Shuri 11. Yamashita Cho 12. Nazakibaru 13. Minatogawa.

Chronology of the external interaction between the Ryukyu Islands, China, and the main islands of Japan (prepared by Naoko Kinoshita, see pp. 13–40)

Period	China	Main Islands of Japan	Ryukyu Islands - Imported artifacts C[a]	Ryukyu Islands - Imported artifacts J[b]	Ryukyu Islands - Economic Phenomenon over Wide Areas	Ryukyu Islands - Chronology of Okinawa	Historic Events in the Ryukyu Islands
BC 3000	Neolithic age	Prehistoric period / Hunter-gatherer economy / Jomon period				Earliest Shell mound period	
2000	Xia			Late Jomon pottery		Early Shell mound period	formation of fringing reef
	Shang						
1000	Zhou			Latest Jomon pottery		Middle Shell mound period	settlements on plateaus
500	Spring and Autumn Warring States	Protohistoric period / Yayoi period	*Mingdao* coin	Early Yayoi pottery			settlements move to dunes
200	Qin			Middle Yayoi pottery	shell trade with Kyushu Yayoi societies	Prehistoric period / Hunter-gatherer economy / Late Shell mound period	
BC/AD 100	Han		*Wushu* coin	bronze implements iron implements			
			Wushu coin	Late Yayoi pottery			
200							
300	Three Kingdoms	Kofun period					
	Jin				shell trade with Kofun societies of Kyushu and Western Japan		
400	Southern and Northern Dynasty						
500							
600	Sui	Asuka period	iron implements				
700	Tang	Nara period / Production economy	*Kaiyuan tongbao* coin	iron implements	trade of Great Green Turban		
800				salt-making pottery			
900	Five Dynasties and Ten Kingdoms	Heian period		*haji* and *sue* ware	trade of Great Green Turban with Kyushu and Western Japan	Transition to production economy	settlements move to plateaus
1000				smoked *haji* ware			
				steatite vessel			
1100	Song		Chinese white porcelain		trade of Great Green Turban with Kyushu and Western Japan, Circulation of Kamuiyaki ware		
			Chinese celadon				
1200		Kamakura period	Chinese coins			Protohistoric period / Production economy / Gusuku period	
1300	Yuan						
		Muromachi period	Chinese blue-and-white porcelain	mortar made of tile-clay			giving tributes to Ming
1400	Ming		Southeast Asian stoneware	*Bizen* ware	relay trade	Historic period / Ryukyu Dynasty	
1500							

a) Goods from China b) Goods from the main islands of Japan.

Preface

RICHARD PEARSON
EMERITUS ANTHROPOLOGY UBC VANCOUVER, SAINSBURY INSTITUTE FOR THE STUDY OF
JAPANESE ARTS AND CULTURES, NORWICH UK

This book concerns the archaeology and culture of the Ryukyu Islands, a chain of some 105 islands extending from Kyushu to Taiwan in the East China Sea. The archipelago is sometimes called Okinawa, after the main island, (some 454 square miles in area), and is also called the Ryukyu Islands, referring to its old Chinese name (Liuqiu or Loochoo). Sitting in the midst of the Kuroshio (Black Current), the sub tropical islands are noted for their fringing coral reefs, which are the product of the warm ocean current and relatively stable sea levels for the last 3500 years. The central and southern islands are historically part of an independent maritime kingdom termed the Ryukyu or Chuzan Kingdom, which formally existed from 1421 to 1879 and had antecedents going back into the 13th century. In 1609 the kingdom came under control of the Satsuma Fiefdom of Kagoshima, southern Kyushu. In 1879 the kingdom became part of the modern nation of Japan. Today the southern half, from Okinawa Island to Yonaguni Island is part of Okinawa Prefecture while islands from Yoron Island to Kyushu are part of Kagoshima Prefecture. The present population of Okinawa Prefecture is 1.3 million persons.

The island of Okinawa was devastated and one third of its population died during the battle of Okinawa in 1945. Present Okinawa Prefecture was a United States Territory under military government from 1945 to 1972. Following reversion to Japan in 1972, an extensive program of archaeological investigation and site protection was initiated as part of Japan's national program. This has produced literally hundreds of excavation reports and the preservation of a substantial number of sites including the World Heritage Sites of Shuri Castle and related sites. Despite the huge amount of research, very little has been available to international scholarship. This book is an attempt to rectify the situation by encouraging local archaeologists to present their discoveries and interpretations at the University of London and to make all of their papers available in English.

Eight authors from Okinawa, the Japanese main islands, and Norway presented new data and interpretations. The papers were given at a symposium entitled *Kingdom of the Coral Seas; A symposium on the Archaeology and Culture of the Ryukyu Islands* at the School for Oriental and African Studies, University of London, on November 17, 2007. Following a succinct orientation and overview by Shijun Asato, Hiroto Takamiya covers the early colonizing populations of the islands and ancient subsistence practices. It appears that while humans inhabited the region some 30,000 to 20,000 years ago, this ancient population became extinct some time after 18,000 years ago and the islands were re-colonized by several groups from about 7,000 years ago. Naoko Kinoshita describes trade connections with the main islands of Japan and Korea in the Latest Jomon, Yayoi, and Kofun Periods. Trade in tropical shells and other items began about 800 BC and continued until about 1200 AD. It is characterized by changing internal structure, trading partners and products. New information on the production of grey stoneware on the island of Tokunoshima for inter-island trade from the 11th to 14th centuries, along with imported Chinese ceramics, is provided by Akito Shinzato. Susumu Asato describes the establishment of the first royal capital at Urasoe in the 13th century and the excavation of the royal mausoleum, showing early relations with South China, Korea, and the main islands of Japan. Kamei Meitoku reviews new information on Yuan Dynasty blue and white trade ceramics in sites on Okinawa and Kume Island which confirms that Okinawa was a major receiver of these wares, on a par with Southwest Asia. The growth of the port town of Naha in the Ko Ryukyu Period, roughly 1250 to 1609, and the establishment of Chinese and Japanese trading communities as well as the construction of shrines, temples, and fortifications are discussed by Takashi Uezato. Although the Ryukyu Kingdom was dissolved in 1879 and subsequently absorbed into modern Japan, the mentality of the kingdom continues in many ways; Arne Rokkum describes the ideas of kingdom and nation in the islands of Yonaguni and Yaeyama. Because of time constraints of a full day symposium, we did not include discussion of the important Sakishima Islands. Hopefully there will be an occasion in the near future to discuss this integral part of the Ryukyus.

Okinawan archaeology has much to say about the archaeology of islands and archipelagoes. Island archaeology is moving in new directions. Broadened perspectives stress islandscapes with shifting boundaries, the archaeology of sea and navigation, and maritime communities linked by the sea (Rainbird 2007). There is a heavy emphasis on social process and human agency as a means for understanding almost all aspects of island communities (Cherry 2004). While most of the authors of this volume follow the perspectives of Japanese archaeology which has different priorities from western or "international" island archaeology, it is clear that their work is relevant to broader considerations. The papers describe maritime communities, linked to each other and to adjacent land masses in variable configurations. Processes of colonization, migration, interaction, assimilation, trade and tribute, commodification and subjugation, have all had effects on the shaping of Ryukyu communities. We are just beginning to search for the natural and human agents which drew islanders together and connected them to the larger land masses of Asia. A further step will be to link the formation of these communities to changes in seafaring.

In the Japanese main islands there is direct evidence of Jomon Period canoes, used on rivers and lakes, from waterlogged deposits but evidence of sea going craft is only indirect, in the form of the remains of deep sea resources and evidence of interaction with the Korean peninsula. In the Yayoi Period there are finds of boat planks and drawings on pottery of boats with many oars and sails, while in the Kofun Period there are clay *haniwa* replicas of boats with raised fore and aft decks (Habu in press). It is possible that the increase in population noted by Hiroto Takamiya at the end of the Jomon Period and in Early Yayoi is related to improved navigation. The rise of trade with China in the 10th to 12th centuries appears to be related to the formidable navigation skills of Song merchants. While each new island appears before sight of the previous island is lost as one proceeds as far south as Okinawa Island (in daylight and good weather!), such 'inter-visibility' is not possible in sailing to the Sakishima Islands. The water compass, recorded in China from the 11th century, must have been a crucial invention for the rise of Ryukyu trade.

The earliest communities in the Ryukyus can be dated to the Late Pleistocene, from roughly 30,000 to 18,000 years ago. Several finds of human bones, without artifacts, have been recorded. Dougome (2007) states that there was a land bridge from the Asian continent to Okinawa from 70,000 to 10,000 years ago. Judging from the recovery of flake assemblages in the northern Ryukyus and the lack of these in the central and southern Ryukyus there may have been two types of assemblages with separate origins in the Ryukyus (Oda 2007). The relation of these finds to actual human communities remains to be explored. After a gap of more than 10,000 years, some time around 7,000 years ago, the first post Pleistocene population appears on Okinawa. Judging from the lack of similarity of the very earliest pottery, which has been termed nail impressed (*tsumegatamon*) but is not identical with the Incipient Jomon nail impressed pottery of Kyushu, the origin of these people is not clear. It seems difficult to believe that the devastating eruption of the Kikai caldera around 7300 cal BP did not have some profound effect on this population. Did they push south in flight from the eruption or did they leave later to escape the extreme devastation which followed (Pearson n.d.)? Around 5,000 years ago, communities using Sobata style pottery arrived. These groups are thought to have moved into southern Kyushu from central Kyushu and to have been part of a migrating group with connections to the Korean peninsula. Evidence of further groups of Jomon migrants is referred to by Shijun Asato in his paper. As with some islands in the Mediterranean and most islands of Caribbean, island settlement occurred before the groups were food producers As in other parts of the world, agriculture was not essential to initial island colonization (Anderson 2004: 262–263). As indicated in Naoko Kinoshita's paper, Ryukyu shell bracelets and/or ornaments were important status markers in Yayoi and Kofun communities and among Korean groups. Professor Kinoshita's research shows that trading relations and the structure of the exchange were dynamic and shifting. From the 7th century, the occurrence of *Kaigen Tsuho* coins in Ryukyu sites raises the possibility of direct contact with Chinese traders, while Kinoshita concludes that at this time trade with the Yamato state declined.

A reorganization of social relations within the Ryukyus is marked by the production of grey stoneware (*kamuiyaki*) on the island of Tokunoshima. As mentioned by Akito Shinzato, its manufacture involved a technology shared with Kyushu and Korea and its exchange involved capital and expertise from Kyushu (see also Pearson 2007). Its distribution throughout the island chain including the Sakishima Islands signified a new cultural and political landscape. Early types of Chinese trade ceramics such as white wares, mark the initial stages of vigorous trade with Song Dynasty Chinese traders and the participation of Ryukyuans in the Chinese trading sphere. The advent of Song navigation technology and knowledge was important in connecting the Ryukyus to other parts of East Asia. The 13th century royal capital of Urasoe as described in Susumu Asato's chapter. Links to Quanzhou (Pearson et al 2002) are of particular significance, as well as participation in the world system of the Yuan Dynasty. The adoption of a palace plan with pond, associated temples, and mausoleum indicates new ways of organizing space to display power. Meitoku Kamei's description of the astonishing amount of large, high quality Yuan Dynasty blue and white vessels found in Shuri, Nakijin, and Kume Island has important implications for understanding the high position of the kingdom in Yuan Dynasty trading networks and diplomacy. Professor Kamei raises the possibility that Ryukyu was a center for distribution of Yuan ceramics to Southeast Asia. While the symposium did not deal with it directly, there is abundant archaeological and historical evidence that the Ryukyus were linked to the islands of Southeast Asia in the 14th to 16th centuries.

New research on the development of Naha, the port of the Ryukyu Kingdom is presented in Takashi Uezato's paper. Foreign enclaves of Chinese and Japanese traders, temples and shrines, and fortifications, show the creation of maritime facilities and participation in Chinese and Japanese commercial and religious networks. The papers on the Ko Ryukyu Period should be read in conjuction with a recent volume of *Acta Asiatica* 95 (2008), which offers new data and interpretations (Acta Asiatica 2008). Studies of the ethnographic account of Yonaguni Island in the 20th century may surprise archaeologists who expect ever expanding and more inclusive social relations within the islands under the power of a kingdom. Yonaguni islanders participated in the kingdom but had limited interaction with neighboring islanders. The archaeology of the Ryukyu Islands has much to contribute to the understanding of Japan and the East China Sea region. From a broader perspective, along with the islands of the Aegean and Caribbean the Ryukyus can help us to understand the life of islanders in general and especially those who live in arcs connecting large land masses.

We should also consider the archaeology of island kingdoms. Many island kingdoms are small scale secondary states using sea lanes to support elites whose land resources may be limited. Port and palace have a particular relationship. Ideologies may include original islanders and later migrants, as well as a paradise across the sea. While the papers in this volume do not touch on all phases of the formation of the Ryukyu Kingdom, they exemplify some of the major approaches used by local scholars. They stress the importance of interaction and shifting alliances, and the arrival of a substantial population in the early mediaeval period (9th, 10th centuries), who brought agriculture. They do not focus on the accumulation of surplus from agricultural intensification, or the role of population growth. They stress the development of secondary states through interrelationships with polities in surrounding areas. The depth of archaeological and historical research on the Ryukyu Kingdom is a valuable resource for scholars beyond the borders of the East China Sea.

I am grateful to the sponsors and organizers of the symposium, The Sainsbury Institute for the Study of Japanese Arts and Cultures, particularly to Dr. Simon Kaner, Assistant Director, and Ms. Kazuko Morohashi, Research and Publications Officer, who devoted a great deal of time and energy to this project. Thanks are offered to the Toshiba International Foundation, the Daiwa Anglo-Japanese Foundation and the Japan Society for their support of this unusual project. Sincere thanks are offered to Ms. Karen Curry, who prepared the text and illustrations for submission, and Dr. David Davison for his assistance in final publication.

Vancouver, December 10, 2008

References Cited

Acta Asiatica
2008   Studies of Mediaeval Ryukyu Within Asia's Maritime Network. *Acta Asiatica* 95. Tokyo: Toho Gakkai

Anderson, Atholl
2004   Islands of ambivalence. In *Voyages of Discovery: the Archaeology of Islands*: 252–273, ed. S. Fitzpatrick. Westport Conn: Praeger.

Cherry, John
2004   Mediterranean island prehistory. What's different and what's new. In *Voyages of Discovery: the Archaeology of Islands*: 233–248, ed. S. Fitzpatrick. Westport Conn: Praeger.

Dougome, Hideto
2007   Ryukyu retto no kyusekki jidai no iseki [Paleolithic sites in the Ryukyu islands]. *Kokogaku Janaru* 564:6–10.

Habu, Junko
n.d.   Seafaring and the development of cultural complexity in Northeast Asia: Evidence from the Japanese Archipelago. In *Global Origins and the Development of Seafaring*, ed. A. Anderson. Cambridge: McDonald Institute Monograph, (under review).

Oda, Shizuo
2007   Ryukyu ko no kokogaku [Archaeology of the Ryukyu arc]. In *Chiiki no Tayosei to Kokogaku: Tonan Ajia to Sono Shuhen [Regional Diversity and Archaeology—Southeast Asia and Vicinity]*: 37–62, ed. Aoyagi Joji Taishoku Kinen Ronbunshu Iinkai. Tokyo: Yuzankaku.

Pearson, Richard, Min Li and Guo Li
2002   Quanzhou Archaeology: A Brief Review. *International Journal of Historical Archaeology* 6:1:23–58.

Pearson, Richard
2007   Early mediaeval trade on Japan's southern frontier: grey stoneware of the East China Sea. *International Journal of Historical Archaeology*. 11:2:122-151

n.d.   *Jomon goes south: Okinawan hunter-gatherers.* Paper presented at the public symposium: The Ancient Jomon and the Pacific Rim, March 20-22, 2008, University of California, Berkeley.

Rainbird, Paul
2007   *The Archaeology of Islands*. Cambridge. Cambridge University Press.

Archaeology of the Ryukyu Islands: Major Themes

SHIJUN ASATO
DIRECTOR EMERITUS, OKINAWA PREFECTURE ARCHAEOLOGICAL CENTER

The Ryukyu Islands form an arc between Kyushu and Taiwan. To the north lie the main islands of Japan and the Korean Peninsula; to the south, Southeast Asia; and to the east, the islands of Micronesia. The nature of the relations between the Ryukyus and these areas in prehistory is an important topic. This is a particular feature of Ryukyu archaeology.

Prehistorians of Ryukyu are studying the nature of pre-state groups, the arrival of people into the islands, their living patterns and their role in the general region. They also examine their social and cultural development and the development of stratified society. These are all topics of great interest.

PALAEOLITHIC PERIOD

The Minatogawa fossils are well known in Ryukyu Palaeolithic studies. They are dated to the Late Palaeolithic, about 18,000 years ago. However, no human artifacts have been found in the several sites yielding the Minatogawa fossils.

Deer bone and antler fragments with forked ends have been found in fossil sites and these have been interpreted as human artifacts termed notched bone tools. These "bone tools" are a special feature of the Ryukyu Palaeolithic. From foreign examples it appears that these tools were created by deer chewing or gnawing bones, and are not human artifacts. On islands close to the Ryukyus, wild deer make the same bone objects by chewing. Thus, the presence of bone tools in the Palaeolithic has been refuted. I believe that no Palaeolithic population can be confirmed for the Ryukyus—instead they are Neolithic people. The dating of 18,000 comes from animal bones in a fissure deposit, not from actual bones. The actual human fossils are typologically similar to very old Jomon individuals.

NEOLITHIC PERIOD

In the Ryukyus, Neolithic sites are abundant. Sites are found on hills near the seashore, the foot of cliffs, and sand dunes. The islands are surrounded by shallow coral lagoons abundant with fish and shellfish. People were maritime-focused, their daily activities centering on the lagoon. Behind them the mountain forest provided wild boar. Abundant shells, shellfish and animal bones were found in shell middens. Their subsistence pattern involved both the sea and the island interior.

Since stone adzes are found in sites where the raw material is not available, it is clear that there was free interaction by sea among the islands. Also, wild boar bones are found in shell middens on very small islands where wild boar could not live in the wild. People must have traveled to Okinawa Island to hunt, or exchanged wild boar meat among groups.

North and South: Two Cultures in the Neolithic

(Neolithic is used here to indicate cultures with pottery and polished stone tools). Two different areas with different cultures of different origins were present in the Ryukyus in the Neolithic. In the area of Amami Oshima and Okinawa, a people and culture with origins in the Jomon of Japan existed while in the Southern Ryukyu culture area, the culture was probably derived from Southeast Asia. Human movement in the Ryukyus was limited to inter-visible islands and at this stage there was no sea travel completely out of sight of land. Between Okinawa main island and Miyako Island there is a distance of 260 km, which formed the boundary between the two culture areas.

Thus the islands in the northern group (and from Miyako to Yaeyama and on to Taiwan, the islands of the Bashee Strait, and the Philippines), were also within sight of each other. This geographical situation affected the development of the two culture areas.

The Neolithic of the Northern Ryukyus

The First People to Arrive in the Northern Ryukyus

Around 6500 to 7000 years ago human groups moved into the Northern Ryukyus. These people brought with them so-called *tsumegatamon* (lit. thumb nail impressed) pottery and edge ground stone adzes. They lived near the seashore relying on reef fish and wild boar for food, establishing a basic pattern of subsistence for Ryukyu Neolithic people. Population was very small and they did not establish long-term settlements. There appear to be gaps or interruptions in habitation. Although sites are evident in several regions of the Ryukyus, they are very few.

Their pottery resembles the *tsumegatamon* of the incipient Jomon of the Japanese main islands, but there is a large chronological gap between the two kinds of pottery. The prevalent opinion is that they are not related. However, it is most likely that the place of origin of the Ryukyu pottery is Japan. Why is there no apparent connection between the two kinds of pottery and is there a possible connection with some other area—these are puzzling riddles in archaeology.

If the Ryukyu *tsumegatamon* were actually related to the pottery of the incipient Jomon from Kagoshima, then older, contemporaneous sites should be found in the Ryukyus. In the Korean Peninsula, pottery connected to the *tsumegatamon* has been found. There are counter interpretations that within Jomon there must be other ceramics that are the same as *tsumegatamon* from Ryukyu and there are moves to look for this possibility.

Also there is one case in which plain pottery has been found below the cultural layer bearing *tsumegatamon* pottery. The nature of this pottery that is older than *tsumegatamon* is a topic for further study.

The Next Group of Migrants.

About 5000 years ago Early Jomon people of the Sobata Pottery Group migrated to the Ryukyus. These people lived in coastal locations in the Japanese main islands and had the motivation to move southward to the Ryukyus by boat. Sobata pottery is also found on the Korean Peninsula to the north, indicating that these people were maritime people with extensive patterns of exchange. These people lived on the seashore, leaving shell middens. Judging from the large numbers of sites their population was considerable. Their pottery has basically the same motifs as that of the main islands of Japan. For a short period of time their pottery remained the same as the pottery they had brought with them and their sites show short occupation spans. They did not seem to stay long enough to begin to make distinctive local styles. Up to this time it seems that small groups of people came to the Ryukyus but did not form stable groups that produced later descendants. They were not ancestral to later Ryukyu people.

Successful Adaptation

About 4000 years ago another group came from the main islands of Japan, successfully adapting their living patterns to the coral reefs. This was the Omonawa Zentei group. Their pottery is derived from Jomon pottery. The center of development was in the Amami Islands. One group of these people moved to the Okinawa Islands. There were several changes in pottery styles, suggesting that their group continued to live for a long time. However they developed in only one region of the Ryukyus.

The Spread to Many Islands

3500 years ago prehistoric people had spread to almost all of the islands of the Ryukyus and had consolidated their adaptation to the reef environment. Their pottery, descended from Late Jomon pottery of Kyushu, developed distinctive local styles based on straight-line motifs. They formed one large group of interaction. The Okinawa Islands produced pottery types known as Iha and Ogido.

There was free movement within the Ryukyus, indicated by the finding of identical pottery over a wide area and the sharing of raw material for stone tools that were absent on some islands. Wild boar bones appear on islands not suitable habitats, indicating frequent inter-island contacts. Human population increased, although the population of each site remained small and the number of house remains is very low. In this period people made many pendants of shell and bone. These were not only ornaments but were considered to have magical properties.

The Development of Villages

At about 2700 or 2500 years ago people lived in flat areas on the tops of hills. Population increased and villages had about 10 houses each. The floor was dug into the ground as a house depression outlined by stones and the thatched roof was supported by posts dug into the ground.

Stone adzes were abundant and were used for digging and house construction. Nuts and roots were processed with abundant mortars and pestles, indicating knowledge of plant food preparation.

Shell middens have not been found from this period and shells, fish bones, and wild boar bones are rare. It is possible that they did not practice a great deal of hunting and fishing. And yet at this time period there was an exchange of obsidian spear points from the main Japanese islands, so it is clear that they used the bow and arrow.

Also the scale of sites was large and villages were formed. Increased population is clearly indicated. It appears that food must have been more abundant than in previous times. What were the most important food resources?

The reason for the lack of shell midden may be because of poor preservation around living areas located on red tropical (acidic) soils. Alternatively, marine food resources may have been scarce or people may have practiced primitive horticulture. The latter idea is supported by the presence of abundant stone tools for plant processing. The types of food eaten in this period remain a puzzle because of poor preservation.

In this period Okinawa and Amami Oshima are included in the same pottery stylistic area. The neck of the vessel is expanded and there is little decoration on the vessel. This type of utilitarian pottery is found over a wide area in the Central and Northern Ryukyus.

At the end of this period, on the main islands of Japan the Yayoi Period was developing parallel to Ryukyu culture.

Movement Toward the Reefs

About 2,000 years ago, in the latter part of the Neolithic, Okinawan people changed the location of their villages to a place closer to the reefs. In Amami Oshima, coastal habitation occurred in the previous period, and also in the Southern Ryukyus people used coastal locations. In Amami, people lived traditionally in coastal locations since the mountains come close to the sea, limiting areas for settlement. The northern part of Okinawa Island is similar: however in the central and southern area there are many limestone coral terraces that were often used for habitation.

In the Late Shellmound Period, villages developed on the seashore, and living patterns were based on shellfish and fish from the reef. Shell middens have many large shells and fish bones and the scale of the sites is large. At the same time hunting of wild boar from the mountains was common. Of all of the Neolithic sites, these sites produce the most wild boar bones. This is the period in which the use of natural resources was the most developed.

Villages were located on each beach near the reef. One can conclude that each group had title to the resources of its respective reef, in the same way as owning land in the subsequent Gusuku Period.

Shell Artifacts and Shell Exchange

Many of the shells collected from the reef were used for food. They were also used for tools and ornaments. They served as plates, bowls, spoons, ladles, and weights for fishnets, pendants, and bracelets. At this time in the Yayoi Period of the Japanese main islands horticulture and stratified society had been attained. The chiefly class were fond of wearing bracelets of large shells from the Northern Ryukyus. These bracelets became symbols of political and religious power. These shells were *imogai* (*Conus litteratus*) and *gohora* (*Tricornis latissumus*). Yayoi people of Northern Kyushu traveled to obtain these shells in exchange with prehistoric people from the Northern Ryukyus. On the side of the islanders, the people of the Northern Ryukyus collected the shells and prepared them for exchange. Sometimes caches of shells are found in shellmound sites. However shell exchange was ultimately in response to demand from the Yayoi side, and the Yayoi people were the active traders. When the demand for the shells disappeared the exchange declined.

The use of metal artifacts and the adoption of rice cultivation are major features of Yayoi culture. People of the Northern Ryukyus who were engaged in exchange must have known about these activities. Small quantities of metal artifacts have been found in sites; therefore these did spread to a degree, but rice cultivation was not accepted. It seems that the use of wild resources was at a peak at this time, and people of the Northern Ryukyus did not perceive the need for rice cultivation and did not adopt it.

Movement Between the Northern and Southern Culture Areas

From the beginning of the Late Shellmound Period, Chinese Tang coins (Chin. *kaiyuan tongbao*) were distributed in both the northern and southern culture areas. People navigated the length of the Ryukyus leaving coins on various islands. This is at the time of the Japanese tributary missions to Tang, for which the southern route passed through the Ryukyus. Also there were thought to be a group of Japanese traders at that time. It is still not certain but there may have been Chinese traders in the area as well. Ryukyu prehistoric society was divided into two culture areas, but both were contacted from outside which led to the development of an important interaction sphere. In the 11th century the societies of the Northern and Southern Ryukyus reached a profound turning point.

The Neolithic of the Southern Ryukyus

The Neolithic of the Southern Ryukyus is divided into an early and a late period. Their culture was not related to the Jomon and Yayoi cultures: groups of Southeast Asian origin arrived in the Southern Rukyus to be replaced by another group from the south, according to most explanations; however I am the only one who thinks that there was basically one continuous group. Subsistence patterns were basically the same as in the Northern Ryukyus; people were dependent on shellfish and fish from the reef and wild boar from the mountains.

Early Period

From about 4000 years ago people lived on low hills and terraces near the seashore. Pottery called the Shimotabaru type belongs to the Early Period. It is thick, with a wide mouth and round bottom and two lugs for carrying, on the shoulder. It is practically undecorated, occasionally having small curving incisions on the exterior. At first it seems to resemble Southeast Asian pottery but in fact the origin has not been discovered. The type of stone adzes that has polishing only on the bit, with the rest left rough, is frequent. Adzes are particularly abundant, and hand adzes are common. They seem to be related to canoe making.

Late Period

From about 2000 or 2500 years ago people began to live on the beaches. Sites from the period are larger than those from the previous period and may have shell middens. This seems to indicate an increase in population. In addition to edge ground stone tools, there are tools that are completely polished. A particular feature is the lack of pottery. Concentrations of burned stones from hearths indicate that they were cooking on heated stones.

Although they do not occur on all sites, shell adzes of *Tridacna* (Jap. *shakogai*) were used. There is a tendency for large quantities of these to occur on single sites. They are almost always made from the hinge portion of the shell, similar to the method of manufacture in the Philippines. Shell adzes are abundant in Micronesia, where they are made from the thick ridged portion of the back of the *Tridacna* shell. The Southern Ryukyu adzes probably came from the Philippines. However some recent accounts favor an independent internal development. I personally consider that they came from the Philippines.

Is There Lapita Pottery in the Southern Ryukyus?

There are archaeologists who think that there is Lapita pottery in the Southern Ryukyus. The possibility of this is extremely low. Colonizing populations first came to the Southern Ryukyus about 4000 years ago, prior to the dates for Lapita. And the population continued until 2000 years ago. No traces of the Lapita pottery culture can be found. Most likely the prehistoric population of the Southern Ryukyus is a group which came from Southeast Asia before the Lapita migrations to Oceania. Their ancestors are the same as those people who went to Oceania, and their migration to the Southern Ryukyus was one migration to the outer world but they are not the same group which later dispersed to Oceania.

In the case of Oceania, linguistics plays an important role in understanding the patterns of dispersal. However the prehistoric groups in the Southern Ryukyus became extinct and after them groups speaking a Japanese language came into the region. Therefore is it is not possible to use linguistics to study the route of migration or relations to other groups.

Gusuku Period

At the end of the Prehistoric Period and the beginning of the Gusuku Period, about the 11th century, movement from the north brought high-quality ceramic containers to the Ryukyus. These are distributed over a wide area from Amami Oshima to Yaeyama, accelerating the process of joining the Northern and Southern Ryukyu areas into a single Ryukyu culture area. These high quality containers consisted of three types of wares: soapstone cauldrons from Kyushu, Chinese white porcelain, and *kamuiyaki* grey stoneware produced within the Ryukyu culture area on Tokunoshima in the Amami Islands. This marked the end of the prehistoric period and the turning point to the Gusuku Period, which was based on cultivation and class society. Here is a list of the distinguishing features of the Gusuku Period.

1. Scholars differ on the time period, but most propose the period from about the 11th century to the 15th century.

2. In each region fortresses called *gusuku* were constructed on the tops of hills. Most of these have stone-walled enclosures and later the most important ones had stone arches and buildings set on stone platforms.

3. There was a shift from hunting and gathering to the development of agricultural production and village life.

4. Cultivation and livestock raising were diffused to the islands and developed locally.

5. Iron working and metal artifacts were diffused to a certain degree.

6. Class society took form with the emergence of a chiefly class in each area. In every region, warfare developed among chiefs and their castles. These chiefdoms gradually became clustered in large groups, culminating in the formation of the Ryukyu Kingdom.

7. Overseas trade developed, centered in Chinese ceramics and including metal artifacts and coins that were brought to the Ryukyus. In the latter half important castles adopted tiled roofs for the ruler's residence and there were connections to Japan.

8. The Northern and Southern Ryukyus became one area of Ryukyu material culture and moved toward becoming a single political region.

The Ryukyu Kingdom and Later

In the latter half of the Gusuku Period, in the 14th and 15th centuries there were three regions of political power united into a single kingdom. Shortly after, the Southern Ryukyus became a part of this kingdom. During this time cultural influences from China and Japan were strong, bringing cut stone architecture expressed in temple ponds, buildings on stone platforms, royal mausolea, and gardens. At the beginning of the 17th century when political independence came to an end, stone construction of tombs, wells, springs, and roads thrived. Also in the 17th century the Ryukyu Kingdom developed its own ceramics industry.

Recently Okinawan archaeology has opened new specializations, such as the archaeology of the Second World War on Okinawa. Okinawa occupies a unique position within Japan. In Okinawa there are many sites and artifacts from the war. These provide materials for the study of the horrors of war and the nature of social movements for the reaffirmation of peace.

Translated by Richard Pearson

Okinawa's Earliest Inhabitants and Life on the Coral Islands

Hiroto TAKAMIYA
SAPPORO UNIVERSITY

INTRODUCTION

Ask ordinary Japanese about their impressions of the islands of Okinawa and their answer might be one (or several) of the following. *The blue sky.* On sunny days, especially during the summertime, the sky over the islands is clear blue as the Mediterranean or Californian sky, and not like the sky of other parts of Japan. *The ocean with its emerald green color and coral reefs.* When one looks from the blue sky to the horizon, the emerald green ocean and white waves breaking on the coral reef are eye-catching. It is a beautiful scene, like islands in the Pacific, not seen in the rest of Japan. *A slow life.* Sometimes this is known as "Okinawa time". Life on the islands seems to be slow, and mainland Japanese might feel that Okinawan people are free from stress.

A prefecture of long-lived people. Japan is known for the longest life expectancy in the world. Among all of the prefectures in Japan, the longest life expectancy is recorded from the islands of Okinawa. *Healthy food.* It has been reported that one of the reasons contributing to the long life expectancy is diet. Accordingly, for a decade or so, Okinawan food has become very popular in the rest of Japan. Thus, recently for many Japanese, the islands of Okinawa seem to be one of the most attractive regions in this country. Consequently, in 2006 more than 5.5 million people visited the Okinawa islands for sightseeing, and more than 50,000 people decided to move into the region.

Imagine life on the coral islands. Now, imagine life on the coral islands in prehistoric times. Without airplanes, automobiles, and ships, the sky must have been bluer, and the ocean must have been more emerald green. People might have been more stress-free while they might have been shorter lived than today (because of no access to modern developed medical technology). Archaeological data collected and analyzed until recently seem to suggest that the prehistory of the region was peaceful with abundant natural resources (Nitta 1982; Asato 1985; Toizumi 2003; Kinoshita 2006). It must have been a heaven on earth.

Or was it? This paper will examine the way of life for prehistoric people in Okinawa, mainly focusing on their subsistence economy. Was it a stress-free peaceful region with abundant natural food throughout prehistoric times? Before examining this question I will first discuss who lived there and who were the earliest inhabitants on the coral islands, since without the leading actors and actresses, the picture of the life on the coral islands is incomplete.

WHO WERE THE EARLIEST INHABITANTS ON THE CORAL ISLANDS?

The islands of Okinawa first witnessed the presence of *Homo sapiens* during the late Pleistocene. The Yamashita-cho No.2 cave site yielded human fossil remains of a six-year-old girl dating to approximately to 32,000 BP. The Minatogawa fissure cave also yielded at least five fossil human remains, said to date to about 18,000 BP. In addition, five other sites are known as Palaeolithic sites with *Homo sapiens* fossil remains, although these remains are fragmentary (Okinawa Prefectural Archives 2003). With these and other archaeological findings, the following chronology has been established for the Central Ryukyu region (Table 1—dates are approximate since the number of 14C dates is inadequate).

TABLE 1. CHRONOLOGY OF THE CENTRAL RYUKYU REGION (WITH APPROXIMATE DATES)

PERIOD	APPROXIMATE DATES
Gusuku	AD12th~15th cent.
Late Yayoi Heian	AD5/6th~ 12th cent.
Early Yayoi Heian	3rd BC~AD 5/6th cent.
Final Jomon	3000~2400 BP
Late Jomon	4000~3000 BP
Middle Jomon	5000~4000 BP
Early Jomon	6000~5000 BP
Initial Jomon	10000~6000 BP
Palaeolithic	32000~10000 BP

Were the Palaeolithic people the earliest inhabitants in this region? The answer to this question must be yes. However, if human beings existed there during the late Pleistocene, at least two further questions must be asked. The first question is whether or not the region consisted of islands like today, during the late Pleistocene? Two hypotheses on possible geomorphology during this period have been proposed. One is by Kimura (1991) who believes that the islands of Okinawa were part of a land bridge extending from southeastern China through Taiwan to this region. Another attempt to reconstruct palaeogeomorphology was carried out by Hiroe Takamiya (1999). According to him, the islands in the Okinawa Archipelago were not part of Kimura's (Kimura 1991) proposed land bridge but combined together to form one big island. In either case, it is not likely that the geomorphology of the region was similar to that of today during the late Pleistocene. Furthermore, while there are not enough data to reconstruct the late Pleistocene environment, considering the climate of the late Pleistocene worldwide, it is likely that coral environment did not exist during this period.

The second question is whether or not these earliest inhabitants were direct ancestors of the modern Okinawan people? Many anthropologists and archaeologists, without doubt, seem to believe that there is a direct biological continuity between the late Pleistocene human groups and the modern Okinawa people. However, recent study indicates population discontinuity after the late Pleistocene (Hiroto Takamiya 1996a). One obvious explanation for this is because no site has been reported which dates between ca. 18,000 years ago and ca. 6,500 years ago, the date of the earliest Holocene site. That site, Toguchi Agaribaru, is well known for yielding the earliest pottery in Okinawa (Okinawa Prefectural Archives 2003). There is more than 10,000 years of hiatus between the dated sites of the late Pleistocene and earliest Holocene, implying that no human populations were living there during this hiatus period.

What happened to the late Pleistocene population? What happened in Tasmania, King, and Flinders Islands, located south of Australia, likely happened in Okinawa. During the Pleistocene, these islands were connected to Australia by a land bridge. Archaeological data reveal that *Homo sapiens* was on these three islands when the land bridge existed. However, as the sea level rose and present island geomorphology was forming, people disappeared from the King and Flinders Islands. According to Jones (1977), Tasmania is a large enough an island to sustain hunter-gatherers from the Pleistocene until recently but not the other two islands. Tasmania is little smaller than Hokkaido, while King Island is slightly smaller and the Flinders is slightly larger than the main island of Okinawa. If the archipelago of Okinawa was a part of land bridge, then more than 70% of land was submerged by the end of the Pleistocene. On the other hand, if the archipelago formed one large island, in this case, more than 50% of land disappeared. This geomorphological change caused a rapid decrease in carrying capacity. Accordingly, the late Pleistocene population either moved to somewhere else or died out in the region as the present day islands were forming (Hiroto Takamiya 1996a).

Then, were the Initial and Early Jomon people successful colonizers of the islands? While several sites dating to the Initial and Early Jomon Periods are known today (Okinawa Prefectural Archives 2003), their inhabitants were not likely successful colonizers of the island environment. When human population (or other species as well) successfully adapts to an island environment (or any new environment), rapid population growth is expected (Kirch 1984). It is also known that the population growth rate decreases as it approaches to the carrying capacity of the environment. Kirch (1984) calls this kind of population trajectory a *logistic model*. In addition to the logistic model, what Kirch (1984) explains as the *step model* is also expected if a human population successfully adapts to an island environment. In the step model, population first logistically increases toward the original carrying capacity. If the level of carrying capacity increases for some reasons (for example, climate change or cultural invention), then the population increases again logistically toward the higher level of carrying capacity.

While it was difficult to estimate the actual number of people during the prehistoric and proto historic times, an attempt has been made to reconstruct population pattern from the Jomon to the Gusuku Periods, assuming that the number of sites reflects the paleo-demography. The result obtained has suggested three conclusions. First, the Initial and Early Jomon population probably did not successfully colonize the island environment (Hiroto Takamiya 1996a; but see Itoh 2006). Second, it was most likely that human groups who finally and successfully colonized the islands were those who came to the region during the later part of the Middle Jomon to the Late Jomon Periods since the expected population increase appears to occur during the Late Jomon Period (Hiroto Takamiya 1996a). This period of successful colonization will be expressed as the Late Jomon Period in this presentation. Third, the islands witnessed a population explosion during the Gusuku Period (Hiroto Takamiya 1996a). Overall, the population pattern reconstructed resembles Kirch's step model, indicating that during the Gusuku Period carrying capacity rose to another level. Thus, the initial inhabitants of the coral islands were not the Palaeolithic people nor the Initial and Early Jomon people, but people who came to the region ca. 4000 years ago.

Now another interesting question is this—were the people in the third group, who successfully colonized the island environment for the first time, the ancestors of the modern Okinawan population? In other words, have human beings continuously occupied the islands since the Late Jomon Period? It was shocking to propose the discontinuity between the Palaeolithic people and modern Okinawans (Ikeda 1998). Therefore, it might be more shocking if the following hypothesis is proposed: there might be a great gap between the Late Jomon people and their descendants and the Gusuku and their descendants, including modern Okinawans.

It was Naomi Doi (Doi 1997) from the University of Ryukyu who first recognized osteological differences between the prehistoric people and a group termed "recent people," who were the direct descendants of the Gusuku population, and who were in turn the direct ancestors of the modern day Okinawans. According to her, the prehistoric people were characterized as short, slender, and round-headed. On the other hand, the group termed recent people were tall, robust, and long-headed. These differences should not be ignored. Furthermore, Dodo (1993) has published an important paper. He analyzed non-metric characteristics of the Jomon, Ainu, migrant Yayoi, historical mainland Japanese, and recent Okinawans, as well as other populations in continental Asia and North America. The result has demonstrated that the Jomon and Ainu clustered together. However, the recent Okinawans, believed to have belonged to the Jomon and Ainu cluster, are not grouped together with this cluster but joined the group of the migrant Yayoi and their descendants. While the result was astonishing and not accepted readily, Dodo's (1993) result has been supported by Pietrusewsky's (1999) analysis. With metric methods, he analyzed many human groups from prehistoric and historic period in Asia and Pacific. Here again, the Jomon and Ainu clustered together, but the recent Okinawans were grouped together with the migrant Yayoi and their descendants. What do these osteological data imply?

In addition to the osteological data, linguistic data have provided significant information. Since the Meiji Period, linguists have noted similarity between the mainland Japanese dialects and Okinawan dialects while for the speakers of the former dialects, the latter dialects are unintelligible today. Chamberlain, as early as 1886, stated that these two dialects are closely related (in Kawamura 1999). Hattori (1999) compared three mainland Japanese dialects and five Okinawan dialects. Both groups show close internal relationships. According to him, the language distance between the two dialect groups is closely related. Furthermore, Hokama (1977), who studied the mainland Japanese and Okinawan dialects, obtained the results which supports Hattori and other linguists' opinions. Hokama (1977) and also Hudson (1994) insist that the Okinawan dialects derived from mainland Japanese. Hattori (1999) proposes the timing of the derivation was about 1400 years ago. Hokama (1977) suggests this timing was between 2nd/3rd and 7th/8th century AD.

One of my research themes is when and how food production began in this region. This is what is known at present. First, the earliest evidence of agriculture is dated to 8th/9th to 10th century AD at the Nazakibaru site, located in Naha City (Hiroto Takamiya 1996*b*). The site has yielded a small amount of cultigen seeds: two rice grains, three wheat grains, two barley, and two foxtail millet. Also, while it is not still determined whether they are wild or domesticated, several legumes were recovered. The evidence suggests that domesticated plants were known by the inhabitants of the site. The next question is whether or not they were cultivated at or near the site or imported from somewhere else. If one just considers the recovered cultigens, the most adequate explanation would be that these domesticated plants were obtained through exchange with farming societies. However, other plant remains, which accompanied the domesticated plants, do not support this explanation. These include grass seeds, some of which according to Hatushima and Amano (1977), grow in open habitat or agriculture fields. The presence of these plant remains suggests that these domesticated plants were cultivated on or near the site. Furthermore, nuts, which have been considered as important source of carbohydrate during the prehistoric times (eg. Pearson 1981), were not present among the plant remains. This also implies that people at the site depended on domesticated plants. In addition, more than 250 hoe marks as well as two lines of ditches, which have been interpreted as agriculture related, were recovered. These lines of evidence indicate people at the site practiced food production (Hiroto Takamiya 1996*b*).

When these results were obtained, it was thought that the Nazakibaru agriculture was the foundation for the Gusuku agriculture. However, if the Nazakibaru people were successful farmers, one would expect rapid population growth after the acceptance of food production. Archaeological data do not demonstrate such population increase. Rather, at the present time, the period between the 10th and 12th century AD is archaeologically the least understood period. Therefore, it is suggested that not only the Nazakibaru agriculture was an ephemeral one but also the foundation of Gusuku agriculture was most likely introduced into this region after the Nazakibaru Period, probably between the 10th and 12th century AD (Hiroto Takamiya 2005). Furthermore, if this interpretation is supported, it implies that agriculture began rather abruptly in the region.

Why did it begin suddenly? During the 1960s and 1990s, the most popular hypotheses for explanation of the spread of agriculture were the population pressure and the competitive feasting hypotheses (eg. Binford 1971; Hayden 1990). Does one of them adequately explain the beginning of food production in Okinawa? No archaeological data seems to support either hypothesis. The osteological and linguistic data discussed above do seem to provide a new explanation. The key word here is that the food production began "abruptly." Why did it begin abruptly? The most adequate hypothesis seems to be the migration of farmers from Kyushu area (also Hokama 1977; Hudson 1994). These new people were not only farmers but also spoke old Japanese and morphologically characterized by "tall, robust, and long headed." If the new groups were successful with the new subsistence economy, rapid population growth is expected. This exactly happened during the Gusuku Period. As a result of the successful colonization by farmers, the indigenous population became either a minority or was replaced by the newcomers. While genetic data does not seem to strongly support this hypothesis (Saito 2005; Shinoda 2007), and it needs more examination, it does well explain other phenomena such as human morphological change, the origin of the Ryukyu dialects, and the abrupt beginning of food production in this region.

The results suggest that at least four human groups existed in the region: the late Pleistocene, the Initial/Early Jomon, Late Jomon and their descendants, and the ancestors of the modern Okinawans. Now let us discuss life on the coral islands, especially focusing on the first successful colonizers of the islands and their descendants.

THE LIFE ON THE CORAL ISLANDS

The islands of Okinawa have witnessed no human population continuity but discontinuity since the Palaeolithic Period. How did they live in this region? Palaeolithic subsistence strategies are not clear at this time. While this is one of the most important research themes, the way of life of Palaeolithic people has not been understood at all, except that they were probably dependent upon wild resources for their living. This subsistence economy probably lasted until prior to the 10th to 12th century AD. Then agriculture and domesticated animals were introduced into this region. During the Jomon to the Yayoi-Heian Period, it seems to have been believed that the subsistence economy based on hunting and gathering was stable. Was it stable throughout prehistoric times? The following paragraphs first examine hunting and collecting (animal use) and briefly gathering (plant use) from the Late Jomon (when the islands were successfully colonized) to the Early Yayoi-Heian Periods. For the animal utilization, I will first discuss on the vertebrate and then shellfish.

Animal Utilization

Vertebrate Utilization

Why has it been believed that the animal utilization was stable during the prehistoric times? Probably the main reason for this belief is because the reports on faunal remains recovered from the prehistoric sites consist of almost all wild species, and similar animal species are listed. For example, among terrestrial mammals, wild boar is the most common species. For fish remains, coral reef fish species such as parrot fish are frequently listed. Cone shells and giant clams are identified from many archaeological sites. Consequently, the results of faunal analysis have given impression that there was no change in subsistence economy. However, this observation appears to have been superficial. While hunting and collecting of wild animals were the basis for the subsistence economy, detailed reanalysis of faunal remains has demonstrated that there were shifts in subsistence strategy during the prehistoric times (Hiroto Takamiya 2000, 2004).

For the vertebrate remains, the analysis was conducted on the class level with the sites which yielded at least 1000 NISP vertebrate bones. The commonly recovered classes were mammals, bony fish, and reptiles. The species included in these classes consist of the similar species throughout prehistoric times. Thus, it is difficult to perceive changes in vertebrate utilization on the species level. However, on the class level analysis, a different picture of animal utilization has emerged. The Late Jomon people appear to have relied on bony fish for the source of protein. On average, the bony fish occupied more than 80% during this period. The difference between the bony fish class and the second ranked class is more than 20%, suggesting the importance of the bony fish class.

What was characteristic of the Late Jomon vertebrate utilization? The most significant observation is that the first ranked bony fish almost totally consists of coral reef fish species. Among all available protein source species, the coral reef fishes are the most predictable, stable, and the least risky species. In other words, these fish species were the most cost-effective protein sources in this region. Since this subsistence strategy is the most cost-effective, this must have been the most ideal subsistence strategy, and thus it is expected that the descendants of the Late Jomon people should have continued with this strategy. However the analysis demonstrated otherwise.

During the Final Jomon, the bony fish class decreases to 60% on average and other classes increase. I interpret this change in vertebrate utilization as the collapse of the Late Jomon system and the transition to the Early Yayoi-Heian system. Indeed, at some Final Jomon sites, the vertebrate utilization is similar to that of the Late Jomon; at other sites, it is similar to the Early Yayoi-Heian. Then what does characterize the Early Yayoi-Heian vertebrate utilization? One obvious tendency is that the average percentage of the bony fish class further decreases to 50%. The difference between the first ranked bony fish whenever ranked first and the second ranked class is less than 10%. Moreover, at some sites, the bony fish class is replaced by other classes. Thus, the most cost-effective class for the source of protein was no longer the priority during the Early Yayoi-Heian Period.

Which class then became an important source of protein? Instead of the bony fish class, the mammal or reptile class increases. Here, I would like to focus on the class of mammals. Among this class, throughout prehistoric times, wild boar constantly occupies highest proportion, often more than 90%. Thus it can be stated that the wild boar was the most important mammal food species (Hiroto Takamiya 2004). However, when the wild boar utilization during the prehistoric times is further examined within the context of vertebrate utilization, an interesting pattern has emerged. During the Late Jomon Period, it occupies only 5% of all vertebrate remains. However, during the Early Yayoi-Heian Period, it increases to approximately 25%. Wild boar is probably the least stable, the least predictable,

Figure 1. Shell species collected from prehistoric sites, showing some of the large shellfish species mentioned in the text.

and the riskiest species available on the islands. In other words, the vertebrate consumption system employed during the Early Yayoi-Heian Period was the most costly one. Thus while the prehistoric people mainly targeted similar vertebrate species, the reanalysis has revealed that the vertebrate utilization system became costly as time went by. How about non-vertebrate (ie. shellfish) utilization?

Shellfish Utilization

From archaeological sites, shellfish remains often outnumber vertebrate remains (Figure 1). While many archaeologists collected and identified shellfish remains, and sometimes attempted to understand what kind of microenvironment prehistoric people used to obtain shellfish (eg. Kurozumi 1988), the shellfish utilization system during prehistoric times had not been clearly understood. It appears that no changes in shellfish utilization had been recognized, giving an impression that the shellfish utilization system had been stable. However, when shellfish remains were reanalyzed, an interesting picture of shellfish utilization strategy emerges (HirotoTakamiya 2000). First of all, *Turbo argyrostomus* (medium gastropod), *Atactodea striata* (small bivalve), and *Strombus luhuanus* (medium gastropod), appeared to have been constantly utilized from the Late Jomon to the Early Yayoi-Heian Periods. Therefore, these three species have been considered the "core" species. These three species became the core species probably because they are comparatively easy to collect and provide reasonable amount of return. The shellfish utilization system consisted of these core species and non-core species.

During the Late Jomon Period, the non-core species were *Nerita albicill* (small gastropod), *Lunella coronata granulata* (small gastropod), and *Gafrarium tumidum* (small bivalve). These shellfish species are small but easy to collect. Even today young and old can easily gather them. Thus, the shellfish utilization system during this period is characterized by the most cost-effective one, and must have been the ideal system. However, like the vertebrate utilization system, the shellfish utilization system was not stable. While the Final Jomon people continued to consume *Gafrarium tumidum*, *Nerita albicill* and *Lunella coronata granulata* were replaced by *Geloina coaxas* (medium bivalve), *Meretrix lamarckii* (medium bivalves), and *Asaphis violascens* (medium bibalve). Furthermore, these non-core species of the Final Jomon were replaced by *Tridacna maxima* (large bivalve), *Tridacna crocea* (large bivalve), and *Trochus niloticus* (large gastropod) as the non-core species of the Early Yayoi-Heian (Figure 1).

How can the change in shellfish utilization in prehistoric times be explained? When the Late Jomon shellfish utilization system and that of the Early Yayoi-Heian are compared, the following observation emerges. The former system is probably the most cost-effective shellfish gathering system. On the other hand, that of the Early Yayoi-Heian is probably the most costly shellfish gathering system. The non-core species for the Late Jomon require the least cost and risk for collection. Contrary to the Late Jomon system, the non-core species consumed during the Early Yayoi-Heian are the most costly and often involve high risks in order to obtain them. For example, Table 2 shows the size and weight of the core and non-core species. As it is clearly seen, the average weight of the Late Jomon species is only 4.4 grams while that of the Early Yayoi-Heian is 121.2 grams. Thus, the latter strategy must have required more than 30 times transportation cost than that of the former if one has to travel the same distance. Also, it should be mentioned that in the case of bivalves, Table 2 shows only one side. Therefore, if one considers the weight of the other side of the bivalves and meat weight, the transportation cost must have been more than 50 times.

Table 2. Core and Most Common Invertebrate Species of Each Period

Species name	Size (cm)	Weight (g)
Core species		
Marmarostoma argyrostoma	4-8	29.3
Strombus luhuanus	4-8	16.1
Atactodea striata	4-8	1.6
Average		15.7
Non-core species in the Late Jomon		
Lunella coronata granulata	4-8	1.6
Theliostyla albicilla	2-4	2.1
Gafrarium tumidum	2-4	9.6
Average		4.4
Non-core species in the Final Jomon		
Geloina papua	4-8	14.9
Meretrix lamarcki	4-8	N/A
Gafrarium tumidum	2-4	9.6
Asaphis dichotoma	4-8	3.9
Average		9.5
Non-core species in the Early Yayoi-Heian		
Tectus maximus	8-16	31.3
Tridacna maxima	16-32	223.4
Tridacna crocea	16-32	109.0
Average		121.2

For details, see Takamiya 2000

At the present time, I cannot provide an adequate explanation for the Final Jomon shellfish utilization system. However, if one only considers the weight, the Final Jomon people spent slightly higher transportation cost than the Late Jomon people. Therefore, like the vertebrate utilization system, it is most likely that the shellfish utilization system had not been stable during the prehistoric times. Furthermore, it should be stated that the shellfish utilization system, like that of the vertebrate, is characterized by changes from the least costly system to the most costly one. Finally, this paper briefly introduces what kind of plant food these inhabitants ate during prehistoric times.

Plant Consumption

Prior to 1992, plant remains were accidentally recovered from a handful sites. These plant remains suggested that prehistoric people depended upon wild resources, especially nuts. However, based on the inadequate amount of plant remains, one could not deny possibilities of presence of agriculture during prehistoric times. Consequently, as of 1993, at least seven agriculture hypotheses had been proposed: the Gusuku agriculture hypothesis, the Early Yayoi-Heian agriculture hypothesis, the Final Jomon agriculture hypothesis, the Late Jomon agriculture hypothesis, the "Late" Jomon hypothesis, the Ocean Road hypothesis, and the New Ocean Road hypothesis (summary in Hiroto Takamiya 2003).

Since 1992, the flotation method has been introduced to the Okinawan archaeology in order to systematically collect plant remains. While the number of sites on which this method was applied is only about twenty, the results indicate that the prehistoric people were mainly hunter-gatherers, except at the Nazakibaru site mentioned above. The Initial/Early Jomon wet site of the Aragusuku-shichabaru Dai 2 (Hiroto Takamiya 2006a) and Ireibaru C (Tomon 2000) yielded only wild species. The Mebaru site, the Late Jomon wet site, unearthed again all wild species (Omatsu and Tsuji 1999; Hiroto Takamiya 1999). At this site, a large amount of acorns was recovered. The Sumiyoshi shellmidden, located on Okinoerabu Island, also yielded only wild plant remains (Hiroto Takamiya 2006b). Furthermore, the Takachikuchibaru site, the Early Yayoi-Heian Period site, where flotation was applied for the first time in Okinawa, unearthed only wild species, mainly consisting of nutmeats, nutshells and Indian chestnut (Hiroto Takamiya 1998). Plant remains recovered from three sites in northern Amami Oshima Island, namely, Yomisaki, Arago, and Matsunoto, and one site on Ie Island in the Okinawa Group, Nagarabaru Higashi, dated to the 5th to 10th century AD, consisted of wild species (summary in Hiroto Takamiya 2003 and 2006c). These results seem to deny the presence of prehistoric agriculture on the coral islands. At the same time, the results seem to indicate that plant use from the Initial Jomon to the Yayoi-Heian had been stable. However, this indication is most likely based on inadequate amount of data. With the increase of plant data in the future, the change in plant use will likely be detected like the animal utilization discussed above.

Conclusions

Was the life on the coral islands in prehistoric times easy with abundant natural resources as many people, including scientists, are inclined to imagine? This paper examined mainly two themes. The first examined who were the earliest inhabitants of the coral islands. Traditionally, it had been believed that the earliest inhabitants of the region were those who lived there during the late Pleistocene. While they were indeed the earliest inhabitants in the region, they were not likely living on the coral islands. Recent analysis suggests that the earliest inhabitants on the coral islands were not the Initial/Early Jomon, but people who attempted to colonize the region during the later part of the Middle Jomon and Late Jomon Periods. Furthermore, recent studies implies that they were not the direct ancestors of modern day Okinawans. Their ancestors were probably people who moved into this region just before the Gusuku Period. This means at least four human groups lived there and in turn is interpreted as how difficult it was to live and survive on the islands.

The second theme examined whether or not subsistence economy was stable during the prehistoric period. Since an attempt to systematically collect plant remains using flotation was just introduced into this region, it is difficult to inquire changes in plant use. The only thing becoming clear is that people were mostly gatherers of the wild plants during the prehistoric times. On the other hand, while prehistoric people were hunters and collectors of wild animals, the reanalysis of animal remains both on vertebrates and shellfish has revealed new insight concerning the animal utilization in the past. The Late Jomon people established the most cost-effective system, which likely disintegrated during the Final Jomon Period. The animal utilization system during this period seems to be also the transition to the Early Yayoi-Heian system, which is characterized by the most costly system in the environment. This tendency strongly suggests that people were experiencing food stress. Given limited amount of natural resources in the region and possible population growth after successful colonization, this conclusion is not astonishing but expected.

The results obtained from two examinations indicate that the prehistoric people on the coral islands were experiencing harsh times as time went by after successful colonization of the islands. It was not a heaven on earth. Most visitors to the islands today only perceive and experience one aspect of the life on the coral islands. In fact, modern Okinawan people are having hard time living on the islands. By the same token, the past might be viewed as a heaven from present day people. But the reality was likely not.

Acknowledgement

I would like to thank Dr. Richard Pearson and Dr. Simon Kaner for inviting me to this symposium and giving me the opportunity to publish this paper.

REFERENCES CITED

ASATO, SHIJUN
1985 Okinawa gusuku jidai no bunka to dobutsu [Okinawa gusuku culture and animal use]. *Kikan Kokogaku* 11:68–70.

BINFORD, LEWIS
1971 Post-Pleistocene adaptations. In *Prehistoric Agriculture*: 22–49, ed. Stuart Struever. New York: Natural History Press.

DODO, YUKIO
1993 Ainu to Okinawajin wa [The Ainu and Japanese]. *Asahi Wan Tema Magajin* 14:73–84.

DOI, NAOMI
1997 *Okinawa Chiho ni okeru Jinkaku Keisei no Chiikiteki/Jikanteki Hensen ni tsuite [On Regional and Historical Changes in Osteological Development in Okinawa]*. Nishihara: University of Ryukyus.

HATTORI, SHIRO
1999 *Nihongo no Keifu [A genealogy of Japanese]*. Tokyo: Iwanami Shoten.

HATUSHIMA, SUMIHIKO AND TETSUO
1977 *Ryukyu Shokubutsu Mokuroku [Flora of the Ryukyus]*. Naha: Deigo Shuppan Sha.

HAYDEN, BRIAN
1990 Nimrods, piscators, pluckers, and planters: The emergence of food production. *Journal of Anthropological Archaeology* 9:31–69.

HOKAMA, SHUZEN
1977 Okinawa no gengo to sono rekishi [Language of Okinawa and its history]. In *Iwanami Koza, Nihongo 11 Hogen*: 181–233, eds. T. Shibata et al. Tokyo: Iwanami Shoten.

HUDSON, MARK
1994 The linguistic prehistory of Japan: Some archaeological speculations. *Anthropological Science* 102 (3): 231–255.

IKEDA, JIRO
1998 *Nihonjin no Kita Michi [The route where the Japanese came from]*. Tokyo: Asahi Sensho.

ITO, SHINJI
2006 Jomon bunka no minami no kyokai [The border of the Jomon culture in the south]. In *Higashi Ajia ni okeru Nihon Kiso Bunka no Kokogakuteki Kaimei*: 1–14, eds. Shinji Itoh and N. Yamazoe. Tokyo: Kokugakuin Daigaku 21 Seiki COE Puroguramu Daiichi Gurupu Kokogaku-han.

JONES, RHYS
1977 Man as an element of a continental fauna: The case of the sundering of the Bassian Bridge. In *Sunda and Sahul*: 317–386, eds. J. Allen, J. Golson and R. Jones. London: Academic Press.

KAWAMURA, TADAO
1999 *Nanpo Bunka no Tankyu [Research on the Southern Culture]*. Tokyo: Kodansha Gakujutsu Bunko.

KIMURA, MASAAKI
1991 Onpa tanchiki kara mita Ryukyu Ko no Daiyonki rikkyo [Quaternary land bridges of the Ryukyu Arc detected on seismic reflection profiles]. In *Nakagawa Hisao Kyoju Taikan Kinen Chishitsugaku Ronbunshu*: 109–117. Sendai: Toko Insatsu.

KINOSHITA, NAOKO
2006 Kai koeki kara mita ibunka sesshoku [Intercultural contacts evaluated from shell trade]. *Kokogaku Kenkyu* 52 (2): 25-41.

KIRCH, PATRICK V.
1984 *The Evolution of the Polynesian Chiefdoms*. Cambridge: Cambridge University Press.

KUROZUMI, TAIJI
1988 Nantai dobutsu izontai [Mollusk remains]. In *Chibazukabaru Iseki*: 95–115, ed. Motobu Town Board of Education. Motobu: Motobu Town Board of Education.

NITTA, JUSEI
1982 Umi ya yama ni shokumotsu o motomete-kaizuka kara hakkutsu sareru shokuryo zanshi [Searching for food in the ocean and mountains-food remains recovered from shellmiddens]. *Shin Okinawa Bungaku* 52:28–39.

OKINAWA PREFECTURAL ARCHIVES (OKINAWA KEN KOBUNSHOKAN)

2003   *Okinawa Ken Shi Kakuron-hen 2 Kokogaku [The history of Okinawa, a detailed examination 2 archaeology]*. Haebaru: Okinawa Ken Kobunshokan.

OMATSU, SHINOBU AND SEIICHIRO TSUJI

1999   Mebaru iseki kara sanshutsu shita ogata shokubutsu itaigun [Macro botanical remains recovered from the mebaru site]. In *Mebaru Iseki*: 223–241, ed. Ginoza Village Board of Education. Ginoza Village: Ginoza Village Board of Education.

PEARSON, RICHARD

1981   Environments of Kume and Iriomote, with reference to prehistoric settlement. In *Subsistence and Settlement in Okinawan Prehistory—Kume and Iriomote*: 8–19, ed. Richard Pearson. Vancouver: Laboratory of Archaeology, University of British Columbia.

PIETRUSEWSKY, MICHAEL

1999   A multivariate craniometric study of the inhabitants of the Ryukyu Islands and comparisons with cranial series from Japan, Asia, and Pacific. *Anthropological Science* 107(4): 255–281.

SAITO, NARIYA

2005   *DNA Kara Mita Nihonjin [Japanese seen from DNA]*. Tokyo: Chikuma Shinsho.

SHINODA, KEN-ICHI

2007   *Nihonjin ni Natta Sosentachi [The Ancestors Who Became Japanese]*. Tokyo: NHK Books.

TAKAMIYA, HIROE

1999   Shoto no kyusekki jidai [Palaeolithic period in the archipelago]. *Yomitan Sonritsu Rekishi Minzoku Shiryo-kan Kiyo* 23:1–29.

TAKAMIYA, HIROTO

1996a   Initial colonization and subsistence adaptation processes in the late prehistory of the island of Okinawa. *Indo-Pacific Prehistory Association Bulletin* 15:143–150.

1996b   Kodai-minzoku shokubutsugaku teki apurochi ni yoru Nazakibaru Iseki no seigyo [Subsistence economy of the Nazakibaru site based on paleoethnobotanical approach]. In *Nazakibaru Iseki*: 83–100, ed. Naha City Board of Education. Naha: Naha City Board of Education.

1998   Shokubutsu itai kara mita Yanagita Kunio "Kaijo no Michi" setsu [Yanagita Kunio's ocean road hypothesis: Evaluation based on plant remains]. *Minzokugaku Kenkyu* 63(3): 281–301.

1999   Saibai shokubutsu no tansaku [Search for cultigens]. In *Mebaru Iseki*: 259–277, ed. Ginoza Village Board of Education. Ginoza: Ginoza Village Board of Education.

2000   Hito no tekio kara mita Okinawa no senshijidai to hennen [Prehistory and chronology of Okinawa based on human adaptation processes]. In *Ryukyu/Higashi Ajia no Hito to Bunka Takamiya Hiroe Sensei Koki Kinen Ronshu*: 403–426, ed. Takamiya Hiroe Sensei Koki Kinenronshu Kankokai. Urasoe: Shoseido.

2003   Shokubutsu itai kara mita Amami/Okinawa no noko no hajimari [Beginning of agriculture in Amami and Okinawa based on plant remains]. In *Senshi Ryukyu no Seigyo to Koeki*: 35–46, ed. Naoko Kinoshita. Kumamoto: Kumamoto University.

2004   Okinawa Shoto no senshijidai ni okeru fudo sutoresu ni tsuite [On food stress in the prehistoric Okinawa Archipelago]. *Nanto Koko* 23:51–57.

2005   *Shima no Senshigaku: Paradaisu dewa nakatta Okinawa Shoto no Senshijidai [Island Prehistory: It Was Not A Paradise. An introduction to island prehistory]*. Naha: Boda Inku.

2006a   Shokubutsu itai [Plant remains]. In *Aragusuku Shichabaru Dai Ni Iseki*: 287–294, ed. Okinawa Prefectural Archaeological Center. Nishihara: Okinawa Prefectural Archaeological Center.

2006b   Sumiyoshi kaizuka shutsudo no shokubutsu itai [Plant remains recovered from the Sumiyoshi shellmidden]. In *Sumiyoshi Kaizuka*: 100–107, ed. China Town Board of Education. China: China Town Board of Education.

2006c   Nanto Chubuen ni okeru shokubutsu riyo fukugen no igi [The significance of reconstruction of plant utilization in the central region of the Ryukyu Archipelago]. In *Senshi Ryukyu no Seigyo to Koeki 2*: 89–100, ed. Naoko Kinoshita. Kumamoto: Kumamoto University.

TOIZUMI, TAKEJI

2003   *Sekizui dobutsu itai karamita Amami/Okinawa no kankyo to seigyo* (Environment and subsistence of Amami and Okinawa based on vertebrate analysis). In *Senshi Ryukyu no Seigyo to Koeki*: 47–66, ed. Naoko Kinoshita. Kumamoto: Kumamoto University.

TOMON, KENJI

2000   *Ireibaru C Iseki* [The Ireibaru C site]. *Kokogaku Janaru* 454:26–31.

Shell Exchange in the Ryukyu Islands and in East Asia

Naoko KINOSHITA
Kumamoto University

INTRODUCTION

The long chain of Ryukyu Islands surrounded by coral reefs is located in the southern part of the Japanese archipelago at a latitude of 24 to 30 degrees north. Coral reefs have developed because of the warm and clear water of the Kuroshio—or Japan Current—which flows from equatorial depths along the western edge of the islands. Calcium from growing coral and aquatic creatures builds up as the coral grows toward the ocean surface, creating an elevated area. The minimum ocean temperature is not less than 20° C. There are coral reefs in Hainan and eastern Taiwan, and small reefs are found south of Tsushima Island and south of the Boso Peninsula (Japan). Otherwise, there are no reefs along the coasts of the main islands of Japan, the Korean Peninsula, or China where coral reef growth is inhibited by muddy water and/or low ocean temperature. The Ryukyus are separated from these areas by the deep sea.

In comparison with the shells of other areas, the species found in the Ryukyu Islands are larger, thicker, shinier, and more highly-colored. Therefore, they were curiosities for people from regions where such shells could not be found. Since Neolithic times, these people came to the Ryukyus in order to acquire these shells to make luxury items. The inhabitants of the main islands of Japan were most eager to acquire shells while people from the Korean Peninsula obtained them through Japan and treated the shells as valuables. It seems that people from China sailed across the sea to get shells from the Ryukyus. In this article I refer to this activity as "shell exchange." I trace shell exchange from the second half of the first millennium BC to the 13th century AD using archaeological evidence.

STAGES OF SHELL EXCHANGE

The formation of coral reefs in the Ryukyus was essential for shell exchange to take place. I will present a spatial and temporal framework before offering concrete explanations about the shell exchange.

Chronological Framework and Shell Exchange

The chronology of the interaction between the Ryukyu Islands and China and the main islands of Japan from 3,000 BC to AD 1,500 is summarized in Figure 1. It is difficult to compare directly the chronological framework of the main islands of Japan with the Three Age System of Europe. The concepts used for the chronological framework of the Ryukyus differ from them. Therefore in Figure 1, I use historical records and information about economic development for the comparison of China and the main islands of Japan.

Formation of the "Coral Reef World"

The coral reefs of the Ryukyu Islands are located at the northern limit of the world distribution of coral reefs and most of the reefs are termed "fringing reefs." Fringing reefs are formed on an outer rise-shaped bank termed "*hishi*" and the shallow lagoon (shallower than 5 m) on the inner side is termed "*ino*" in Amami and Okinawan dialect (Figure 2).

The *hishi* barrier weakens the waves of the open sea, creating quiet conditions in the *ino*. Various creatures inhabit the severe environment of the outer reef and the quiet conditions of the lagoon, and they move between them according to tidal flows and seasons. The coral reefs were highly prized by the islanders. The reefs were rich in life and natural resources, and provided protection from violent marine waves.

The coral surrounding reefs of the Ryukyu Islands began to form during the Holocene Period, around 8,500 BP for the Sakishima Islands and 7,700–7,000 BP for the Amami and Okinawa Islands. In Okinawa and its satellites, hereafter called the Okinawa Islands, the deposition began at a depth of around 10–20 m; the *hishi* appeared at 5,000 BP, and then each of the islands was surrounded by a fringing reef about 3,500 to 3,000 BP. The reef functioning as a buffer against waves was completed through this formation process (Kan et al. 1997).

Period	China	Main Islands of Japan	Ryukyu Islands			Chronology of Okinawa		Historic Events in the Ryukyu Islands
			Imported artifacts C[a]	Imported artifacts J[b]	Economic Phenomenon over Wide Areas			
BC 3000	Neolithic age	Prehistoric period / Hunter-gatherer economy / Jomon period				Prehistoric period	Earliest Shell mound period	
2000	Xia			Late Jomon pottery			Early Shell mound period	
	Shang							formation of fringing reef
1000	Zhou			Latest Jomon pottery			Middle Shell mound period	settlements on plateaus
	Spring and Autumn Warring States	Yayoi period	*Mingdao* coin	Early Yayoi pottery				settlements move to dunes
500								
200	Qin		*Wushu* coin	Middle Yayoi pottery bronze implements iron implements	shell trade with Kyushu Yayoi societies			
BC/AD 100	Han	Protohistoric period	*Wushu* coin	Late Yayoi pottery				
200							Late Shell mound period	
300	Three Kingdoms	Kofun period						
400	Jin Southern and Northern Dynasty				shell trade with Kofun societies of Kyushu and Western Japan			
500								
600	Sui	Asuka period	iron implements					
700	Tang	Nara period / Production economy	*Kaiyuan tongbao* coin	iron implements salt-making pottery	trade of Great Green Turban			
800								
900	Five Dynasties and Ten Kingdoms	Heian period		*haji* and *sue* ware smoked *haji* ware steatite vessel	trade of Great Green Turban with Kyushu and Western Japan		Transition to production economy	settlements move to plateaus
1000								
1100	Song		Chinese white porcelain Chinese celadon		trade of Great Green Turban with Kyushu and Western Japan, Circulation of Kamuiyaki ware	Protohistoric period / Production economy	Gusuku period	
1200		Kamakura period	Chinese coins					
1300	Yuan							
1400	Ming	Muromachi period	Chinese blue-and-white porcelain Southeast Asian stoneware	mortar made of tile-clay *Bizen* ware	relay trade	Historic period	Ryukyu Dynasty	giving tributes to Ming
1500								

a) Goods from China b) Goods from the main islands of Japan.

Figure 1. Chronology of external interaction among the Ryukyu Islands, China and the main islands of Japan.

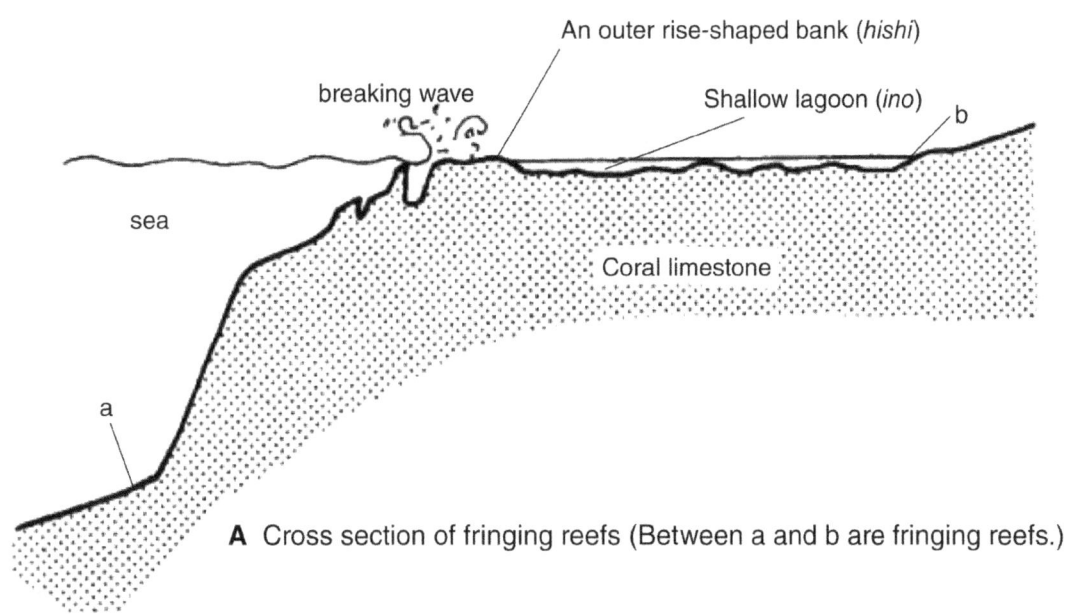

A Cross section of fringing reefs (Between a and b are fringing reefs.)

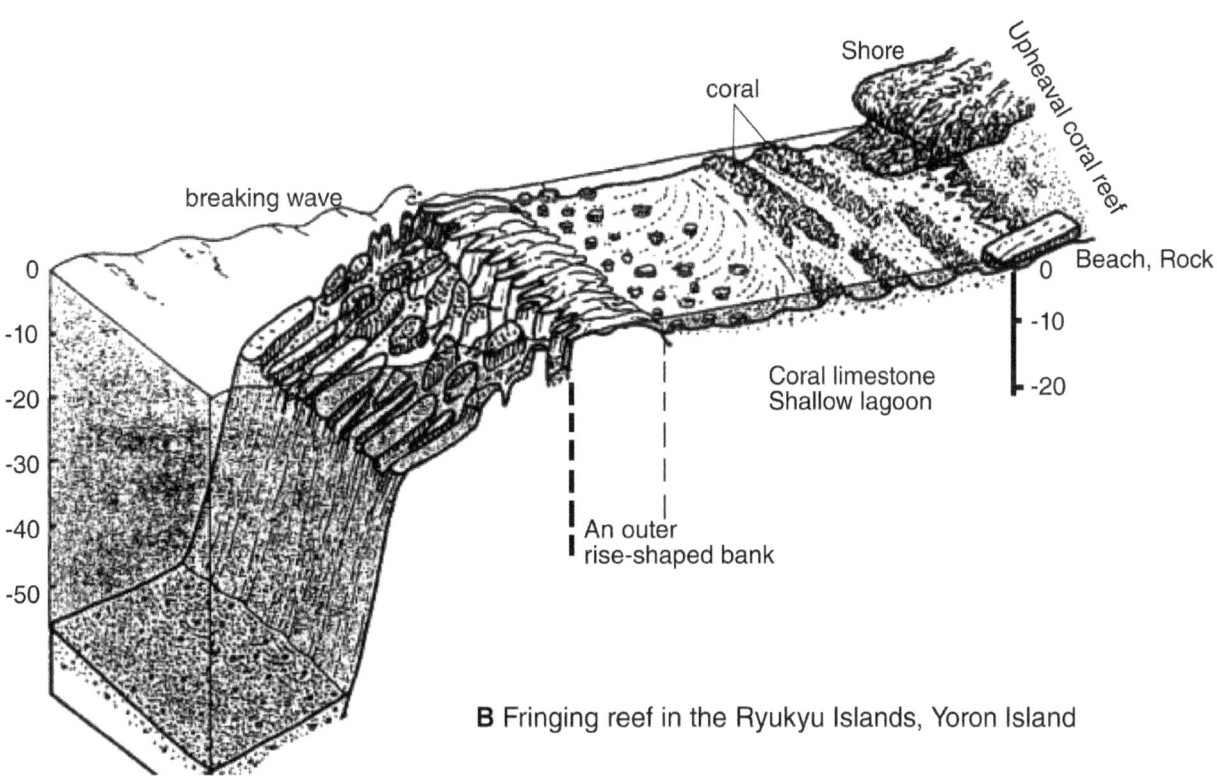

B Fringing reef in the Ryukyu Islands, Yoron Island

Figure 2. The coral reef of Yoron, as an example of Ryukyu reefs (Kaizuka et al. 1985:115).

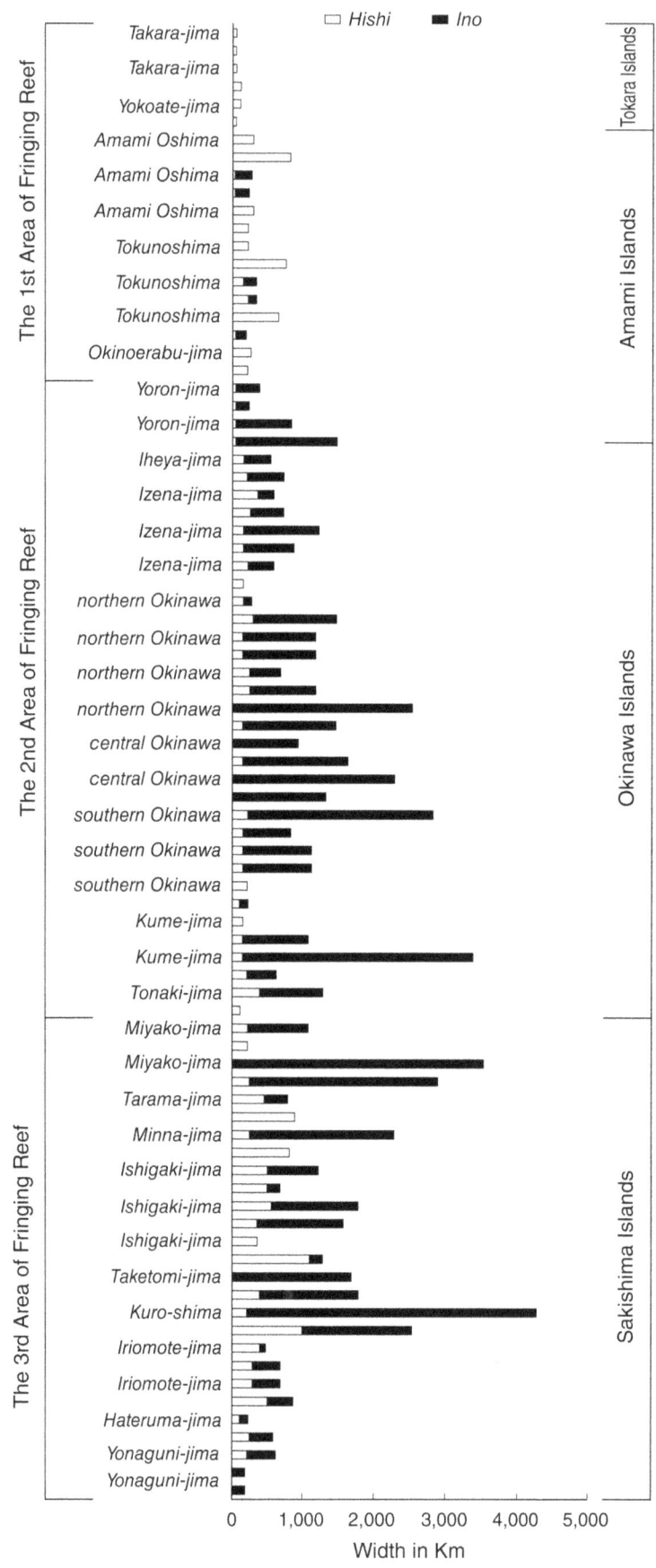

Figure 3. Width of barrier reef and lagoon from north to south in the Ryukyus.

The time lag of coral reef development between the Northern and Southern Ryukyu Islands also manifested in differences in the formation of the coral reefs (Hori 1980). Figure 3 shows the width of 83 coral reefs divided into *hishi* (barrier) and *ino* (lagoon) around the Ryukyus based on topographic maps of 1/50,000.

Hori (1990), Kagoshima Ken (1983), Mezaki (1985), Okinawa Ken (1983), Nakamori and Ota (2001), and Shimabukuro and Toguchi (1990) were referred to for details on Ryukyu coral reefs. In Figure 3 the islands are arranged from north to south latitude. Most islands in the Tokara Group (north of Amami Island) and the Amami Islands have coral reefs with a maximum width of 1,000 m. In these islands the *hishi* expands while the *ino* does not. I refer to these as Area 1. The number of islands with coral reefs wider than 1,000 m increases from the south of the Amami Islands to the south of the Okinawa Islands, and they have both barrier and lagoon. This region is termed Area 2. The Sakishima Islands have the widest coral reefs, some having a *hishi* wider than 1,000 m and an *ino* wider than 3,000 m. Thus the scale of coral reefs increased from north to south within the Ryukyus and lagoons exist mainly south of Okinawa.

Formation of Coastal Dunes

Site location in the prehistoric Ryukyus is roughly classified into three patterns: coastal sand dune and low seashore; cliff bottom, rock shelter and cave; and terrace and hill (Kishimoto et al. 2000). Figure 4 shows the types of location of 841 sites in Okinawa and surrounding islands.

The total number of sites increased gradually at each stage and increased rapidly in the Gusuku Period. The rapid increase of sites in the Gusuku Period corresponds to the beginning of agriculture on natural terraces. In the Late Shellmound Period the number of sites located in sand dunes and coastal lowlands increased. Just before the beginning of the Late Shellmound Period, the function of coral reefs to buffer against wave action was achieved, so the reefs must have protected the islands against tidal waves. This feature must have been related to the subsequent shift of site locations to the coast. Although it is considered that the fringing reefs were formed around 3,500–3,000 BP, in this formative period the function of the fringing reefs as buffers against the waves was probably imperfect. The settlements of Okinawa in this stage were still located on the terraces. In addition Kawana (2006a, 2006b), a geographer, has pointed out that large tsunamis occurred all over Ryukyu Islands 3,400 years ago. Therefore, it is considered that the settlements moved to the sand dunes some time after fringing reefs formed.

Abundant shell remains have been excavated from sites on coastal sand dunes in the Late Shellmound Period, in comparison with the amount of shells from earlier sites. Although many of the shells are food residue, shells that were selected as material for everyday tools were also recovered. For people in the Late Shellmound Period, shells were used in various aspects of their life—from the tools of production to accessories (Kinoshita 1988)—showing how life in those days was closely linked to the coral seas. It was at this stage that people who lived in the main islands of Japan, especially Yayoi people of Kyushu, learned of the existence of the large univalve shells of the Ryukyu Islands.

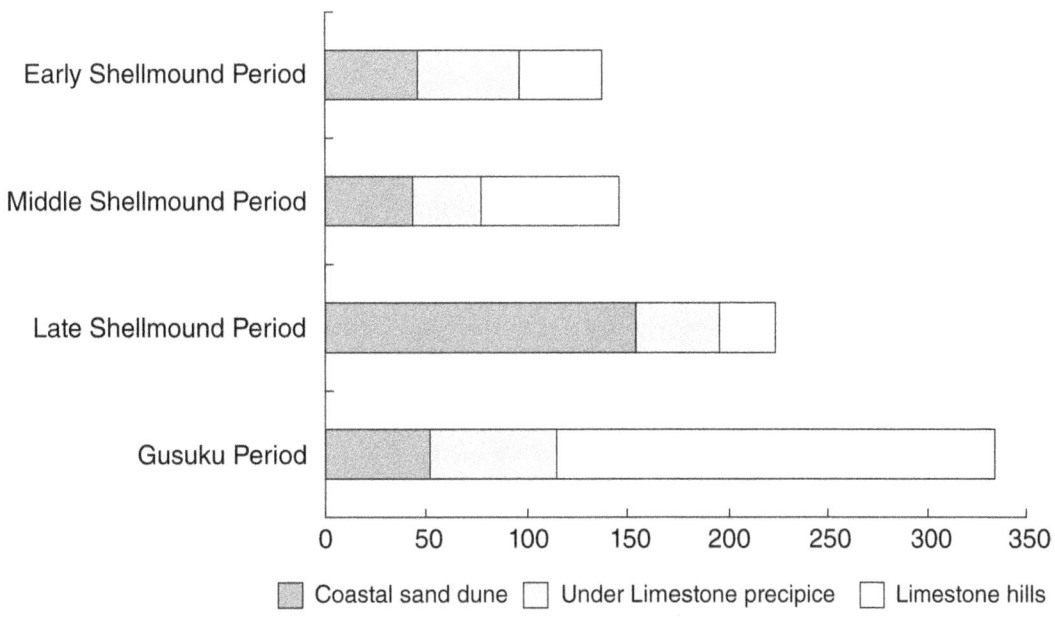

Figure 4. Location of sites in the Okinawa Island Group (841 sites).

THE ACTUAL CONDITIONS OF SHELL EXCHANGE

The Beginning of Shell Exchange

The Birth of Bracelets Made from Ryukyu Shells

The Yayoi Period is considered to be the period of wet rice agriculture in the main islands of Japan. In the first half of the 1st millennium BC, a culture based on agriculture and metal artifacts in the southern Korean Peninsula spread to northern Kyushu and Jomon people of northern Kyushu accepted new immigrants and culture. Radiocarbon dating has recently shown that it took about 500 years for the acceptance of the new culture to result in the beginning of Yayoi culture. New technology and people spread from Kyushu to various districts of Japan where some attempts were made to form agricultural societies. During this long period of preparation, bracelets using Ryukyu shells appeared in Kyushu Yayoi society.

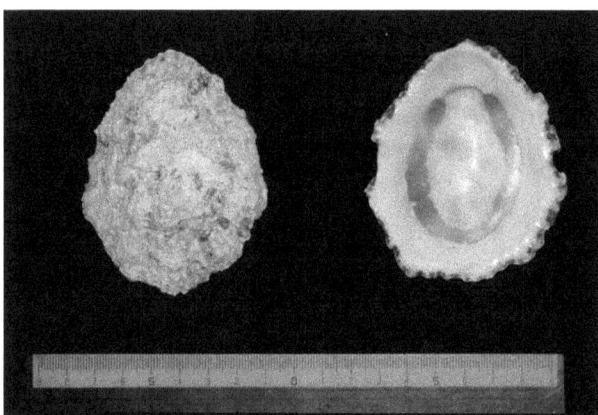

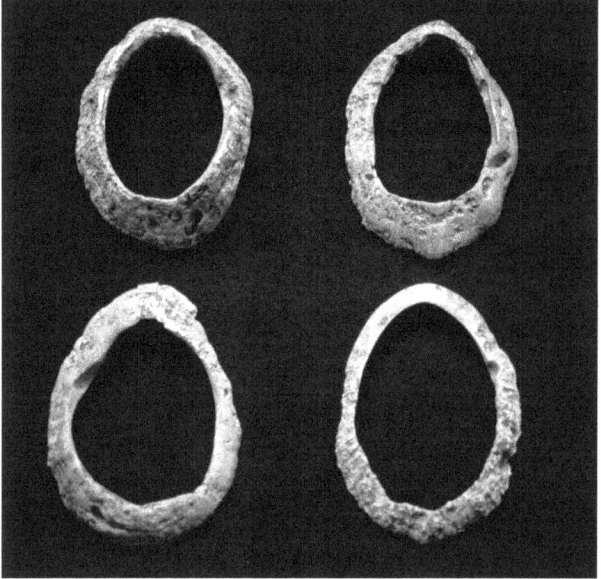

Figure 5. True Limpet Shell and bracelets of True Limpet Shell in the Early Yayoi Period. (Upper) Interior and exterior of recent True Limpet Shell. (Lower) Bracelets of True Limpet Shell from Burial No. 1, Matsubara Site, Nagasaki. The interred female wore two bracelets on each arm.

The first people to use bracelets of Ryukyu shells lived on the seashores of northern Kyushu and western Japan and were half and half occupied with farming and fishing. The characteristic shell bracelets appeared in the Earliest and Early Yayoi Periods. Bracelets were made of large Ryukyu univalves—Broad Pacific Conch, Lettered Cone, and True Limpet. Broad Pacific Conch *Strombus latissimus*; *Strombus* (*Tricornis*) *latissimus* Linnae is one of the large-sized univalve shell belonging to the Strombidae family, and *Strombus thersites* also known as *Tricornis thersites* Swainson, a smaller species, was also used. As for Lettered Cone shell (Conidae), many *Conus litteratus*; *Conus* (*Lithoconus*) *litteratus* Linnaeus and *Conus leopardas*; *Conus* (*Lithoconus*) *leopardas* Hwass were used. True Limpet shell *Patella* (*Penepatella*) *optima* Pilsbry is one of the limpets belonging to the Patellidae family. The classification of the shellfish in this paper depends on Habe (1975) and Abbott and Dance (1985). Among coastal people, males wore bracelets of Broad Pacific Conch on their right arms, females wore bracelets of Lettered Conch or True Limpet on their left or both arms, and children wore Limpet bracelets on the left or both arms. Such a bracelet system is not seen in the Jomon Period. It is important that many of them were buried in graves of styles peculiar to the Korean Peninsula, such as dolmens, and it can be considered that these new bracelets appeared with other cultural aspects from the Korean Peninsula. Examples of use of the shell bracelets in the early stages are as follows. In the Matsubara Site, Nagasaki Prefecture, a female from a dolmen burial (No. 1) wore two or more shell bracelets made of True Limpet shell, and another female from a pit burial (No. 1) wore two shell bracelets made of True Limpet shell on each arm (Uku Machi 1997). In the Nakanohama Site, Yamaguchi Prefecture, a female from a stone-covered grave (ST905) wore a shell bracelet made of Lettered Cone shell on the left arm. In the Otomo Site, Saga Prefecture, a male from a dolmen burial (57A) had two shell bracelets made of Broad Pacific Conch on the right arm, and an infant from a grave (II-No. 50) wore a shell bracelet of True Limpet shell on each arm. The oldest type of shell bracelet was made of True Limpet during the Earliest Yayoi Period (9th to 10th centuries BC) (Figure 5).

True Limpet inhabits fringing reef Area 1 (Kurozumi 1994). First coastal people of northern Kyushu received knowledge of the True Limpet. Subsequently, they acquired information about the Broad Pacific Conch and Lettered Cone, which occurred in Area 2, through contact with people in central and southern Kyushu. The Lettered Cone shell inhabits the lagoon. The Broad Pacific Conch and the *Strombus thersites* inhabit the deep part of the lagoon or on the sand of the deep seabed in the outside of barrier (Takamiya and Chinen 2004: 6–7). These people had been accumulating knowledge of the Ryukyu Islands since the Final Jomon Period. Some Amami-style pottery is found on the Satsuma Peninsula and the Tokara Islands in the Final Jomon Period. Pottery of southern Kyushu in this stage also influenced domestic pottery all over the Amami and Okinawa Islands, and jade and obsidian were brought to

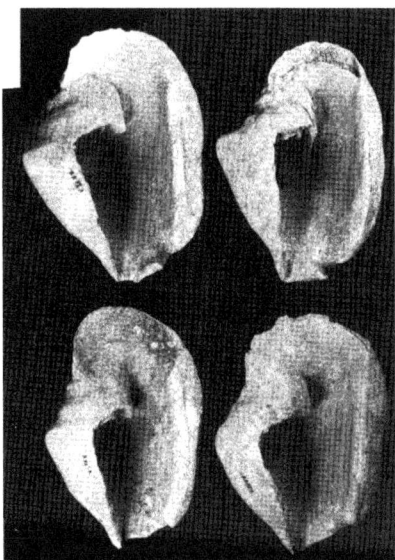
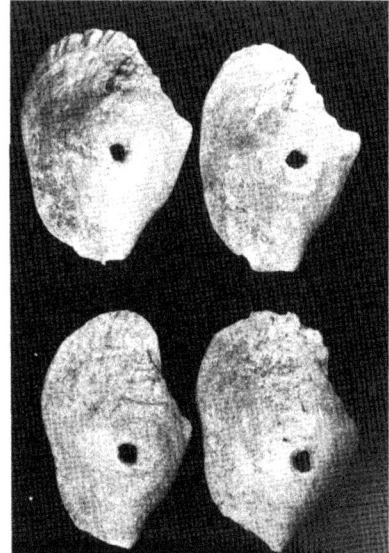

Figure 6. Broad Pacific Conch in the early stage of exchange of the Yayoi Period. Cache of Broad Pacific Conch in the Ohara Site, Locality A, Kume Island. The inner (central) portions of the eight shells were removed.

the Ryukyu Islands from Kyushu. It can be concluded that there were frequent cultural interactions between southern Kyushu and the Ryukyu Islands of the Final Jomon Period (Obata, Morimoto, and Kadobuchi 2004). Among coastal people, shell bracelets were worn by a few special persons. Why did they begin to make bracelets using shells brought from the distant islands? Round and thin bracelets made from bronze or jade used by elites in China and the Korean Peninsula provide a helpful suggestion about this question. The bronze bracelets are called the "Lelang-style bronze bracelets" (Oda 1974). Although there were not many jade bracelets, they were used in the Chinese Lelang commandery in the northern Korean Peninsula (Umehara 1959). It is thought that the coastal people of northern Kyushu and western Japan learned about these bracelets in the process of accepting Chinese and Korean culture in the Jomon-Yayoi transition, and that they transposed bronze and jade to shell from the Ryukyus.

The Beginning of Shell Exchange

Caches or concentrations of Broad Pacific Conch and/or Lettered Cones were made in the Okinawa Islands from the end of the Middle Shellmound Period paralleling the Early Yayoi Period. Pits containing Broad Pacific Conch have been found in the Ohara (Locality A) Site, Kume Island (8 Broad Pacific Conch) (Okinawa Ken 1980); the Furuzamami Shellmound, Zamami Island (22 shells of Broad Pacific Conch), and the Atta Shellmound II, Onna Village, Okinawa (3 Broad Pacific Conch) (Figure 6).

Eleven Broad Pacific Conch (from a total of 33) were punched and opened with a hole on the surface of the shell, and the inner portion of the shell was removed, leaving only the outer part. These are definitely semi-processed shell bracelets. Each of the other twelve nearly perfect Broad Pacific Conch shells also has a hole 1–2 cm in diameter at the almost same part. This hole is thought to have been used for stringing and carrying the shells. Eight or more pits containing Lettered Cone shells were also found at the Momenbaru Site, Yomitan-son, Okinawa. This kind of pit containing semi-processed shells had not been found previously in any sites in the Okinawa Islands. All species of shell cached in the Okinawa Islands correspond to species used in Kyushu Yayoi groups, and the form of these semi-processed shells corresponds to the form of the shell bracelets used in Kyushu (Figure 7). In addition, the temporal duration of such shell deposits in the islands corresponds to that of the shell bracelets in Kyushu. It is thought that the caches of shells in the islands appeared because of the demand for shell bracelets in Kyushu (Kishimoto and Shima 1985). In the Early Yayoi Period shell exchange took the form described above.

Continuation of Shell Exchange

Expansion of Consumption

The custom for coastal Yayoi people to wear round shell bracelets spread to agricultural people on the inland Kyushu plain, and shortly after they also came to make their own bracelets of Ryukyu shell. Coastal peoples' bracelets differ from those of the inland peoples', which are three dimensional, thick, and unusual in shape (Figures 8 and Plate 1).

These bracelets are classified into "Kanenokuma type," "Doigahama type," and "thick type." Among the agricultural people, males wore bracelets of Broad Pacific Conch on the right arm, females wore Lettered Cone bracelets on the left or both arms, and infants wore bracelets of *Strombus thersites* or Lettered Cone (Figures 9 and 10). These bracelets were worn by a few special

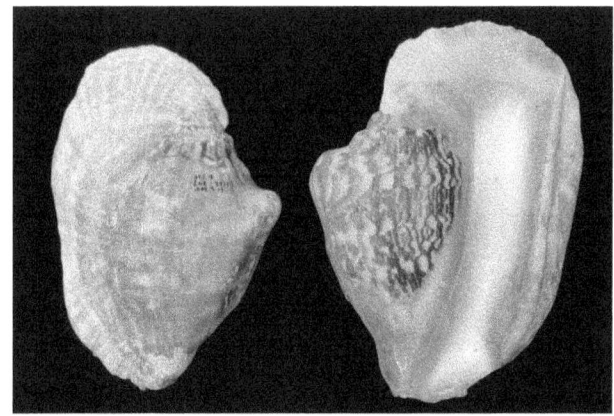

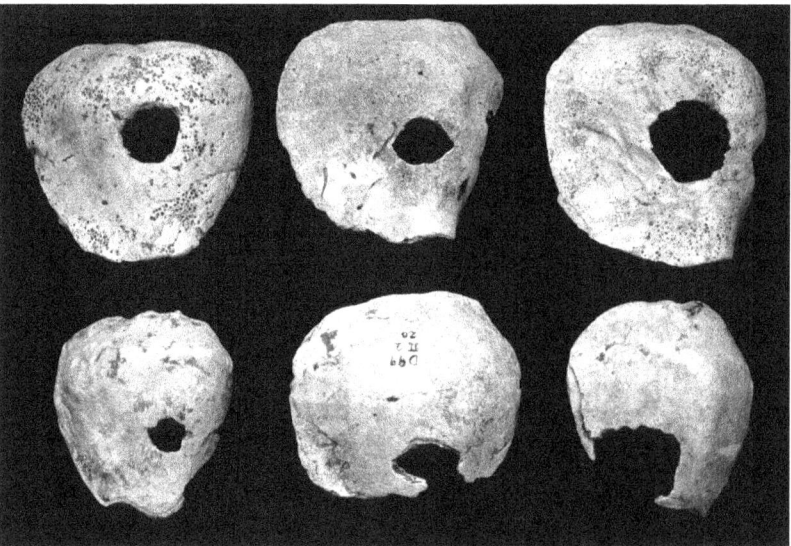

Figure 7. Broad Pacific Conch and Broad Pacific Conch bracelets in the Early Phase of the exchange. (Upper) Recent Broad Pacific Conch. Left: dorsal view. Right: ventral view. (Lower) Semi processed bracelets of Broad Pacific Conch. Dorsal use type. Takahashi Shellmound, Kagoshima. Early Yayoi Period

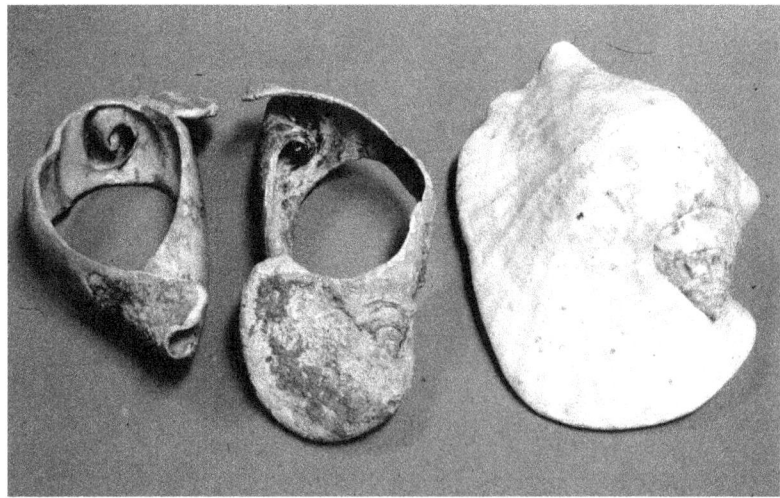

Figure 8. Bracelets of Broad Pacific Conch of agricultural people. Right. Recent Broad Pacific Conch. Left and middle : Bracelets of Broad Pacific Conch from Kanenokuma Site, Fukuoka.

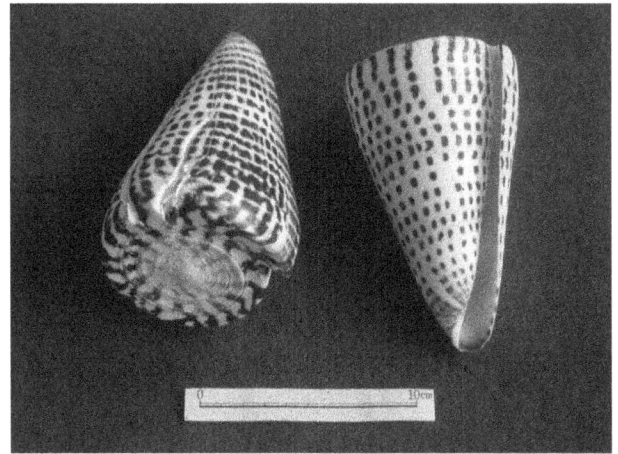

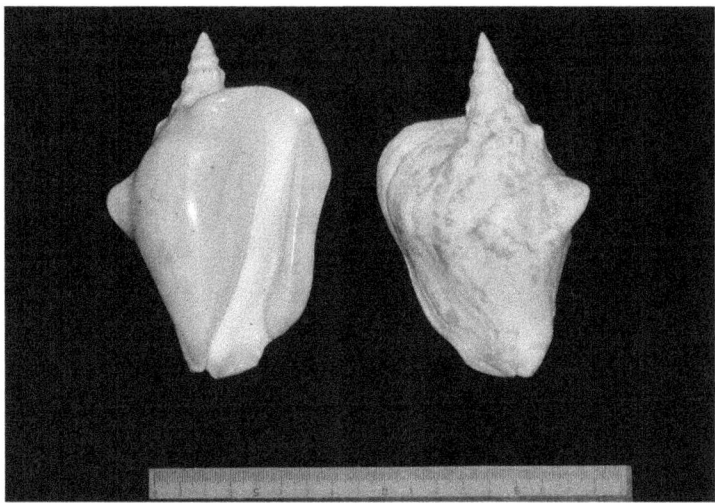

Figure 9. Lettered Cone, bracelet of Lettered Cone, and *Strombus thersites*. (Upper left) Recent Lettered Cone Shell (*Conus litteratus*). (Upper right) Bracelets of Lettered Cone, Matsunoo Site, Kagoshima Prefecture. (Lower) Recent *Strombus thersites* Left: ventral. Right: dorsal.

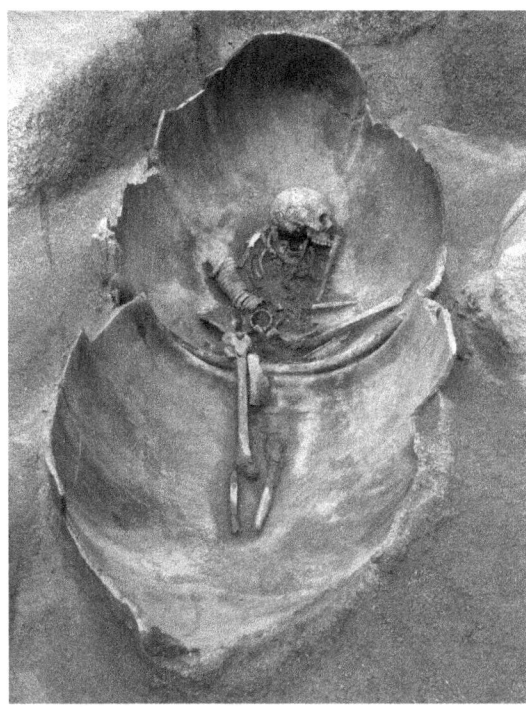

Figure 10. Females wearing Lettered Cone bracelets. (Left) Female 15-16 years of age wearing 18 Lettered Cone bracelets on the left arm, in jar burial. Hanaura site, Saga Pref. Middle Yayoi Period. (Right) Female wearing modern replicas of Lettered Cone bracelets (Wajinden no Michi Kenkyukai 1980, 94).

Figure 11. Storage caches of Lettered Cone Shells (*Conus litteratus*) at the Anchinoue Site, Sesoko Island, Okinawa.
(Upper) Left: No. 3 Cache of Lettered Cone 77 Shells. Right: No. 4 Cache of 117 Lettered Cone Shells.
(Lower) Lettered Cone Shells from No. 4 Cache.

persons among the agricultural people, so that they are thought to have been special accessories. Takakura (1975) noted that there was an exclusive relation between the shell bracelets and bronze weapons and mirrors in burials. He thus suggests that weapons and mirrors signified persons with political prestige while bracelets signified religious specialists (Takakura 1975). Infants wore the same shell bracelets as the adult's bracelets, indicating the presence of individuals whose social roles had been determined from childhood.

In the early stages, one or two bracelets were worn on one arm while later the number of them increased to six or eight. In the latter half of the Middle Yayoi Period, the largest number of them on one arm was 21 bracelets of Broad Pacific Conch and 25 of Lettered Cone. Up to now, 55 sites containing a total of 671 bracelets using Ryukyu shells, dating to the Yayoi Period, have been found in the main islands of Japan. The use of bracelets of Ryukyu shell increased on the plains from the latter half of the early Yayoi Period, exceeding substantially the use of bracelets among coastal peoples. If we include the number of undiscovered bracelets and the number broken in production, the number of shells transported to the Japanese main islands must have been huge.

The Situation at the Place of Origin

Storage caches of unprocessed shells, the raw material for bracelet production, have been found in many parts of the Okinawa Islands, dating to the Middle Yayoi Period (Late Shellmound Period), when bracelets prevailed in Yayoi society. These cache pits contain different proportions of shell species. The shells were buried in sand to facilitate the decay of the soft parts and to eliminate the odor of the decaying animals. While it is possible to remove the animal by heating, this damages the shell. In typhoons, shifting sand may have hidden the cached shells forever. Some shells may have been left behind because they were too small or too thin, and therefore unsuitable for exchange. Also shells already dead at the time of harvesting are of poor quality. In 40 cache pits found in the Kajyo Shellmound, Urasoe, Okinawa, 23% of Broad Pacific Conch were dead at the time of harvesting and 53% were young, while 58% of *Strombus thersites* were dead. The diameter of many Lettered Cone shells from this site is 5.5–6.0 cm, too small for making bracelets (Shimabukuro 2004). Lettered Cone shells found in the Anchinoue Shellmound, Motobucho (Figure 11), the main island of Okinawa (Morimoto 2005) and thought to be raw materials for bracelets were 77 pieces from No. 3 pit and 117 pieces from No. 4 pit.

Figure 12. Broad Pacific Conch as raw material, Kajo Shellmound, Okinawa, period parallel to Middle Yayoi Period.

Up to 2004, 106 shell cache pits have been found in 32 sites (Shimabukuro 2004). In 83 shell pits of 26 sites, in which shell species and number are given, there are 220 individuals of Broad Pacific Conch and *Strombus thersites* and 819 pieces of Lettered Cone.

Pits of earlier stages have Broad Pacific Conch while those of later stages have many Lettered Cones. This tendency corresponds to the consumption trend in Kyushu, where the proportion of shell bracelets made of Broad Pacific Conch was high in the early stages and the rate of Lettered Cone was high from the latter half of Middle Yayoi. The cache pits found in Okinawa and its surrounding islands are not found in the Amami Islands. This kind of pit definitely corresponds to differences in the development of coral reefs in both areas.

The Appearance of Semi-Processed Shell Bracelets

If the materials were chosen in the place of exchange, probably people of the Okinawa Islands knew the final form of the bracelets as finished goods, and endeavored to offer suitable materials. Shell bracelets of the Middle Yayoi agricultural people of northern Kyushu came to be limited to a few regular forms instead of the variety of forms in Stage 1. At the same time shells as raw materials were no longer exported, but instead, semi-processed bracelets, approximating the form of the finished bracelets, were produced in the Okinawa Islands. Each semi-processed bracelet had a hole punched open on the surface of the Broad Pacific Conch, needing only to be enlarged by abrasion and polishing to be completed. The hole could be enlarged to fit the size of each user's arm and some external finishing of the outside would complete the bracelet. I term these "roughed or semi-processed" bracelets (Figure 12). Yayoi people were able to fashion a set of shell bracelets that matched the size of each user's arm because of these semi-processed forms, and people wore many bracelets (Figure 13). The region had access to semi-processed

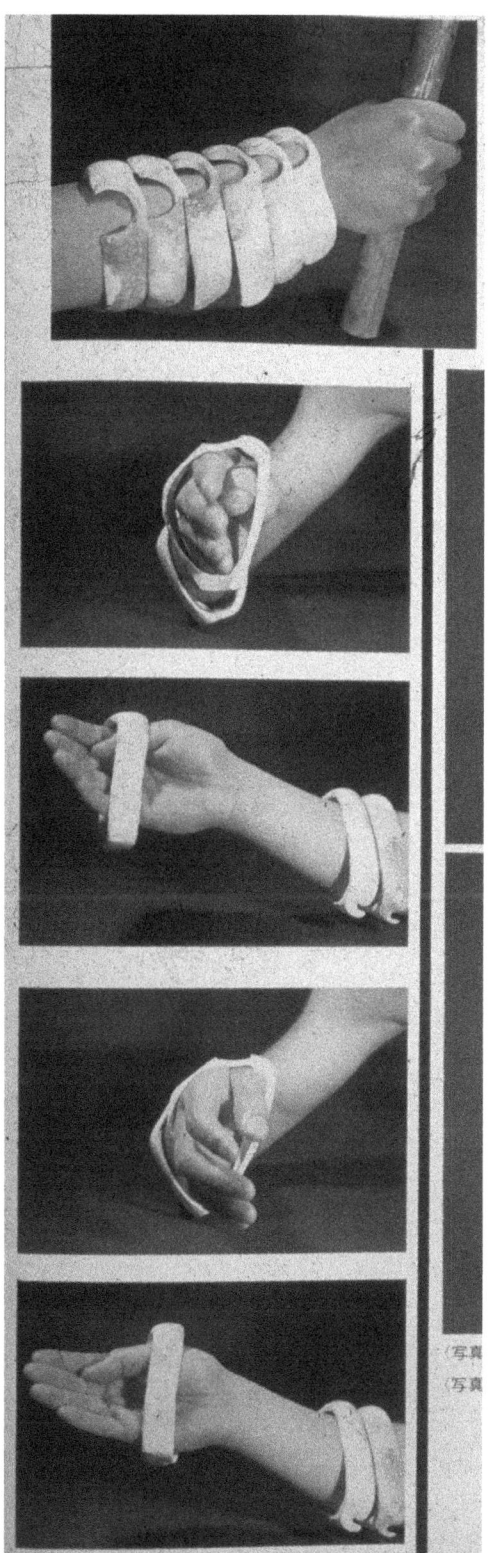

Figure 13. Tests of wearable sizes of bracelets of Broad Pacific Conch (Nagai and Kokubu 1978, Plate 12).

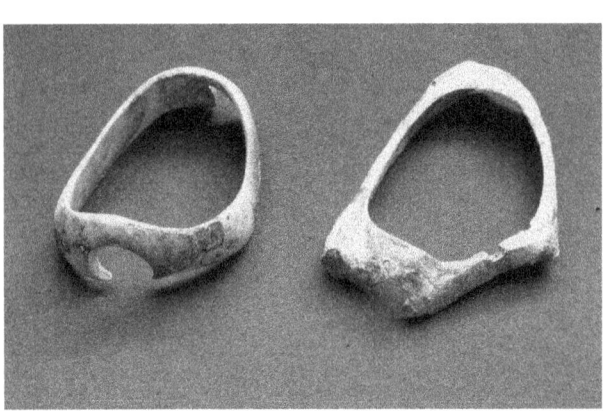
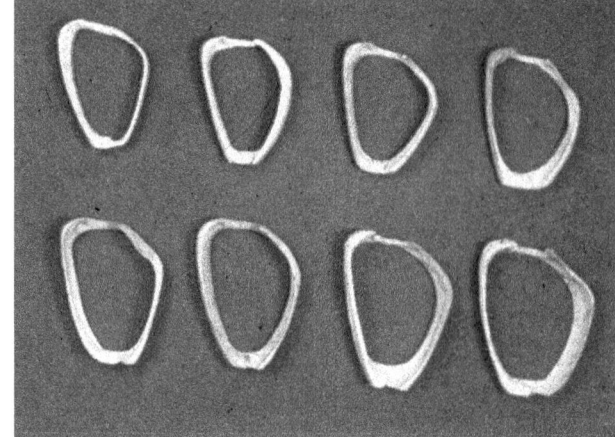

Figure 14. Finished bracelets of Broad Pacific Conch. (a) Bracelets, left, Moro-oka Site, Fukuoka Prefecture; right, Tateiwa Site, Fukuoka Prefecture. (b) Bracelets of Broad Pacific Conch worn by one individual, Moro-oka Site, Fukuoka Prefecture (Tateiwa Iseki Chosa Iinkai 1977, Fig. 8)

bracelets of Broad Pacific Conch and finished them as bracelets expanded in the latter half of the Middle Yayoi Period (Figure 14 and Plate 2). There was a close relation between the areas of production and consumption (Figures 15, 16, and 17).

Exchanging the Shells for Goods

For what were the shells exchanged? Artifacts brought to the Okinawa Islands from Yayoi societies were iron axes and Chinese-type bronze arrowheads dating to the Warring States (475–221 BC) and Han Dynasty (202 BC to AD 220). There were also recycled parts of bronze daggers, Chinese *Wushu* (Jap. *Goshu*) coins, glass beads, jade ornaments etc. (Casting of *Wushu* coins began in 119 BC). It seems however that these items which were not exchanged continuously because only a few of each have been found. Probably there were also cloth and wooden containers, which have already perished. Pottery was the most regularly traded item. As soon as the shell trade was started by Yayoi agriculturalists, pottery of northern Kyushu style appeared in the Ryukyus. In the Middle Yayoi Period it is suggested that the central and southern Kyushu people, in addition to the northern Kyushu people, participated in the shell exchange, because many pottery vessels from these districts of Kyushu are found in various places in the Ryukyu Islands. Food, such as rice and beans is thought to have been stored in these pots for the traders, and to have been regular trade goods; however the actual contents of these pots have not yet been discovered. Many of these Yayoi pots are storage vessels (Figure 18).

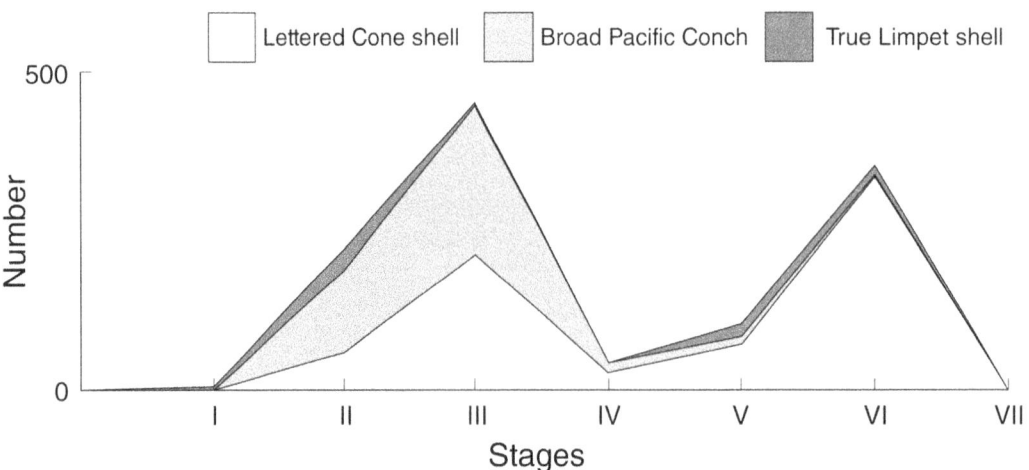

Figure 15. Consumption trend of univalve shells from the Ryukyu Islands in the main islands of Japan and the Korean Peninsula. N=-1175. I. Latter half of Early Yayoi or before (6th century BC or before). II. End of Early Yayoi to the first half of Middle Yayoi (5th to 2nd centuries BC). III. Middle of Middle Yayoi to Late Yayoi (1st century BC to 2nd century AD). IV. End of Yayoi to the first half of Kofun Period (3rd to 4th centuries AD). V. Middle Kofun (5th century AD). VI. Latter half of Kofun Period to the end of Kofun Period (6th to 7th centuries AD). VII. Time of Ritsuryo system (8th century or later).

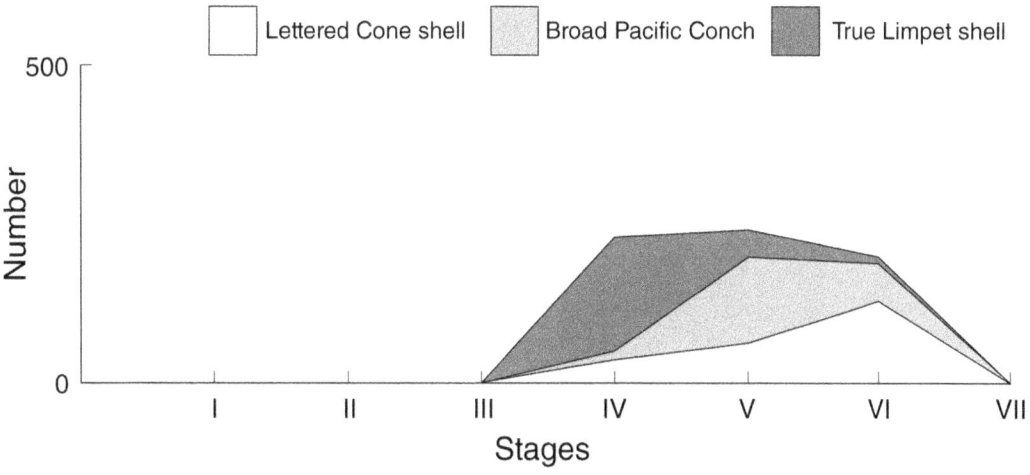

Figure 16. Consumption trend of univalve shells from the Ryukyu Islands on Tanegashima Island N=662.

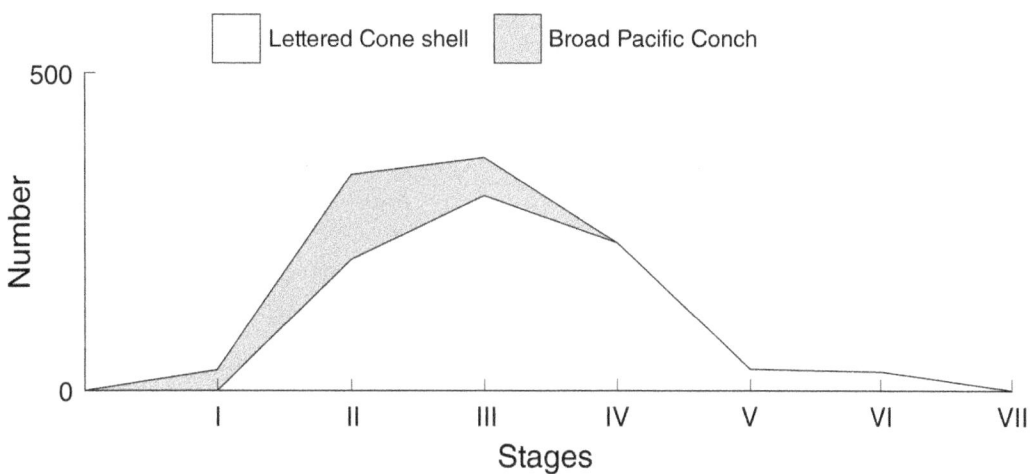

Figure 17. Consumption trend of univalve shells from the Ryukyu Islands in the Okinawa Islands N=1039.

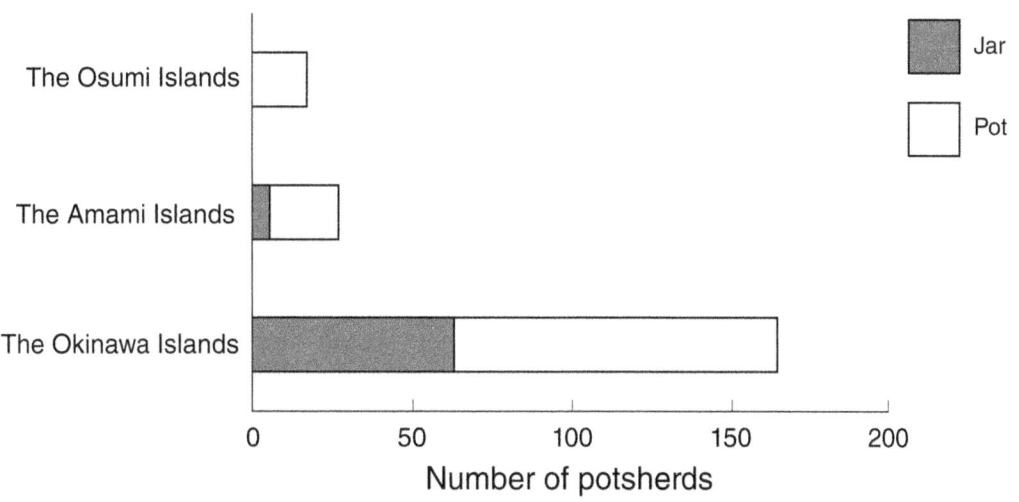

Figure 18. Yayoi pottery found in Ryukyu Island sites (1). N=208.

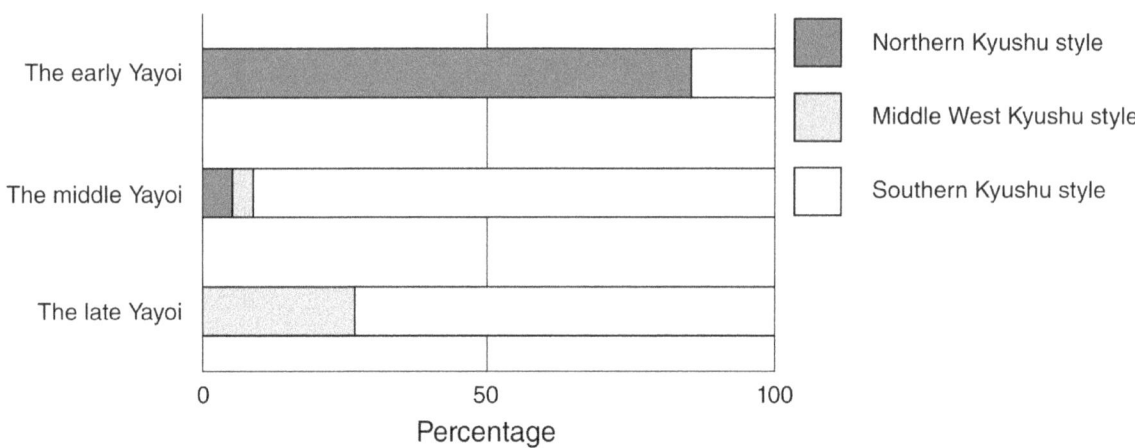

Figure 19. Yayoi pottery found in Ryukyu Island sites (2). N=88.

The Yayoi pottery consists of jars for cooking, pots for storage, and bowls and pedestal dishes for serving. The ratio of pots and jars of Yayoi pottery (208 potsherds), which is found in the Ryukyu Islands, is 7 to 3; where many are pots. On the other hand, at settlement sites in southern Kyushu during the middle Yayoi Period, the ratio of pots and jars is 2 to 8 or 4 to 5; where there are more jars than pots (T. Shinzato 2000). Therefore, the reason for so many pots among the shape categories of the Yayoi pottery in the Ryukyus is the selective use of pottery in the shell exchange. Thus, it is concluded that jars containing grain were exchanged with the empty jars remaining on the sites.

The "Front Line" of Shell Exchange

The first and latter halves of the shell exchange. Yayoi pottery found in every area in Ryukyus tells us the diachronic trading activities of the Yayoi people. In Figure 19, 88 sherds for which the chronological position and form were identified, among 208 sherds of such Yayoi pottery were classified by regional style.

This figure was drawn based on the data of Takayuki Shinzato (2000). The "Kyushu-style Yayoi pottery" includes not only pottery made in Kyushu but also pottery imitating the style of Kyushu. (In this paper, style refers to morphology rather than place of origin.) Yayoi people of northern Kyushu may have prepared pottery for exchange as containers in the early stages of the shell trade. In the middle of the exchange, much of the pottery is of southern Kyushu style. At this time it can be said that central Kyushu people also participated in the exchange. This suggests that the exchange in the later stage was mostly with central and southern Kyushu, These changes show that the location of preparation of trade goods for the Ryukyu Islands changed at the beginning of the latter half of Middle Yayoi. Central Kyushu people became involved in the latter half of the Middle Yayoi. The former half of Middle Yayoi is termed Stage 1 Shell Exchange, while the latter half of Middle Yayoi is termed Stage 2 Shell Exchange.

Participation of northern Kyushu coastal people in the shell exchange. Some graves thought to belong to shell traders have been found from the Tokara Islands to the Okinawa Islands. A typical example is the Momenbaru Cemetery in a coastal sand dune at Yomitan Village, Okinawa main island. Skeletal remains of 17 people were found from 10 graves in the site. Seven graves among them are box-type stone cist graves made of tabular coral. Local pottery imitating Yayoi pottery, finger rings made of shell, and jade beads found in these graves suggest that

Figure 20. Graves of shell traders (Photos courtesy of Yomitan son Kyoiku Iinkai). Box type stone cist graves, Momenbaru Site, Okinawa main island, in the period parallel to the Early Yayoi Period.

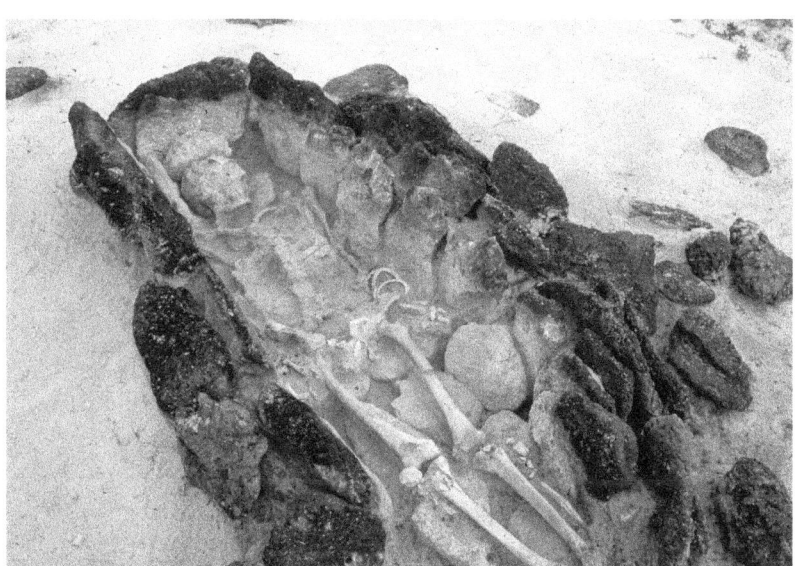

Figure 21. Graves of shell traders (2) (Upper) Oike Site, Takara Island, Tokara Islands, Kagoshima Prefecture. There was a stone cist under the cairn. (Lower) A box type stone cist grave containing a female wearing three bracelets of True Limpet on the left arm.

they are related to Kyushu. This cemetery dates to the end of the Middle Shellmound Period, corresponding to the period when round shell bracelets were worn by coastal Yayoi people. It is notable that among the Momenbaru stone coffin burials there were persons who had physical characteristics of both Ryukyu islanders and Yayoi coastal people (Matsushita 2003) (Figure 20 and Plate 3).

The cist grave was universal among coastal Yayoi people. Considering that the coastal Yayoi people in Kyushu were already using bracelets made of broad Pacific Conch at this stage it seems natural that they themselves went to the Ryukyu Islands and were performing shell exchange in the Early Yayoi Period. Such cist graves have been found at Takara Island, Tokunoshima Island, and the main island of Okinawa. Sites yielding this type of cist grave are the Oike Site Locality B, Takara Island (Takarajima 1995, 1997) (Figure 21) the Omonawa Cave No. 1 (Ushinohama and Dogome 1983) and Tomachin (Shinzato 2005).

Reconstruction of shell exchange. Based on the above descriptions, I will provide a reconstruction of the shell trade in Stage 1, with some conjecture (Figure 22).

Yayoi coastal people accumulated trade goods, such as grain, putting them in beautiful pots. In late autumn with the onset of winds from the north they set out along the west coast of Kyushu, resting on the Satsuma Peninsula, loading provisions and arranging their cargo. Evidence from sites and artifacts show that there were satellite communities from northern Kyushu located on the west coast of the Satsuma Peninsula (Kinoshita 1989). Yayoi coastal people used local pilots and interpreters as they moved southward to the Osumi and Tokara Islands. It must have been difficult to cross the Japan Current (Kuroshio) in the Tokara Strait between Kodakara Island and Akuseki Island without being pushed off course. They proceeded carefully through the islands. Arriving in the Okinawa Islands in early winter they selected and stored shells,

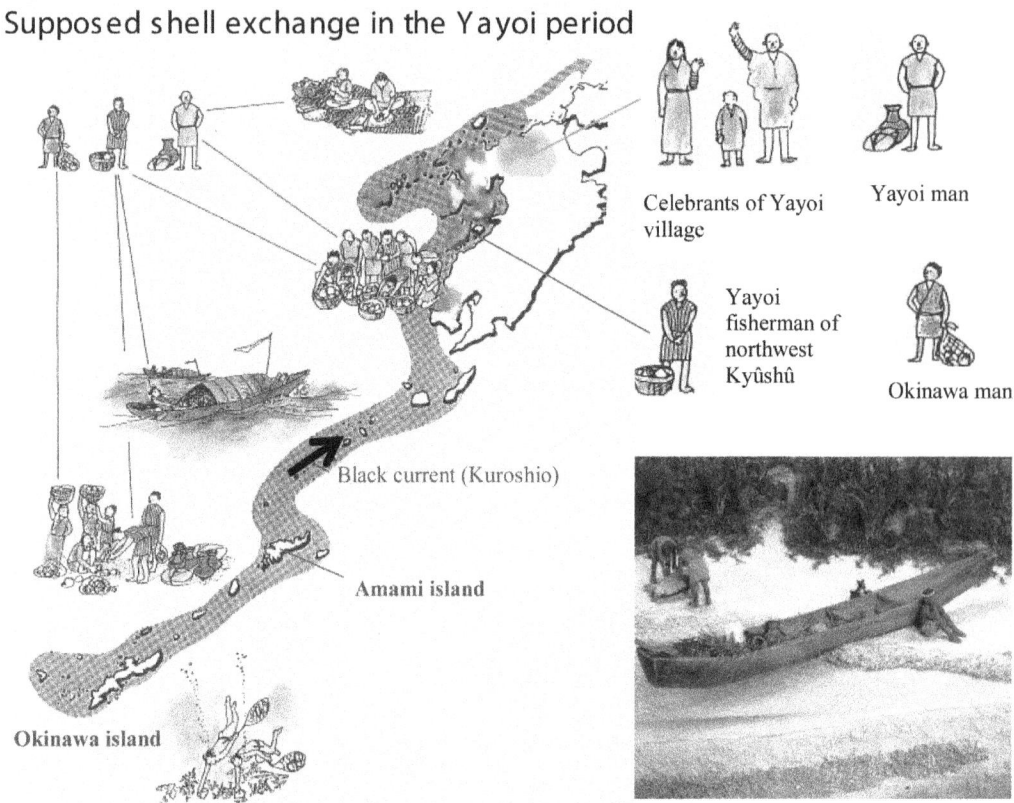

Figure 22. Postulated shell exchange in the Early Yayoi Period.

waiting for spring to come. Some traders intermarried with villagers. With the onset of winds from the south the traders loaded their shells carefully and left for the north, catching the Japan Current and finally arriving at their transit villages on the Satsuma Peninsula. After mending their boats they carried the shells to their final destination in northern Kyushu.

Stage 2 (the latter half) of shell exchange. In the second half of the shell exchange, the northern Kyushu-type of Yayoi pottery is absent and instead there are types from the area of central Kyushu facing the bays of Ariake and Yatsushiro and southern Kyushu. The main areas of shell bracelet distribution are not northern Kyushu but adjacent areas. Shell bracelet distribution shows that they were brought in through the coast of the inland bays of western Kyushu. There are more examples of individuals wearing eight or more bracelets at this stage and there are many more semi-processed bracelets of Broad Pacific Conch. This suggests that coastal people of the west coasts of southern Kyushu and the area of central Kyushu facing the bays of Ariake and Yatsushiro were actively participating in the transport instead of coastal people of northern Kyushu, in Stage 2.

Figure 23 shows the amount of two styles of pottery found in the Okinawa Islands; one style is Yayoi pottery while the other is Amami-style pottery, which imitates Yayoi pottery and was made in the Amami Islands. This figure is based on the data of Takayuki Shinzato (2000). The appearance of Amami-style Yayoi pottery may suggest that Amami people participated in the exchange at this stage. The graph suggests that Amami people replaced Kyushu people as the major agents of shell exchange in the Late Yayoi Period. In Stage 2, Amami people transported shells among the Ryukyu Islands while people of the area of central Kyushu facing the bays of Ariake and Yatsushiro, and northern Kyushu transported the shells within Kyushu.

Changes in Shell Exchange

Shell Exchange in the Kofun Period

With the broad re-organization of Yayoi society in western Kyushu beginning in Late Yayoi (first and second centuries AD) the consumption of shell bracelets in Kyushu declined. It appears that the Ryukyu islanders were not immediately aware of this situation and so the semi-processed shell bracelets continued to be transported and accumulated in the Kyushu coastal villages. They were obtained by the newly emerged class of chiefs in various places in western Japan at the end of the Yayoi Period (the first half of the third century) and the incomplete bracelets were used as new prestige goods. It is important that the role of the shell bracelet changed from a usable accessory to a nonusable symbol of power at this time. When political power formed in the Kinki area in the mid 3rd century, bracelets of Ryukyu shell came to be used as general prestige goods. Then the raw materials for their bracelets, Broad Pacific Conch, Lettered Cone, True Limpet, Spider Conch

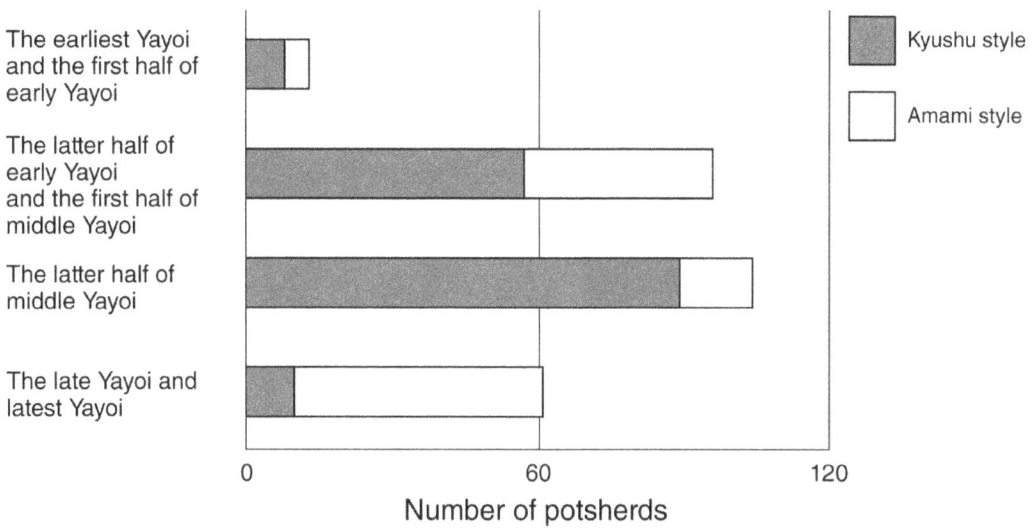

Figure 23. Kyushu style and Amami style Yayoi pottery found in the Okinawa Islands. N=274.

(*Harpago chiragra*), Ram's Murex (*Chicoreus ramosus*), and *Tectus maximus* (also known as *Trochus niloticus*) and others were carried from the Ryukyus in the Early Kofun Period. Spider Conch inhabits the lagoon while the latter two live on the outside of the reef. The coastal people of Amami, the area of central Kyushu facing the bays of Ariake and Yatsushiro, and southern Kyushu continued the shell exchange between the Ryukyus and Kyushu, passing the shells to the maritime people of the Seto Inland Sea. These maritime people carried the shells from Kyushu to the Kinki region of Yamato, the political center (Kinoshita 1996).

Consumption of shell bracelets in the Kinki region declined in the Middle Kofun Period. Then the powerful clans of central and southern Kyushu made bracelets of Broad Pacific Conch, inventing original forms. When the custom of horse riding flourished in the Late Kofun Period (6th century) the use of the top of the Lettered Cone extended to the Kinki Region as material for disk ornaments on saddles and horse trappings.

Consumption of Shells in the Hirota Site

At the end of the Yayoi Period when the consumption of Ryukyu shells declined in Kyushu, shells from Amami and Okinawa began to be used at the Hirota Site of Tanegashima Island, the northernmost island in the Ryukyus. People who wore various accessories made of shell continued to be buried in a cemetery belonging to a settlement dating from the end of the Yayoi Period to the Late Kofun Period (Hirota 2003; Kinoshita 2003; Minami 2007).

Although people of the Hirota site first gathered True Limpets in coastal waters, later they went south to Amami and Okinawa gathering Lettered Cones and Broad Pacific Conch, and produced ornaments such as bracelets, shell plaques and shell pendants with complex patterns in fine relief (Figure 24 and Plate 4). Since the peculiar and

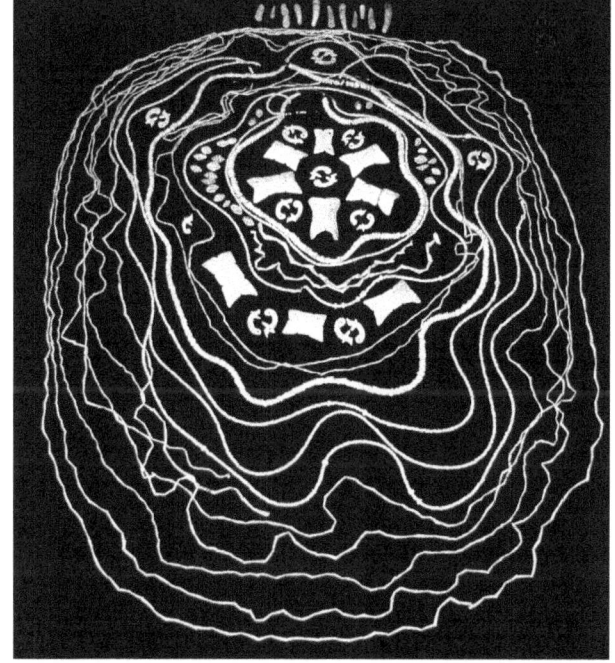

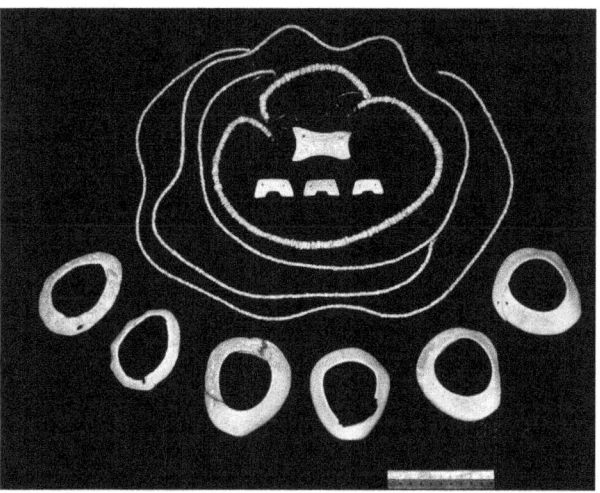

Figure 24. Materials from the Hirota Site, Tanegashima, Kagoshima Prefecture. (Upper) Shell accessories, Hirota Site 4. (Lower) Shell accessories, Hirota Site. D-III.

Figure 25. Great Green Turban shells and their site context.
(Upper) Recent specimen of Great Green Turban.
(Lower) Great Green Turban shells in the Matsunoto Site,
Kagoshima Prefecture, 6th to 7th centuries.

characteristic ornaments of the Hirota Site are found in the Amami and Okinawa Islands and the influence of their artifacts are found in the Hirota Site, there must have been traffic between Hirota and the Islands.

The End of Prehistoric Shell Exchange

Demand for Lettered Cones in mainland Japan decreased sharply and the shell trade concluded at the end of the Kofun Period (7th century). At the same time shell consumption at the Hirota Site declined and the economic relationship between Kyushu and the Ryukyu Islands quickly became distant. In the latter half of the 7th century the central government established a political system leading to the Ritsuryo state with a system of centralized autocracy, taking advantage of political changes in the Imperial Court, introducing Buddhist culture and building many temples. In this way an archaic state of Chinese style was achieved in mainland Japan at the end of the 7th century. Fundamental historical documents of the 8th century mention Ryukyu Islanders. The *Nihon Shoki (Chronicle of Japan)*, an official history of Japan was written in 720 (Kojima et al. 1994). The history from the age of the gods to the end of the 7th century was described. The *Shoku Nihongi (Later Chronicle of Japan)* (Aoki et al. 1989) is also an official history which was completed in 797. The period from the end of the 7th century to the end of the 8th century was described; in these books there are accounts of people living on the southern islands of Tane, Yaku, and other islands as far south as Amami Oshima. There are 7 accounts in the first half of the 7th century, 18 accounts in the latter half of 7th century, 16 accounts in the first half of 8th century, and 10 in the latter half of 8th century.

The fact that the Ryukyu Islands did not appear in the records of the central government until this time (7th to 8th centuries) deserves attention. According to these ancient records, not only Ryukyu islanders but also Ezo/Emishi of northern Japan often appeared in the capital. Scenes of people from remote districts traveling to the capital with interpreters must have epitomized Sinocentrism for the central government, allowing people from remote areas to participate in the high civilization of the center. Moreover contact between the central government and the people from the Ryukyus must have provided some security for Japanese envoys traveling to Tang Dynasty China. What was the significance of these delegations for the Ryukyu side? According to the records, Ryukyu Islanders who went to the capital were trading people on the front line of shell exchange. It is not difficult to imagine that their trip to the capital was aimed at resumption of trade because the 7th century was the time of recent decline of the shell exchange.

Such activity disappeared in the latter half of the 8th century, although the Ryukyu Islanders often sent red sandalwood *akagi*, *Bischofia javanica*, as tribute to the capital. This semi-deciduous tree is similar to rosewood, grows in the tropics and the subtropics. Actual rosewood is a beautiful, hard, red-colored wood used for the wooden pieces of scrolls, musical instruments and other valuable art objects. However it is not found in Japan or the Ryukyu islands. Since the *akagi* timber is also hard and tinged with red, it was regarded as a substitute for rosewood in ancient Japan. At that time true rosewood was imported from China; however *akagi* wood is difficult to work with and was not exchanged on a regular basis. In the latter half of the 8th century, the relationship between the Ryukyu Islands and mainland Japan became distant on both sides.

Ancient and Medieval Shell Trade

Many Great Green Turbans (Figure 25) were gathered in the region centering on Amami Oshima in the 7th century when trade between the Ryukyus and Yamato was declining (Takahashi 2000). Over 3,000 specimens of

Great Green Turbans have been excavated and analyzed from four settlement sites on Amami Oshima Island. As a result it became clear that there were great size differences in the shells. By counting and measuring the *operculi* (lids) which should give the same number as the actual shells, it became clear that there were great differences in the size of the shells gathered from each site. These shells were randomly gathered regardless of size and were accumulated at certain sites for export (Kinoshita 2006, 2007). Although it is difficult to understand the unusual attraction of the Great Green Turban for Amami Islanders, there was a certain kind of trade in them. When production of domestic mother-of-pearl, using the glossy inner surface of the Great Green Turban which originated from China in the 7th to 8th century, began in Japan in the latter half of the 9th century, various handicrafts made from mother-of-pearl on plain and lacquered wood were circulated in China and abroad. In the 10th century mother-of-pearl products became trade goods between Japan and Song China because Japanese mother-of-pearl was of the quality admired in China (Nakazato 1995, 1996). Another shell of interest was the Triton Shell (*Charonia tritonis*), a univalve inhabiting the deep seabed outside the reef. When use of Triton shells in esoteric Buddhist temples of Japan increased, demand for these large conch shells from the Ryukyus also increased (Figure 26).

It is thought that merchants from mainland Japan went to the Ryukyus to secure the Great Green Turbans and Tritons in order to satisfy this demand (Kinoshita 2002b). *Sue* (grey stoneware), *haji*, (reddish earthenware) and salt-making pottery from Kyushu appeared suddenly in the Amami and the Okinawa Islands around the 9th to 10th centuries (Ikeda 2005; Ikehata 1998) as a result of the commerce in shells. From the 11th to 12th centuries consumption of domestic mother-of-pearl grew gradually, increasing as the number of trading ships from Japan came to the Ryukyus. Stone cooking vessels made of steatite and imported porcelain, which were in fashion in mainland Japan were brought in succession to the Ryukyus as goods for exchange. Japanese mainland house styles also affected the design of houses in the Ryukyus during this stage (Nakasone 2004). By such stimulus from Japan the cultivation of grain began on the main island of Okinawa, during the 9th to 10th centuries (Naha Shi 1996) and production of medieval stoneware began on Tokunoshima Island (latter half of 11th century) (Isen Cho 1985a, 1985b, 2001, 2005; Ikeda 2000; A. Shinzato 2002, 2003). A set of stoneware is considered to be necessary for cooking and storing cereals. Thus, the long prehistoric period of the Okinawa Islands came to a close. It is also in this stage that large trading ships reached the Sakishima Islands for the first time (Asato and Harunari 2001), and as the result of this economic behavior the Kerama Gap, a strait of about 200 km between Okinawa and the Sakishima Islands, was overcome. Ancient and medieval shell exchange is regarded as the main factor in ending the prehistoric society of the Ryukyu Islands Kinoshita 2002b).

Figure 26. Triton shell trumpets. (Upper) Buddhist monk playing Triton shell trumpet. (Lower) Triton shell trumpets, Horyuji Temple, Nara Prefecture.

SHELL TRADE WITH THE KOREAN PENINSULA AND CHINA

Shells from the Ryukyu Islands in the Korean Peninsula

In the Korean Peninsula there have been about 100 large tropical conch artifacts found up to now. Most of them are decorative pieces of Lettered Cone that sit in metal decorative pieces attached to straps for saddles and bits where they cross each other. The metal pieces include circular plaques with four or more protuberances fixed to straps on the rear of the horse to keep the saddle in place. These artifacts date from the 5th to 7th centuries. At this time, traffic between the Korean Peninsula and mainland Japan was frequent and since many similar shell pieces were also found in mainland Japan it is clear that these Lettered Cones were brought to the Korean Peninsula from mainland Japan. Earlier than these examples, two Lettered Cones were found in the northern Korean Peninsula in the period parallel to the Yayoi (first century AD). Also raw materials from processing Lettered Cones, personal ornaments, containers and spoons of Great Green Turban, and accessories of *Tectus pyramis*, a shell inhabiting the deep seabed of the lagoon are found from a period parallel to the Kofun Period (Table 1 and Figure 27).

TABLE 1. LARGE-SIZED UNIVALVE SHELL GOODS IN THE KOREAN PENINSULA

STAGE	DISTRICT	KIND OF SHELLS	SHELL ARTIFACT (N)
I Middle of 1st century	Lelang	Lettered Cone Shell	Grave goods put into a bronze jar (2)
II 3rd–4th centuries	Geumgwan Gaya	Lettered Cone shell	Processing scrap material (1), accessory (1)
III 5th century – latter-half of th century	Daegaya	Lettered Cone shell	Decorative parts of hose implement (about 90), ritual decorations
	Baekje (Mohan)	Broad Pacific Conch	Kyushu-style bracelet from a grave (1)
	Silla (Apdok)	Great Green Turbans	Spoon as grave goods (1)
	Unified Silla	Green Top	Ornament (1)

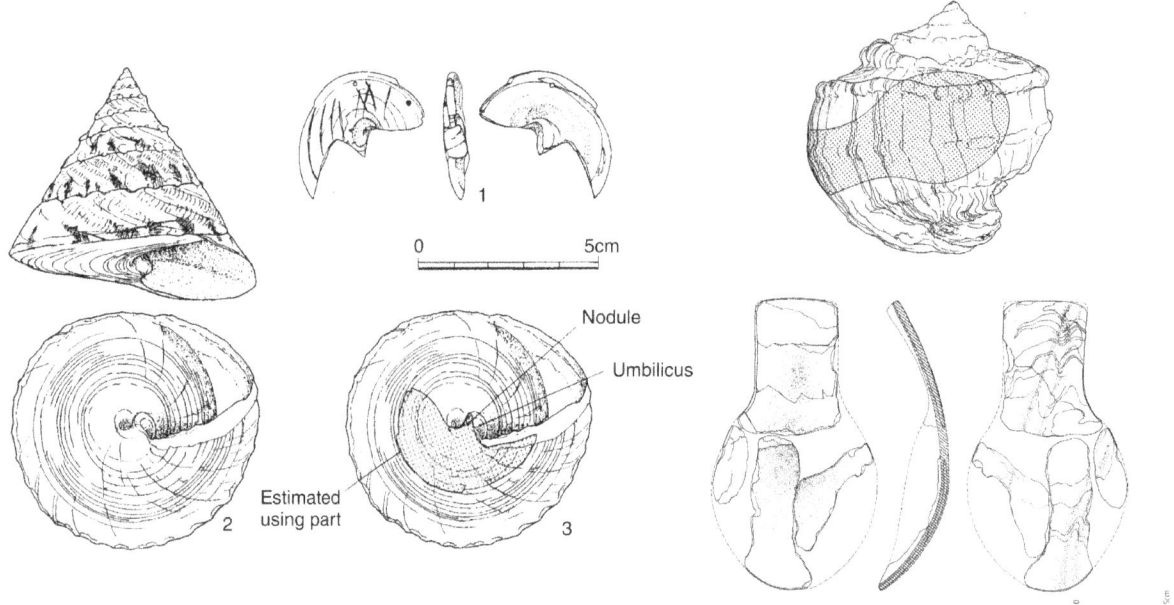

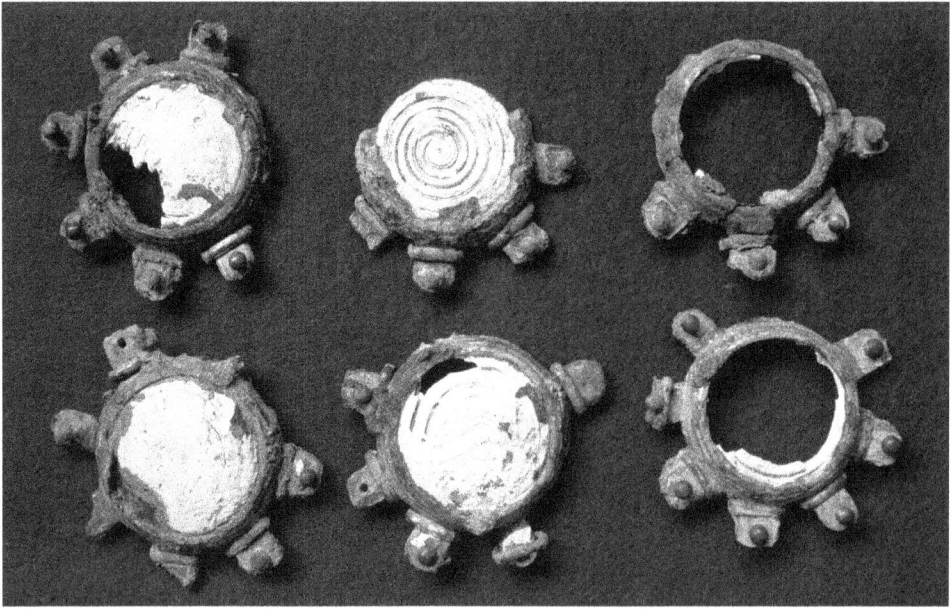

Figure 27. Shell artifacts recovered from Korean sites. (Upper left) 1. Processed fragments of Green Top Shell. 2. Specimen of whole Green Top Shell. 3. Portion used for ornaments, Limdan-dong, Gyeongsan Si, Korea, 4th to 5th centuries. (Upper right above) Diagram showing portion of shell used. Tomb No. 44, Jisan-dong, Goreong-gun, Korea. (Upper right below) Spoon of Great Green Turban. (Below) Lettered Cone shell ornaments for horse gear, Dancung eup, Sancheong gun, Korea, 6th century

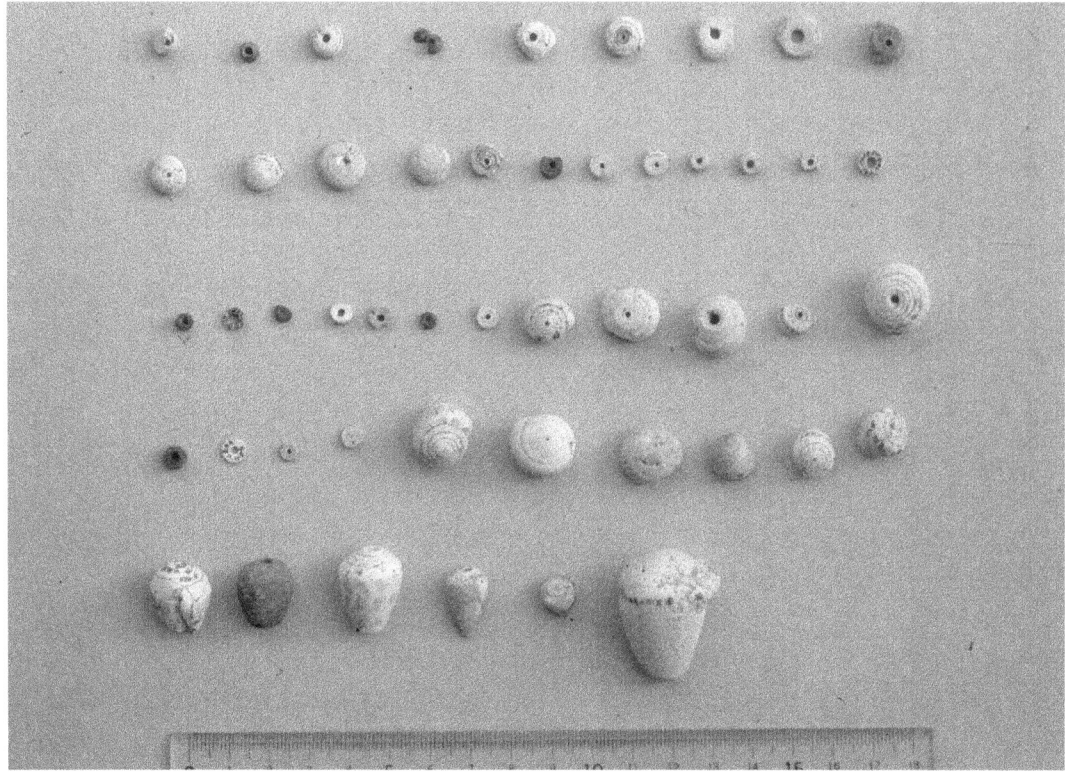

Figure 28. Shell beads, Shimotabaru Shellmound, Hateruma Island, Okinawa, about 1600-1500 BC.

All of these tropical shells are not found near the Korean Peninsula and it is unlikely that they were taken from the Ryukyus through China to Korea. It is more likely that they were sent from the Ryukyus to Korea through Kyushu. Many of them are decorated with unique motifs although a few have the same designs as those from Japan. Horse decorations using Lettered Cone Shell material also appeared in the Silla Dynasty and spread to Japan (Figure 27).

Figure 29. *Kaiyuan tongbao* coin, Yomisaki Site, Amami Oshima Island, Kagoshima Prefecture, 7th century AD. Diameter 24.1 mm, weight 3.35 g. (Kumamoto Daigaku 1996).

Although most of the raw materials for conch artifacts in the Korean Peninsula were from the Ryukyu Islands sent through Japan, people of the Korean Peninsula made types of artifacts to suit local taste and did not copy Japanese types. Cultural differences are clear. Even though they were able to obtain shells, they had no more interest in the large shells and their use ended in the 7th century (Kinoshita 2002*a*).

Shells from the Ryukyu Islands in China

Two subjects concerning relationships between China and the Ryukyus through shells are currently under investigation. The first concerns the use of large quantities of cowry shells in North China from the 13th to 8th centuries BC. Analysis of cowries from Anyang, Henan Province began in 2001 as a joint project between Japan and China and raised the possibility that the east coast of Taiwan was the source of production (Kurozumi 2003). The Yaeyama Islands, from which one can occasionally see the high mountains of Taiwan, may also be included as part of the source area. Small shell beads which commonly appeared in sites from parts of Taiwan where there are coral reefs and in sites in the Yaeyama Islands from this period seem to hint at a solution (Kinoshita 1999, 2002*c*) (Figure 28).

The second subject is the already described Great Green Turban. The interpretation that they were fashioned into spoons and exported from Amami Oshima to mainland Japan is based on analysis of artifacts and historical documents (Takanashi 2000). There is another hypothesis that Great Green Turbans were exported to China, based on the distribution of some 40 Chinese *Kaiyuan tongbao (Jap. Kaigen tsuho)* coins and Chinese *Wushu (Jap. Goshu)* coins in the Ryukyus, which overlaps with the distribution of sites dating to the 7th to 9th centuries AD, where Great Green Turbans have been excavated in large quantities (Kinoshita 2000). The *Kaigen tsuho* coin, which is circular with a square hole in the center, is a typical coin of the Chinese Tang Dynasty. Its casting was begun in 621 and circulated for 286 years (Figure 29).

TABLE 2. SUMMARY OF EXCHANGE OF RYUKYU SHELLS

STAGE	MAIN SHELLS FOR TRADE	PURPOSE OF USE	MAJOR CONSUMER	MAJOR SUPPLIER	INTERMEDIARY OR TRADER
1ST STAGE Yayoi period (9th century BC – 3rd century AD)	Broad Pacific Conch, *S. thersites*, and Lettered Cone shell	Bracelet	Main islands of Japan	Okinawa Islands	Coastal people of Kyushu and Amami people
2ND STAGE Kofun period (3rd–7th centuries AD)	Broad Pacific Conch, Chiragra Spider Conch, and Lettered Cone shell	Prestige goods Horse trapping	Main islands of Japan Korean Peninsula	Okinawa Islands	Coastal people of Kyushu and Amami people
3RD STAGE Ancient period (7–9th centuries AD)	Great Green Turban	Material for mother-of-pearl inlay	Main islands of Japan or China	Amami and Okinawa Islands	
4TH STAGE Ancient and medieval periods (9–15th centuries AD)	Great Green Turban and Conch shell	Material for mother-of-pearl inlay and conch-shell horn	Main islands of Japan	Amami and Okinawa Islands	Japanese merchants

SIGNIFICANCE OF THE SHELL EXCHANGE

Characteristics of Shell Exchange

Table 2 summarizes the stages of the shell exchange in the Ryukyu Islands from the Yayoi Period to medieval times. These can be divided into prehistoric exchanges which mainly involved the Broad Pacific Conch and Lettered Cone Shell (Stages 1 and 2) and ancient and medieval trade based on the Great Green Turban (Stages 3 and 4). Exchange in the prehistoric period has a clear structure in which there were consumers in the north, providers in the south, and carriers in the middle area. It was long-distance exchange in which coastal people of northern Kyushu carried goods in the first half and people from Amami, the area of central Kyushu facing the bays of Ariake and Yatsushiro and southern Kyushu, carried trade goods in a relay system in the second half. In the case of Tanegashima, the consumers themselves went to the source of the shells and obtained raw material for shell ornaments without any specific intermediaries. The exchange of ancient (*kodai*) and medieval times, however, differed from prehistoric exchange since merchants who played an important role in the medieval economy over wide areas appeared, except for Stage 3, in which many points are not yet solved. Through examination of the shell exchange, it is recognized that, as in any exchange, the consumer's side had a motive for acquisition, and those people went to the Ryukyu Islands. During extended trade over a long period of time it is important to note that there is little trace that people living in the source area of the shells went north. The exception is the appearance of Ryukyu islanders at the palace in the capital in the 7th to 8th centuries. Although it seems that the Ryukyu islanders intended to ask for the resumption of the trade, it was not actually resumed.

What Did the Shell Exchange Bring to the Ryukyu Islands?

In the shell exchange during the Yayoi Period, many pieces of Yayoi pottery were sent to the Okinawa Islands as their final destination. The pottery, however, hardly influenced domestic pottery of the Okinawa Islands (Shinzato 2004). Moreover evidence that Okinawans themselves went to Kyushu to get more exchange goods, such as grain and metal artifacts, has not been found. On the other hand, the Amami people who transported goods made pottery imitating Yayoi pottery and carried it into the Okinawa Islands. They also changed the form of their domestic pottery to resemble Yayoi pottery (Kinoshita 2005). Through the shell exchange, Amami people changed their living patterns, but on the other hand, Okinawa people seldom changed their lifestyle. Why was there such a difference? One of the reasons is that Amami people as traders were frequently in contact with people from southern Kyushu. The essential reason, however, is the difference in the reef environment between Amami and Okinawa. In contrast to the Amami Islands which belong to Fringing Reef Area 1, an extremely stable life was guaranteed by the reefs of the Okinawa Islands, which belong to Fringing Reef Area 2. It seems that local culture in the Okinawa Islands was stable and resistant to change. The center of gravity of culture was not moved easily.

Shell exchange in ancient and medieval times brought the newest cultural items of mainland Japan throughout the Ryukyu Islands. In this way the Ryukyu islanders began to practice agriculture and accepted Japanese medieval living patterns. Then the prehistoric period of thousands of years in the Ryukyu Islands finished and the door toward formation of the Ryukyu Dynasty opened.

Structure of Shell Exchange

The Ryukyu Islands are "tropical islands" extending in a line north and south in maritime East Asia. Their isolation has given absolute scarcity value to their shells. Growth of the coral reefs yielding these resources took place around 1500 to 1000 BC and was completed after that date. Therefore it can be said that stability in time and space for about 3,000 years was the basis of the shell exchange. The environment of the islands with coral reefs shows a gradual north/south transition creating differences that divided the islanders within the shell exchange, from the prehistoric period, between gatherer and transporter. The history of these two groups diverged. The common environment of the fringing reef created one large habitat for the distribution of Great Green Turbans throughout the islands.

If the islanders had not moved their settlements to the beach at the time of the completion of the coral reefs, creating a field for the shell exchange, and if they had not used various shells, there would not have been activity from people outside the islands, to be stimulated to obtain certain shells. In addition, Ryukyu islanders would not have been asked to supply the Great Green Turban if advanced craft skills had not already developed in the surrounding areas. In the Ryukyu Islands, shell exchange continued for 2,000 years because there was a complementary multi-layered structure of nature and culture.

The original version of this article written in Japanese was translated into English by Yoshimi Kawashukuda, and proofing assistance was afforded by David McMurray at The International University of Kagoshima. Subsequently the article was edited by Richard Pearson.

REFERENCES CITED

ABBOTT, RICHARD T. AND S. PETER DANCE
1985   *Sekai Kaisan Kairui Daizukan [Compendium of Seashells]*. Trans. Tadashige Habe and Takashi Okutani. Tokyo: Heibonsha.

AOKI, KAZUO, KOJI INAOKA, HARUO SASAYAMA, AND REIKO SHIRAFUJI
1989-1998   *Shoku Nihongi [Latter Chronicles of Japan]*. Tokyo: Iwanami Shoten.

ASATO, SUSUMU AND HIDEJI HARUNARI (EDS.)
2001   *Okinawa-ken Odomarihama Kaizuka [The Odomarihama Shell Mound, Okinawa Prefecture, Japan]*. Kokogaku Senshu, 27, Grant-in-Aid for Scientific Research on Priority Areas A (1), The Ministry of Education, Culture, Sports, Science and Technology. Sakura. Chiba: The National Museum of Japanese History.

HABE, TADASHIGE (EDITORIAL SUPERVISOR)
1975   *The Mollusks of Japan, 1*. Tokyo: Gakken.

HIROTA ISEKI GAKUJUTSU CHOSA KENKYUKAI (ED.)
2003   *Tanegashima Hirota Iseki [Tanegashima Hirota Site]*. Kagoshima: Kagoshima Kenritsu Rekishi Shiryuo Senta–Reimeikan.

HORI, NOBUYUKI
1980   Amami Shoto ni okeru gensei sangosho no cho chikei kosei to minzoku bunrui [The microtopological composition and folk-classification of live coral reefs in the Amami Islands]. *Jinrui Kagaku* 32:187–224.

1990   Nihon no Sangosho [Coral reefs in Japan]. In *Nihon no Sangosho Chiiki, Atsui Shizen-Sangosho no Kankoki [Tropics in Japan: Natural history of coral islands, Series of Coral Islands in Japan]*, 1:3–22, ed. Sangosho Chiiki Kenkyu Gurupu. Tokyo: Kokon Shoin.

IKEDA, YOSHIFUMI
2000   Ruisueki kara mita Ryukyu Retto no koeki shi [The exchange history of exchange in the Ryukyu Islands through investigation of *Ruisueki* ware]. *Kodai Bunka [Cultura Antiqua]* 52:34–38.

2005   Kaneku shiki doki hanshutsu gairai doki no keifu to nendai [Genealogy and age of foreign pottery associated with the Kaneku type pottery]. In *Kominato Fuwaganeku Iseki-gun [Kominato Fuwaganeku Sites]* 1:134–148, ed. Naze Board of Education. Kagoshima: Naze Board of Education.

IKEHATA KOICHI
1998   Kokogaku shiryo kara mita kodai no Amami Oshima to minami Kyushu [The ancient Amami Islands and southern Kyushu through archaeological data]. In *Retto no Kokogaku: Watanabe Makoto Sensei Kanreki Kinen Ronshu [Archaeology of the Archipelago: Prof. Makoto Watanabe's Sixtieth Birthday Memorial Essays]*: 733–743, ed. Watanabe Makoto Sensei Koki Kinen Ronshu Kankokai. Iwaki. Fukushima: Watanabe Makoto Sensei Koki Kinen Ronshu Kankokai.

ISEN CHO KYOIKU IINKAI
1985a   *Kamuiyaki Koyoseki-gun [Kamuiyaki Kilns]*, 1. Isen, Kagoshima: Isen Cho Kyoiku Iinkai.

1985b   *Kamuiyaki Koyoseki-gun [Kamuiyaki Kilns]*, 2. Isen, Kagoshima: Isen Cho Kyoiku Inkai.

2001   *Kamuiyaki Koyoseki-gun [Kamuiyaki Kilns]*, 3. Isen, Kagoshima: Isen Cho Kyoiku Iinkai.

2005   *Kamuiyaki Koyoseki-gun [Kamuiyaki Kilns]*, 4. Isen, Kagoshima: Isen-cho Kyoiku Iinkai.

KAGOSHIMA KEN (ED.)

1983   *Kagoshima Ken 1/50,000 Tochi Bunrui Kihon Chosa: Chikei Bunrui Zu [Fundamental Investigation for Land Classification 1/50,000: the Landform Classification Maps [Detached island parts]]*. Kagoshima: Kagoshima Ken.

KAIZUKA, SOHEI, HIROSHI NARUSE, AND YOKO OTA

1985   *Nihon no Heiya to Kaigan [Plain and Seashore in Japan]*. Nihon no Shizen [Nature in Japan] 4. Tokyo: Iwanami Shoten.

KAN, HIRONOBU, NOBUYUKI HORI, TOSHIO KAWANA, AND KIYOSHI ICHIKAWA

1997   The evolution of a Holocene fringing reef and island: Reef environmental sequence and sea level changing in Tonaki Island, the Central Ryukyus. *Atoll Research Bulletin* 443:1–20.

KAWANA, TOSHIO

2006a   Kaigan chikei to shizen saigai [Coastal landform and natural disaster]. In *Senshi Ryukyu no Seigyo to Koeki: Amami Okinawa no Hakkutsu Chosa kara [Subsistence and Exchange in Prehistoric Ryukyus Based on Excavations in Amami and Okinawa]*: 31–39, The Research Report of Grant-in-Aid for Scientific Research (A) (2), 2002–2005, The Ministry of Education, Culture, Sports, Science and Technology, ed. Naoko Kinoshita. Kumamoto: Department of Literature, Kumamoto University.

2006b   Okinawajima tonanbu to sono shuhento no sango shitsu taisekibutsu kara suitei sareru yaku 3400 nen mae no onami no shurai [Invasion of about 3400 cal BP large wave in the southeastern Okinawa Island and the surroundings, the Ryukyus, Japan, as deduced from coralline deposits]. *Bulletin of Faculty of Education, University of the Ryukyus* 68:265–271.

KINOSHITA, NAOKO

1988   Nihon retto no kodai kaibunka shiron [An essay about the ancient shell culture of the Japanese Islands]. *Nihon Kenkyu: Bulletin of International Research Center for Japanese Studies* 18:11–33.

1989   Nankaisan kai udewa koeki ko [A consideration about the trade of shell bracelets produced in the Southern Seas]. In *Seisan to Ryutsu no Kokogaku: Yokoyama Koichi Sensei Koki Kinen Ronbun-shu [Archaeology of Production and Circulation: Prof. Koichi Yokoyama's Retirement Memorial Essays]* 1: 203–249. Fukuoka: Yokoyama Koichi Sensei Taikan Kinen Jigyokai.

1996   Kofun jidai nanto koeki ko [A consideration about exchange in the Southern Islands in the Kofun period]. *Kokogaku Zasshi* 81(1): 1–81.

1999   Dong ya beiju wenhua kao [A consideration about the culture of shell ornaments in East Asia]. In *The Seventh Zhong Liu Li Shi Guan Xi Guo Ji Xue Shu Hui Yi Lun Wen Ji*. Taipei: Zhong Liu Wen Hua Jing Ji Xie Hui.

2000   Kaigen tsuho to yakogai: 7-9 seiki no Ryukyu Chu koeki shiron [Kaiyuan Tongbao Coin and Great Green Turban: An essay about trade between Ryukyu and China in the 7-9th centuries]. In *Ryukyu Higashi-ajia no Hito to Bunka: Takamiya Hiroe Sensei Koki Kinen Ronbun-shu [People and culture of Ryukyu and East Asia: Prof. Hiroe Takamiya's Seventieth Birthday Memorial Essays]*, vol. 1: 187–219, ed. Nishibaru Cho. Okinawa: Takamiya Hiroe Sensei Koki Kinen Ronshu Kankokai.

2002a   Kan hanto no Ryukyu retto san kai seihin: 1-7 seiki o taisho ni [Shell products from the Ryukyu Islands in the Korean Peninsula: During the 1st-7th centuries]. In *Kan-hanto Kokogaku Ronso*: 503–544, ed. Tadashi Nishitani et al. Tokyo: Suzusawa Shoten.

2002b   Koeki to kokka keisei: 9 seiki kara 13 seiki o taisho ni [Shell trade and state formation: During the 9-13th centuries]. In *Senshi Ryukyu no Seigyo to Koeki [Subsistence and Exchange in Prehistoric Ryukyus]*: 117–144, The Research Report of Grant-in-Aid for Scientific Research (B) (2), 1999-2001, The Ministry of Education, Culture, Sports, Science and Technology, ed. Naoko Kinoshita. Kumamoto: Kinoshita Laboratory, Department of Literature, Kumamoto University.

2002c   Kodai Chugoku kara mita Ryukyu Retto no takara gai [Cowries of the Ryukyu Islands in the context of ancient China]. In *Sekai ni Hiraku Okinawa Kenkyu: Dai 4 Kai Okinawa Kenkyu Kokusai Shinpojiumu [Okinawa Studies Opened in the World: The 4th International Symposium for Okinawa Studies]*: 182–191, ed. The 4th Committee for the International Symposium on Okinawa Studies. Naha: The 4th Committee for the International Symposium on Okinawa Studies.

2003 Kai soshingu kara mita Hirota iseki [The Hirota site from the viewpoint of shell accessories]. In *Tanegashima Hirota Site*: 329–366, ed. Hirota Iseki Gakkujutsu Kenkyukai. Kagoshima: Kagoshima Kenritsu Rekishi Shiryuo Senta–Reimeikan.

2005 Kai koeki kara mita ibunka sesshoku- ontai to anettai no sesshoku [Cultural contact from the viewpoint of shell trade: contact between the temperate zone and the subtropical zone]. *Kokogaku Kenkyu: Quarterly of Archaeological Studies* 52(2): 25–41.

2006 Yakogai koeki no kanosei: 6-8 seiki no Amami Oshima mitsu no iseki o taisho ni [Examination of the Great Green Turban trade: Analysis of three sites in Amami Oshima during the 6-8th centuries]. In *Senshi Ryukyu no Seigyo to Koeki: Amami Okinawa no Hakkutsu Chosa kara [Subsistence and Exchange in Prehistoric Ryukyus Based on Excavations in Amami and Okinawa]*: 201–203, The Research Report of Grant-in-Aid for Scientific Research (A) (2), 2002-2005, The Ministry of Education, Culture, Sports, Science and Technology, ed. Naoko Kinoshita. Kumamoto: Department of Literature, Kumamoto University.

2007 Yakogai tairyo shutsudo iseki no kento; 6-8 seiki Amami oshima no yotsu no iseki o taisho ni [Analysis of four sites with the large quantities of Great Green Turbans: Analysis four sites in Amami Oshima during the 6-8th centuries]. *Bungakubu Ronso: Kumamoto Journal of Culture and Humanities* 93:1–22.

KISHIMOTO, YOSHIHIKO, AKIRA NISHIME, HIROKI MIYAGI, AND MITSURU AZUMA

2000 Okinawa hennen koki no doki yoso ni tsuite [Pottery in the Okinawan Late Shellmound Period]. In *Ryukyu Higashi Ajia no Hito to Bunka: Takamiya Hiroe Sensei Koki Kinen Ronbun Shu [People and Culture of Ryukyu and East Asia: Professor Hiroe Takamiya's Seventieth Birthday Memorial Essays]*: 131–152, ed. Takamiya Hiroe Sensei Koki Kinen Roshu Kankokai. Nishihara Cho, Okinawa: Takamiya Sensei Koki Kinen Ronshu Kankokai.

KISHIMOTO, YOSHIHIKO AND HIROSHI SHIMA

1985 Okinawa ni okeru kai no shuseki iko-gohora, imogai chushin [The features consisting of accumulated shells in Okinawa: Broad Pacific Conch and Lettered Cone shell]. *Kiyo [Bulletin of Okinawa Prefectural Board of Education]* 2:49–68.

KOJIMA, NORIYUKI, KAZUTAMI NISHINOMIYA, SUSUMU MORI, AND MASANORI MORI

1994–98 *Nihon Shoki: Shinpen Nihon Koten Bungaku Sosho Zenshu [Chronicles of Japan: Compiled New Edition of Japanese Classical Literature]*, Vol. 2–4. Tokyo: Shogakkan.

KUMAMOTO DAIGAKU KOKOGAKU KENKYUSHITSU

1996 *Yomisaki Iseki: Kenkyushitsu Hokoku 31 [Yomisaki Site: Report of Department of Archaeology 31]*. Kumamoto: Kumamoto University.

KUNAICHO SHOSOIN JIMUSHO

1996 *Annual Report of the Office of the Shosoin Treasure House, 18*. Nara: Office of the Shosoin Treasure House.

KUROZUMI, TAIJI

1994 Otsutanoha no kyokuchi [The supplying district of True Limpet shell]. *Nanto Koko*:14, 57–64.

2003 Kairuigaku kara mita chugoku kodai iseki shutsudo kairui no kyokuchi: takaragai chushin ni [The supplying district of shell excavated from ancient sites in China from the viewpoint of malacology: Mainly cowries]. In *Chugoku Kodai Takara-gai Shiyo to Ryutsu, sono Imi [Cowries in Ancient China, Mainly Shang and Chou Dynasty: Use, Circulation, and Meaning]*: 12–40, Handout of Public Symposium Department of Archaeology, Kumamoto University. Kumamoto: Department of Archaeology, Kumamoto University.

MATSUSHITA, TAKAYUKI

2003 Okinawa Ken Yomitan Son Momenbaru iseki shutsudo no Yayoi jidai jinkotsu [The Human skeletal bones excavated from Momenbaru site, Yomitan-son, Okinawa, in Yayoi period]. *Nanto Koko* 22:67.

MEZAKI, SHIGEKAZU

1985 *Ryukyu-ko o Saguru [Exploring Ryukyu Arc]*. Ginowan, Okinawa: Aki Shobo.

MINAMI TANE CHO KYOIKU IINKAI

2007 *Hirota Iseki [Hirota Site]*. Minami Tane Cho: Minami Tane Cho Kyoiku Iinkai.

MORIMOTO, ISAO

2005 Kairui shuseki iko ni tsuite [Storage caches of shells]. In *Sesokojima Anchinoue Kaizuka [Sesoko Island Anchinoue Shellmound]*: 213–214, ed. Motobu Cho Kyoiku Iinkai. Motobu Cho: Motobu Cho Kyoiku Iinkai.

NAGAI, MASAFUMI AND NAOICHI KOKUBU

1978   Udewa no chakuso [Wearing of shell bracelets]. *Etunosu* 10.

NAHA SHI KYOIKU IINKAI

1996   *Nazakibaru Iseki [Nazakibaru Site]*. Naha: Naha City Board of Education.

NAKAMORI, TORU AND AKI OTA

2001   Gaisetsu [Outline]. In *Nihon no Chikei [Regional Geomorphology of the Japanese Islands]*, 7, *Kyushu Nansei-shoto [Geomorphology of Kyushu and the Ryukyus]*: 220–232. Tokyo: Tokyo University Press.

NAKASONE, MOTOMU

2004   Gusuku jidai kaishiki no hottate bashira tatemono ni tsuite no ichi kosai [One conception of dug post buildings of the beginning of the Gusuku Period]. In *Gusuku Jidai o Kangaeru [Thinking About the Gusuku Period]*: 269–288, eds. Nakijin Son Kyoiku Iinkai. Tokyo: Shin Jimbutsu Oraisha.

NAKAZATO, HISAYOSHI

1995   Kodai raden no kenkyu-jo [Study of ancient mother-of-pearl inlay first part]. *Kokka*, 1199, 3–18.

1996   Kodai raden no kenkyu-ge [Study of ancient mother-of-pearl inlay, latter part]. *Kokka*, 1203, 19–26.

OBATA, HIROKI, ISAO MORIMOTO AND SUSUMU KADOBUCHI

2004   Ryukyu retto shutsudo no kokuyoseki to kagaku bunseki ni yoru sanchi suitei to sono igi [Chemical source analysis and its meaning of the obsidian implements excavated from the Ryukyu Islands]. *Stone Sources* 4: 101–136.

ODA, FUJIO

1974   Nihon de umareta seidoki [Bronze ware made in Japan]. In *Kodaishi Hakkutsu [Excavating Ancient History]* 5:137–149, ed. Takayasu Higuchi. Tokyo: Kodansha.

OKINAWA KEN KYOIKU IINKAI

1980   *Ohara: Kumejima Ohara Kaizuka Gun Hakkutsu Chosa Hokokusho [Ohara: Report of the Excavation of the Ohara Shellmound Group on Kume Island]*. Naha: Okinawa Ken Kyoiku Iinkai.

OKINAWA KEN (ED.)

1983   *Okinawa Ken 1/50,000 Tochi Bunrui Kihon Chosa: Chikei Bunrui Zu [Fundamental Investigation for Land Classification 1/50,000: the Landform Classification Maps]*. Naha: Okinawa Ken.

SHIMABUKURO, HARUMI

2004   Iseki betsu ni nuru Amami, Okinawa no kai seihin [Examination of shell goods according to sites in the Amami and Okinawa Islands]. *Kokoshiryo Taikan* 12:231. Tokyo: Shogakkan.

SHIMABUKURO, SHINZO AND TAKESHI TOGUCHI

1990   Ino no chikei to chimei [Geographical features and place name of Ino]. *Minzoku Bunka [Folk Culture]* 2:234–263.

SHINZATO, AKITO

2002   Kaseki ishinabe no kisokuteki kenkyu [Fundamental study of talc vessels]. In *Senshi Ryukyu no Seigyo to Koeki [Subsistence and Exchange in Prehistoric Ryukyus]*: 163–190, The Research Report of Grant-in-Aid for Scientific Research (B) (2), 1999-2001, The Ministry of Education, Culture, Sports, Science and Technology, ed. Naoko Kinoshita. Kumamoto: Kinoshita Laboratory, Department of Literature, Kumamoto University.

2003   Ryukyu retto ni okeru yogyo seisana no seiritsu to tenkai [Formation and development of pottery-industry production in the Ryukyu archipelago]. *Kokogaku Kenkyu: Quarterly of Archaeological Studies* 49(4):75–95.

SHINZATO, TAKAYUKI

2000   Kyushu, Nansei Shoto ni okeru Yayoi jidai heikoki no doki ido ni tsuite: kisokuteki sagyo [Movement of the pottery in the parallel stage of Yayoi period in Kyushu and the Southwest Islands: A fundamental study]. *Taiga* 7:237–257.

2004   Okinawa Shoto no doki [Pottery in the Okinawa Islands]. *Kokoshiryo Taikan* 12:203–212. Tokyo: Shogakkan.

2005   Tokunoshima Isen Cho Kinen, Saben sakyu itai iseki Tomachin chiku hakkutsu chosa gaiho [Brief report of excavation at Tomachin area in Kinen and Saben dune sites, Isen-cho, Tokunoshima]. *Amami News Letter* 15:5–14.

TAKAKURA, HIROAKI

1975   Migite no fushiyo: nankaisan makigai kai udewa chakuso no igi [Non-use of the right-hand: The meaning of wearing the shell-bracelets made of univalve shell from the Southern Marine]. *Kyushu Rekishi Shiryokan Kenkyu Ronshu* 1:1–32.

TAKAMIYA, HIROE AND ISAMU CHINEN (EDS.)

2004   Kaizuka koki bunka [The Culture of the Late Shellmound Period]. *Kokoshiryo Taikan* 12. Tokyo: Shogakkan.

TAKANASHI, OSAMU

2000   Yakogai no koeki no kokogaku [Archaeology of Great Green Turban trade], *Gendai no Kokogaku [Contemporary Archaeology]*, 5, *Koryu no Kokogaku [Archaeology of Interaction]*: 228–265, ed. H. Ogawa. Tokyo: Asakura Shoten.

TAKARAJIMA OIKE ISEKI HAKKUTSU CHOSADAN

1995   Tokara retto Takarajima Oike iseki [Brief report of the excavation of Oike on Takarajima Island, Tokara Islands]. *Bulletin of the National Museum of Japanese History* 60:261–282.

1997   Tokara retto Takarajima Oike iseki tokutei kenkyu "Retto nai shobunka no sogo koryu no kenkyu" 1993 nendo hakkutsu gaiho [Brief report of the excavation of Oike on Takarajima Island, Tokara Islands, "Study of interaction of culture in islands"]. *Bulletin of the National Museum of Japanese History* 70:219–251.

TATEIWA ISEKI CHOSA IINKAI (ED.)

1977   *Tateiwa Iseki [Tateiwa Site]*. Tokyo: Kawade Shobo Shinsha.

UKU MACHI KYOIKU IINKAI

1997   *Uku Matsubara Iseki [Uku Matsubara Site]*. Uku, Nagasaki: Uku-machi Kyoiku Iinkai.

UMEHARA, SUEJI

1959   *Chosen Kobunka Sokan [Conspectus of Korean Ancient Culture]*, 3. Tanba, Kyoto: Yotoku Sha.

USHINOHAMA, OSAMU AND HIDETO DOGOME

1983   *Omonawa Daiichi Daini Kaizuka [Omonawa No.1 Shell Mound and No. 2 Shell Mound]*. Isen, Kagoshima: Isen Cho Kyoiku Iinkai.

WAJINDEN NO MICHI KENKYUKAI

1980   *Yamataikoku e no Michi [The Road to Yamataikoku]*. Fukuoka: Asahi Shinbunsha.

YOBUKO MACHI KYOIKU IINKAI

1981   *Otomo Iseki [Otomo Site]*. Yobuko Machi: Yobuko Machi Kyoiku Iinkai.

Kamuiyaki and Early Trade in the Ryukyu Islands

AKITO SHINZATO
BOARD OF EDUCATION, ISEN TOWNSHIP, TOKUNOSHIMA

INTRODUCTION

A production economy (*seisan keizai*) began in the Ryukyu Islands in the 11th century for the purpose of trading commercial goods in which cultural goods from Kyushu and China were spread as far as the Sakishima Islands. The special feature of cultural unification resulted from this trading throughout the area from the Tokara Islands to Sakishima (Figure 1). It was also in this time period that a hard-fired ceramic termed *kamuiyaki* came to be made in Tokunoshima. It was used throughout the Ryukyu Islands for serving food along with other local and imported ceramics (Figure 2).

The name *kamuiyaki* is derived from the locality where the production sites were discovered, Kameyaki or Kamuiyaki (Figure 3) (Isen 1985a, 1985b, 2001, 2005). The kilns are of subterranean type, made by digging into a slope to make an open space. The entrance of the firing chamber is narrow and the horizontal plan has a fig shape (a narrow entrance with an expanded chamber) (Figure 4). From the dating of the kiln sites, production continued from the 11th century to the 13th century.

The ceramics are blackish grey, and many have a particular wavy incised line decoration. The forms include narrow neck jars (*tsubo*), wide mouth jars (*hachi*), bowls (*wan*), deep jars (*kame*), and spouted ewers (Figures 5, 6, Plate 5). The ceramics are closely related to Japanese medieval grey stoneware (*sueki*). They also resemble Koryo stoneware from the Korean Peninsula, thus having mixed characteristics from Japan and Korea. Yoshioka (2002) termed them Southern Islands Medieval Grey Stoneware. *Kamuiyaki* is the first kiln-fired ceramic of the Ryukyus. It provides archaeological evidence of the achievement of a new economic level of production and exchange in the Ryukyus, In this paper, I wish to consider the analysis of *kamuiyaki* in terms of production, exchange, and consumption and the implications of these for the development of economic relations within the region.

HISTORY OF RESEARCH

Kamuiyaki has been known since the 1950s (Tawada 1956). From the 1960s materials accumulated from the investigation of *gusuku*, resulting in studies using different methods. These studies can be placed into three large groups.

1. Typological studies of sites and artifacts to create a chronology. On the basis of chronology there were studies of Ryukyu economic exchange and the development of political strata, which led to the emergence of the Ryukyu Kingdom, and reconstruction of historical development (Sato 1970; Asato 1975, 1988, 1990, 1991; Onishi 1996).

2. Investigations of the forms of the kilns and techniques of manufacture of the ceramics and the kilns along with the technical derivation and economic conditions (Shirakihara 1999; Nishitani 1981; Akashi 1999; Ogino 1993; Yoshioka 1994, 2002; Shinzato 2004). These two kinds of studies made continuous progress before the discovery of the kiln sites.

3. Studies of the conditions under which the ceramics were discovered, typological grouping and refined studies of kiln distribution and the temporal changes of products, the construction of the kilns, and the nature of the kiln area (Yoshioka 2002; Shinzato 2003a, 2003b; Ikeda 2005). These have continued from the discovery of the kiln in 1983 (Gi and Yotsumoto 1984) to the investigation of the production sites (Isen Cho 1985a, 1985b, 2001, 2005). Recent studies have been devoted to the understanding of the actual nature of production. There have been natural scientific studies along with the archaeological studies, and analysis of the clay paste of the ceramics from various parts of the Ryukyus. There have also been studies of production and consumption (Mitsuji 2001) and studies which combine themes in archaeology and natural science, which prepare the basic research environment of *kamuiyaki*.

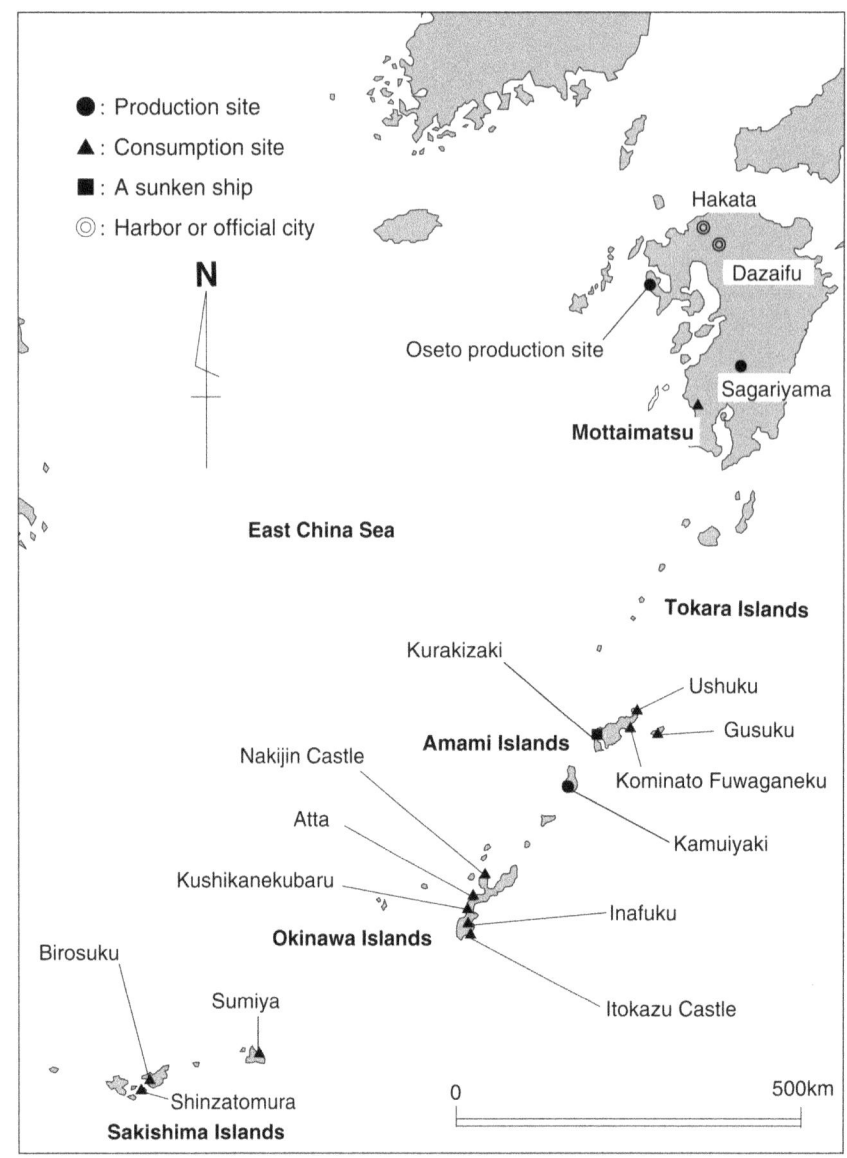

Figure 1. Sites mentioned in the text.

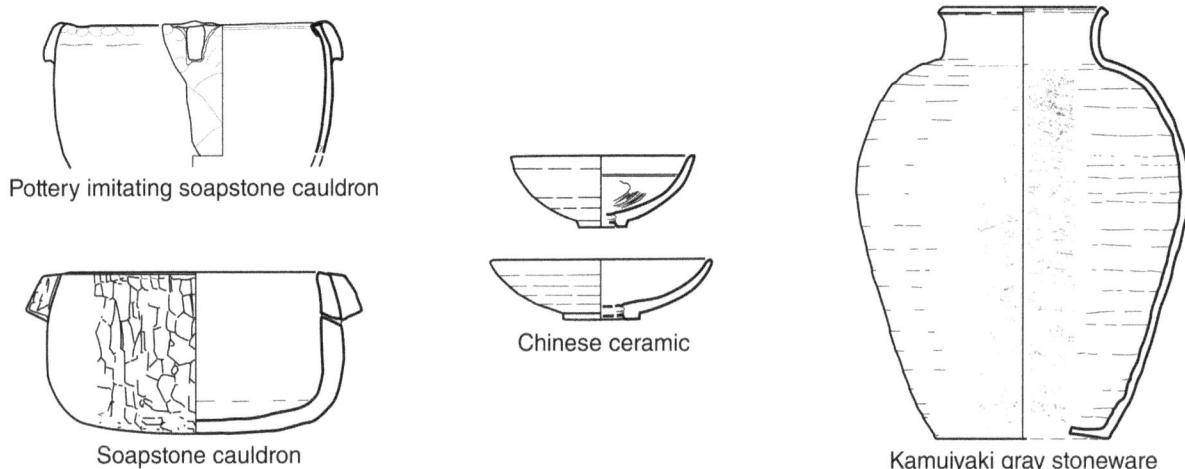

Figure 2. Food serving wares found in the Ryukyu Islands.

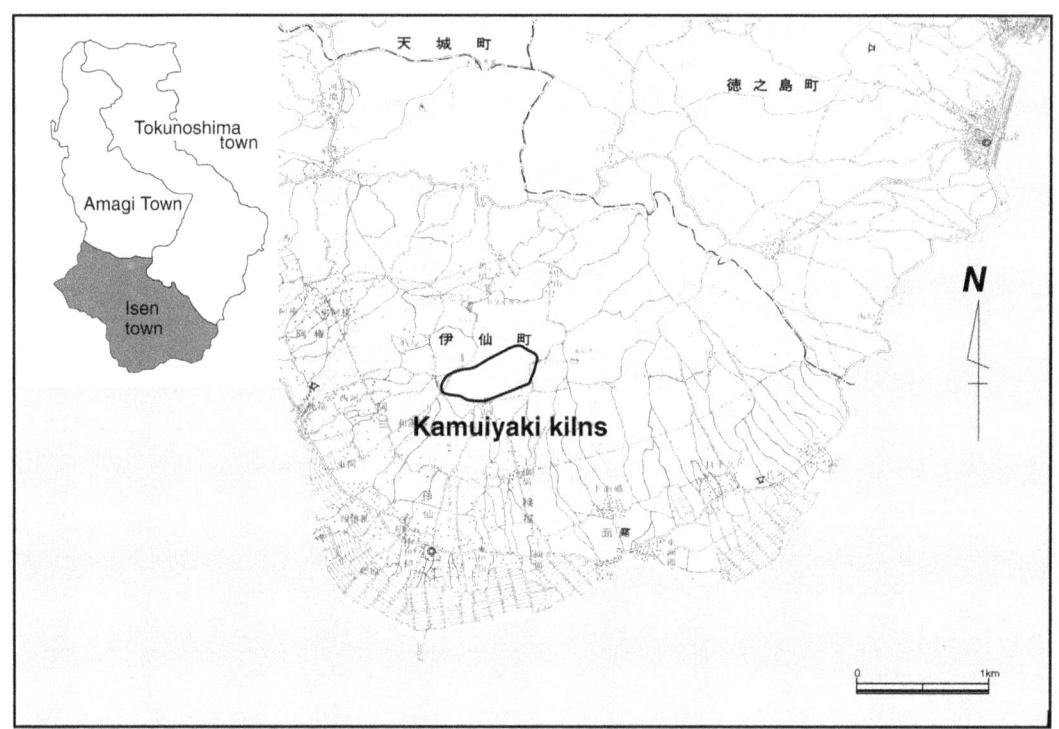
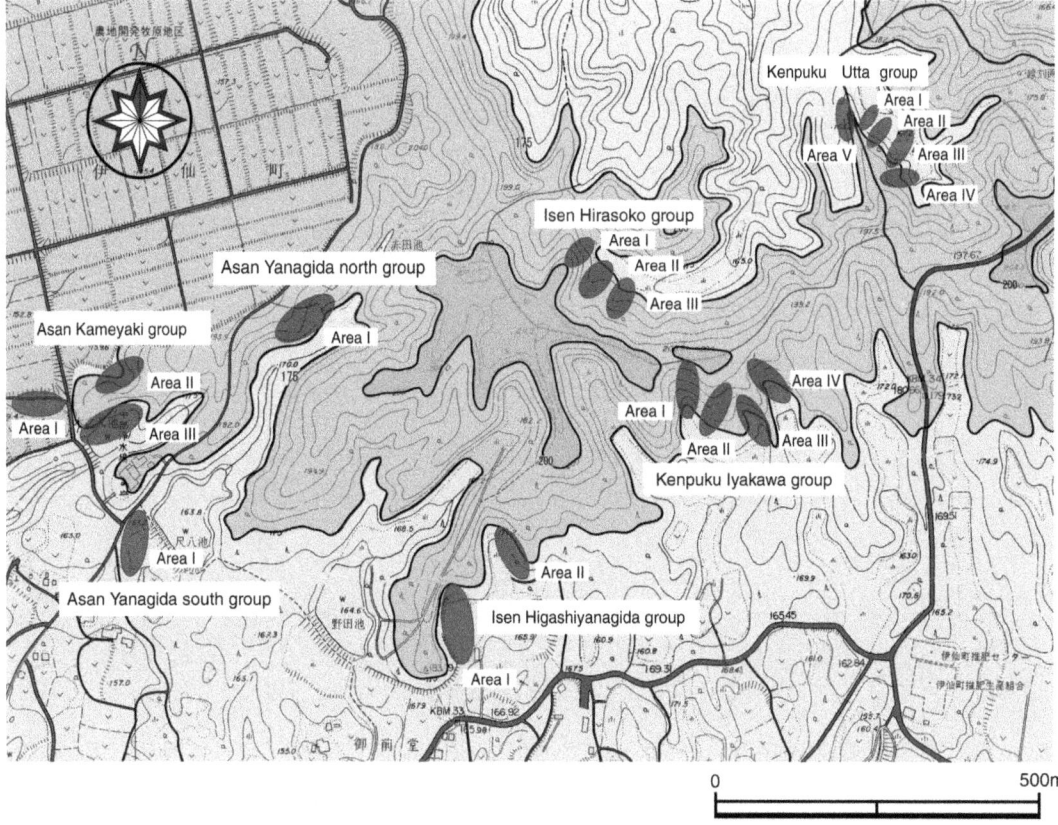

Figure 3. Location of Kamuiyaki kilns.

Up to the present, studies of *kamuiyaki* production, exchange, and consumption have shown that Ryukyus circulation changed step-by-step. I've reviewed below the results of these studies up to the present, organizing production and consumption into stages and proposing the ways in which the form of the exchange changed. From there I examined the distribution of vessel types in different areas of the Ryukyus.

PRODUCTION OF *KAMUIYAKI* CERAMICS

In order to understand *kamuiyaki* production, investigation has proceeded in the following manner. *Kamuiyaki* can be divided into two broad types. Temporal typological changes of the two types are shown in Figure 6. In Group A the vessel wall is thin, the firing is hard and fine, there are traces of stamping on the surface, and the interior surface shows traces of crossing lines made by stamping and wiping. Vessel forms are narrow neck jars (*tsubo*), wide mouth jars (*hachi*), and bowls (*wan*). Group B is thick walled, and the exterior stamping has been erased by wiping and scraping. The interior surfaces have fine horizontal lines. On the narrow neck jars of Group A, clay

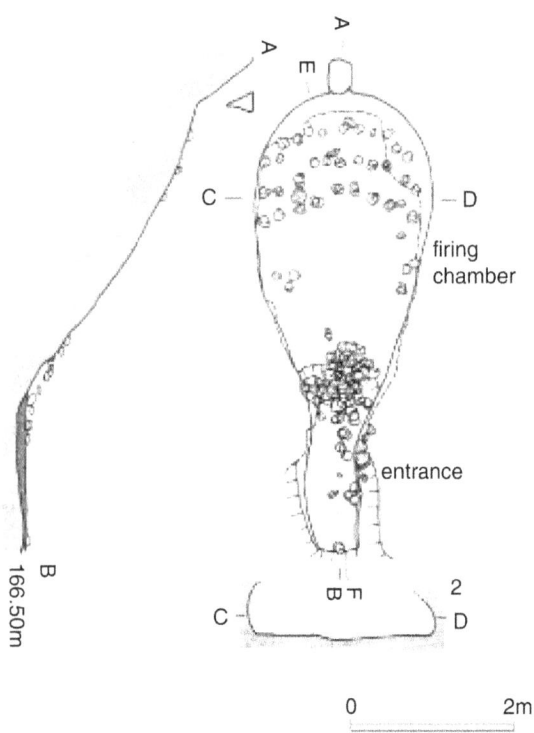

Figure 4. Diagram of kiln.

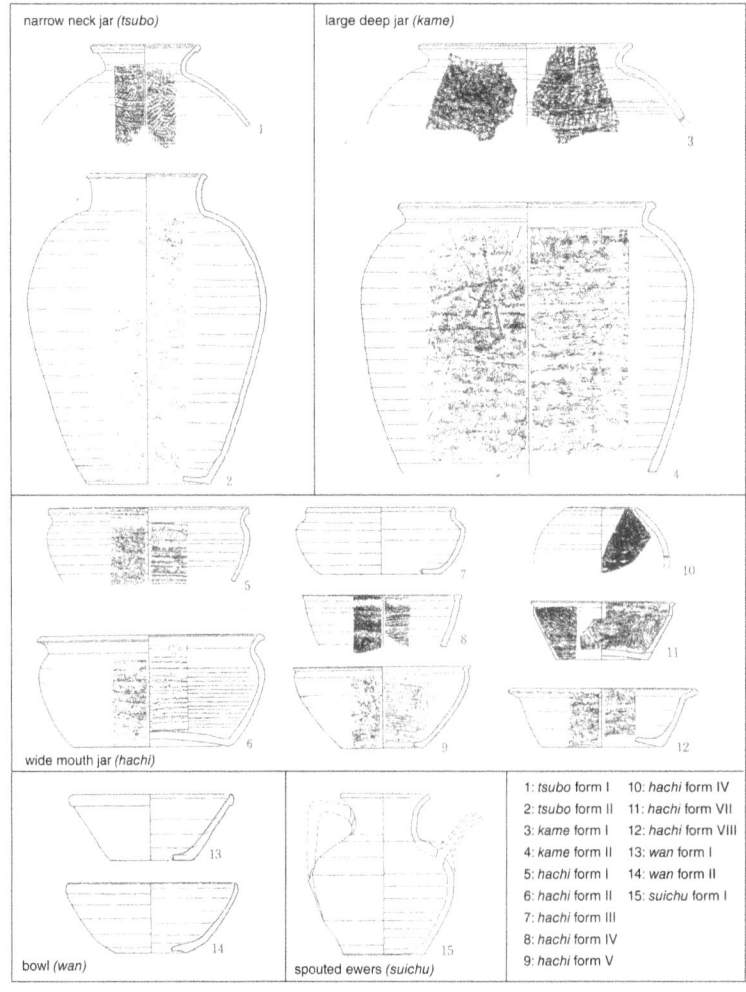

Figure 5. Vessel forms of *kamuiyaki*.

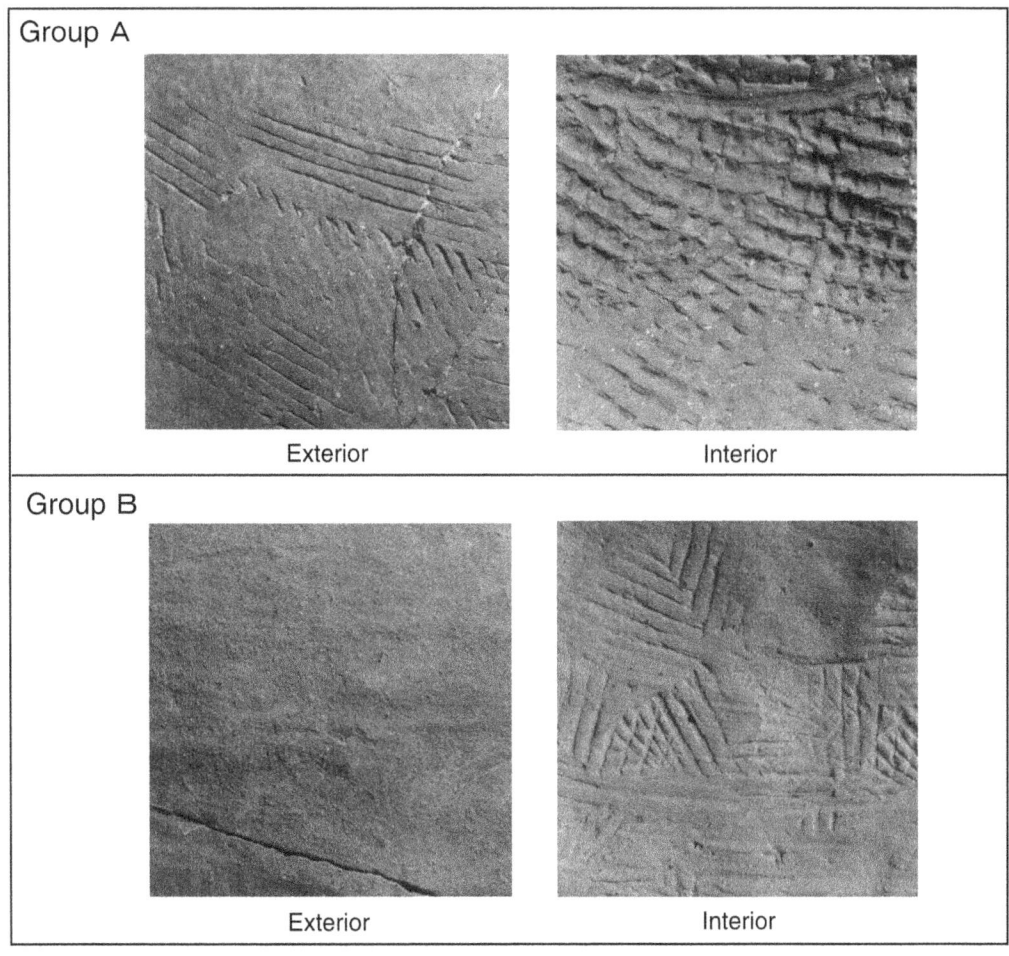

Figure 6. Exterior and interior surface treatments of *kamuiyaki* ceramics, Groups A and B.

has been applied to the inside of the shoulder of the vessel and the neck has a wide curve. In the narrow neck jars of Group B, clay has been added to the extreme upper edge of the shoulder and the outer edge of the lip stands straight up. These features indicate that the method of manufacture of A and B were different, the finishing method and the shape of the lip showing linked changes in manufacture. The vessel forms consist of narrow neck jars, wide mouth jars, deep jars, and ewers.

Up to now studies such as Sato (1975) and Asato (1991), have been based on the shape of the mouth of vessels from production sites. There are 6 major types and 36 sub types (Figure 7). These are based on temporal changes in the cross section of the rim. Types 1 to 4 are in Group A and 5 and 6 are in Group B.

In investigating the relative temporal positions of Groups A and B, the relative quantities of ceramics from kiln sites were examined (Figure 8). In Asan Kamuiyaki Group Area No. 2, successive kilns cut into each other. And from the ash deposit it became clear that there was a sequence from Kiln No. 2 to Kiln Nos. 3 and 7, to Kiln No. 4, to Kiln No. 6, and Kiln No. 5. Also on the east side of the investigation area there were 4 layers of accumulated ash deposit, and a stratigraphic excavation was conducted (Isen 1985*b*).

From these different kiln groups A and B, I examined the numbers of sherds of Groups A and B from the upper layers to the lower layers. Group A was found in older kiln sites than Group B. The classification of Sato and Asato had the purpose of establishing the chronology of *gusuku* and village sites throughout the Ryukyus, and compiling information on trends in consumption sites, was a useful step for other studies. From an examination of trends in consumption sites, since Group A occurs with Chinese Song porcelain, (11th to the middle of the 13th centuries) while Group B occurs with Yuan ceramics (latter half of 13th to 14th century), Group A is older than Group B. This can be confirmed by the finding of ceramics from consumption sites.

If we look at the composition of each group (Figures 9 and 10) in both Groups A and B, *tsubo* are an important product with no difference but Group A has *hachi* and *wan*. On the other hand, in Group B the production of bowls declines and *hachi* and *kame* increase. This indicates change in the composition of Groups A and B.

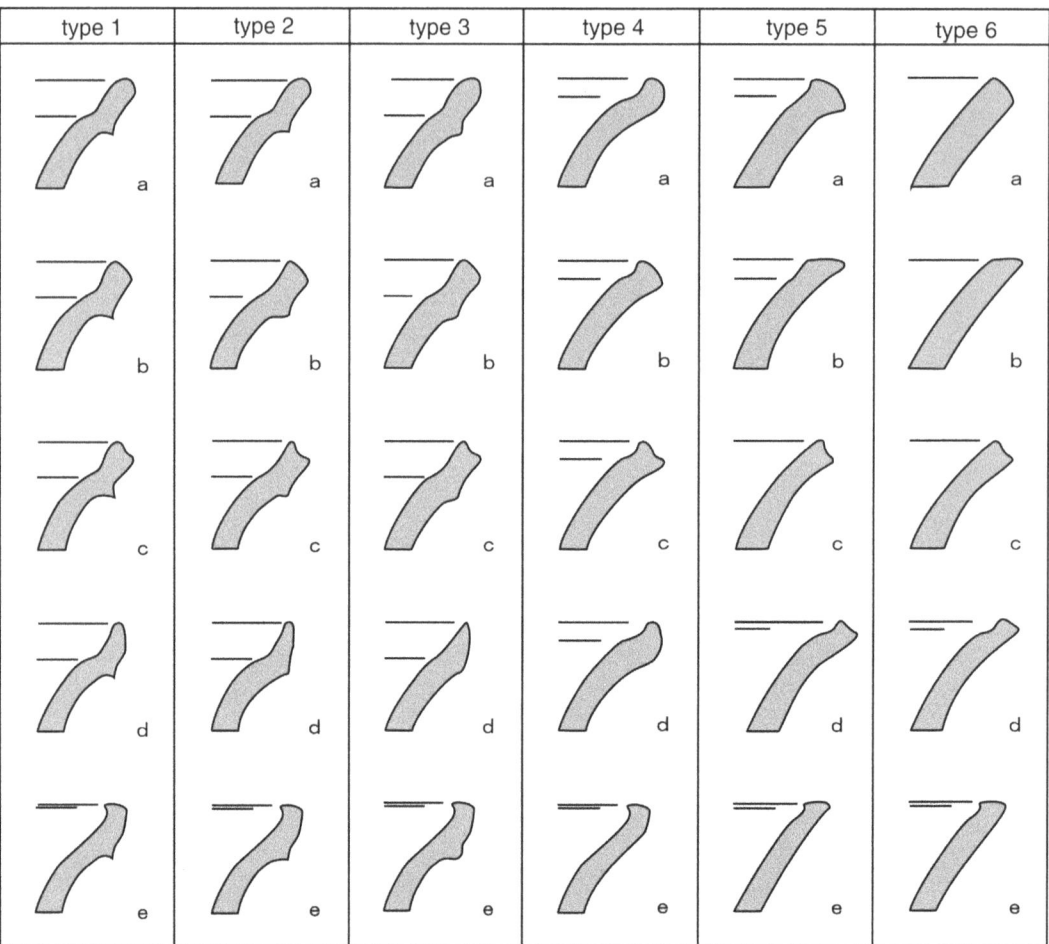

Figure 7. Typological classification of rim shapes of narrow neck jars (*tsubo*).

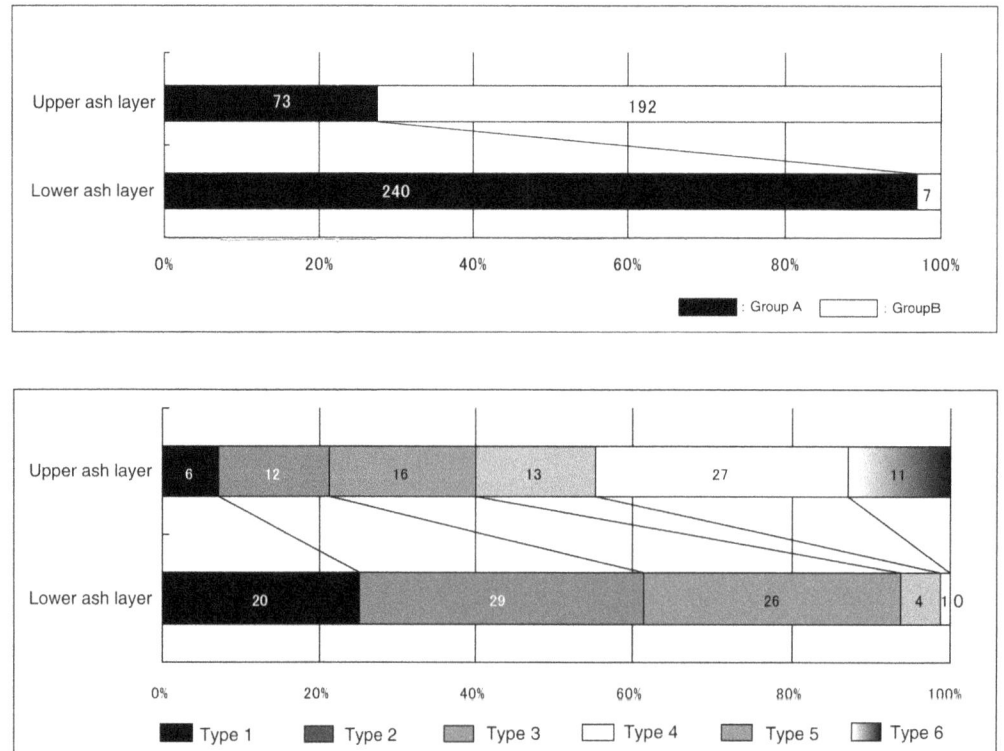

Figure 8. Excavated finds from ash layers at Kamuiyaki kilns.

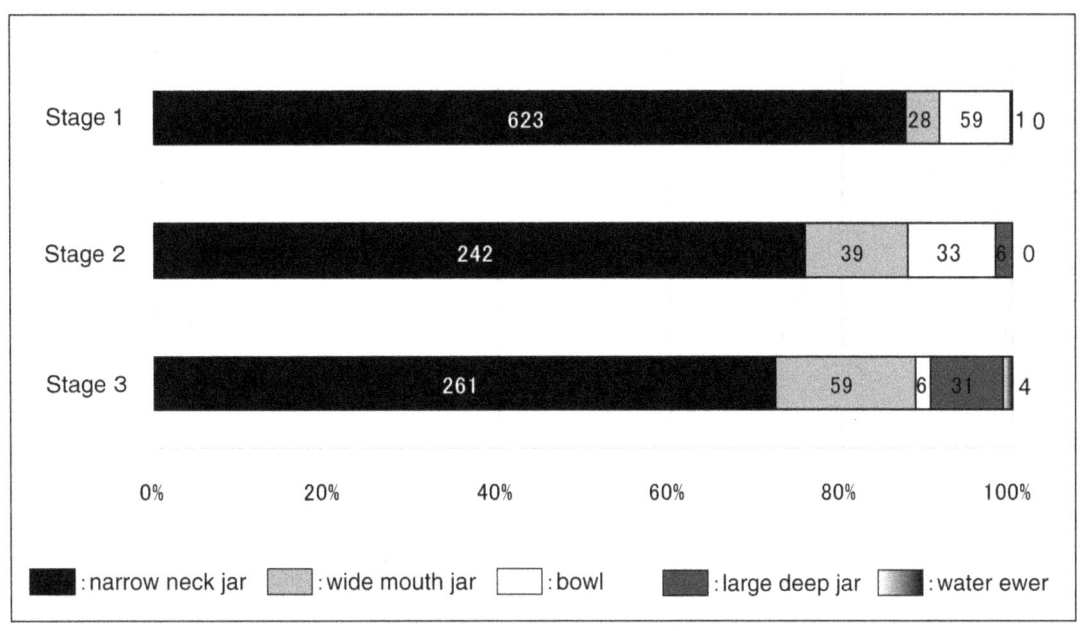

Figure 9. Changes in frequency of vessel forms of *kamuiyaki* ceramics.

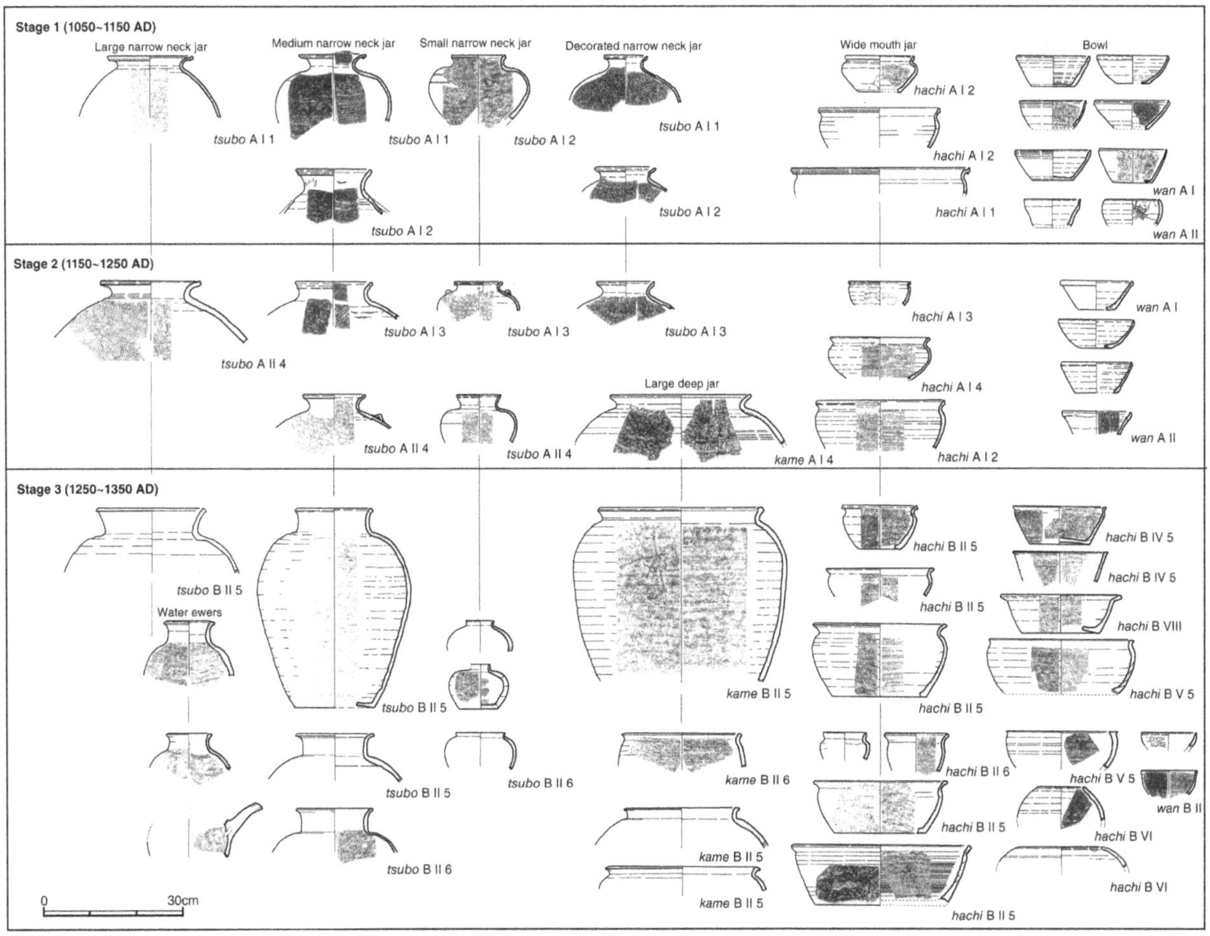

Figure 10. Relative chronology of vessel forms of *kamuiyaki* stoneware-vessel shapes.

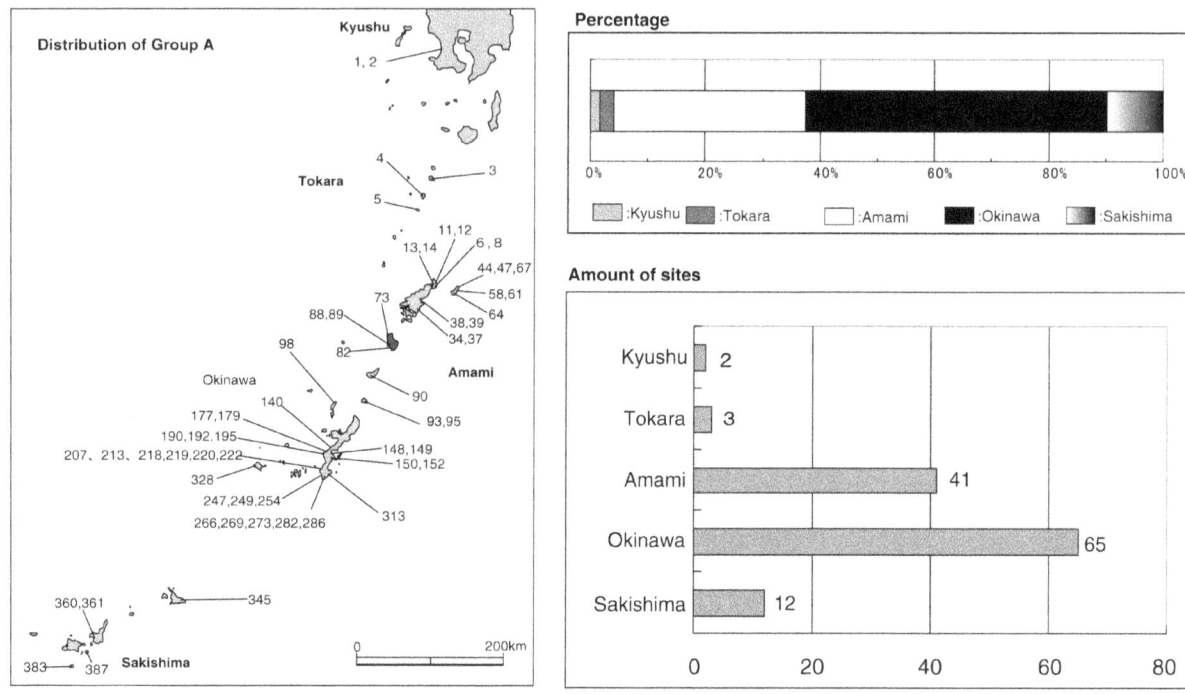

Figure 11. Distribution of Group A of *kamuiyaki* ware.

CONSUMPTION OF *KAMUIYAKI* CERAMICS

It is confirmed that *kamuiyaki* has been found on 300 sites (Ikeda 2003*a*; Shinzato 2003*b*), from southern Kyushu to Sakishima. The distribution of sites in this area is shown in Figure 11. Group A was consumed over a wide area from Kyushu to Sakishima (Figure 10). From the beginning of production it spread quickly from southern Kyushu throughout the Ryukyus, a distance of some 1200 km. The area with the most sites yielding *kamuiyaki* is the Okinawa Islands but there are also many sites in the Amami Islands as well. With the center of production sites in Tokunoshima, the area of consumption of Group A includes the Amami and Okinawa Islands. On the other hand, Group B does not occur north of the Tokara Islands or in Kyushu (Figure 12). It is decidedly rare in the Amami Islands. In contrast to the distribution of Group A from Kagoshima to Sakishima, Group B is found further to the south. The center of consumption shifted to the south to the Okinawa Islands.

PRODUCTION, DISTRIBUTION, AND CONSUMPTION

Regarding production and consumption the following points are proposed.

1. Groups A and B were produced at different times. Group A was produced from the latter half of the 11th century to the first half of the 13th century while Group B was produced from the latter half of the 13th to the 14th century.

2. In the time period of Group A, bowls were produced in quantity, while in the time period of Group B, bowl production declined sharply and wide mouth jars and ewers increased, as the assemblage became more complex.

3. Since Group A is distributed up to Kyushu, it is proposed that there were economic connections to Kyushu. The center of consumption was Amami and Okinawa.

4. Since Group B is not found in Kyushu, it appears that there was no economic connection to Kyushu. The rate of occurrence in Amami Oshima decreases and consumption is greater in the Okinawa Islands.

5. From these points, there was a difference in time periods, production, in the size of the region of exchange, and in consumption. Changes in production and circulation were related.

OTHER KINDS OF FOOD VESSELS IN THE RYUKYU ISLANDS

As mentioned above the production and consumption of *kamuiyaki* were related. What was the nature of the circulation and consumption of other types of ceramics used for food? In every area of the Ryukyus, *kamuiyaki* was accompanied by soapstone cooking vessels for boiling and Chinese ceramics for serving food. What was the economic context in which these ceramics functioned?

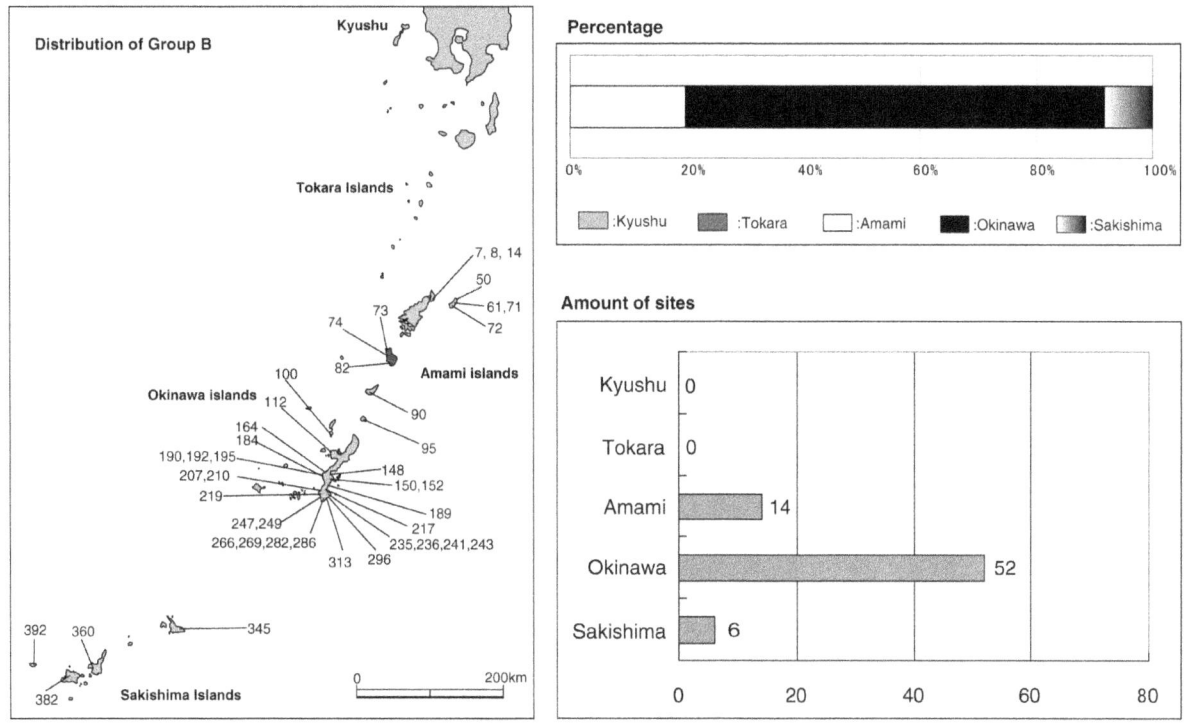

Figure 12. Distribution of Group B of *kamuiyaki* ware.

The Circulation and Consumption of Soapstone Vessels in the Ryukyus

The largest production site of soapstone vessels made of soft steatite, was located on the Nishi Sonogi Peninsula, Nagasaki Prefecture. A detailed study of site distribution showed 14 production sites (Oseto Cho 1980; Higashi 2003). Soapstone cauldrons are found as far north as Aomori Prefecture and as far south as Hateruma Island. In medieval times, they were the typical utensil for boiling in Japan. In the region to the south of Kyushu, soapstone fragments have been recorded from 900 sites (Shinzato 2002). The study of the typology and chronology of soapstone cauldrons has become very advanced (Kido 1982, 1993; Morita 1983; Suzuki 1998). Three periods of change occurred. In the 11th century there were two opposing square lugs near the mouth; in the latter half of the 12th century there was a flange or brim around the exterior of the mouth; and in the 13th and 14th centuries the base contracted and the flange atrophied. The square lug is abundant in Kyushu while the flanged form is widespread to the east of the Inland Sea. Within Kyushu there are morphological differences. The form with the lugs attached is common in the port of Hakata and the administrative city of Dazaifu. In the latter half of the 12th century the flanged form spread throughout Kyushu (Shinzato 2002) (Figure 13). In the Ryukyus, the form with external lugs is frequent and the flanged form is rare (Shinzato 2003a). The old type with external lug is older in the Kyushu area and was distributed to the south, while the new flanged form later spread throughout Kyushu (Shinzato 2002) (Figure 14).

In recent years from continuing excavations at the Gusuku Site of Kikaigashima, many non-local food utensils have been found with unusual types of external lug soapstone vessels. This site appears to have been a base for trading (Sumida and Nozaki 2007). The lugged stone cauldrons were distributed throughout the Ryukyus from the centers of Hakata, Dazaifu, and Kikaigashima, judging from the scattered distribution of fragments (Ikeda 2003b). It is thought that rather than being goods for trade, the cauldrons were spread through the Ryukyus as items of daily use of Hakata traders (Suzuki 2006, 2007). They provide evidence of the economic activities of the Hakata traders and the economic relations between the Ryukyus and the center of Hakata. The soapstone cauldrons produced in Kyushu were closely tied to Hakata and were circulated in the Ryukyus. At the same time, within the economic exchange in the Japanese Islands, there are indications that the Amami Islands were a leading center.

The Circulation of Chinese Ceramics in the Ryukyus

Chinese and Southeast Asian ceramics are found in large quantities in *gusuku* and village sites in the Ryukyus. This was established before World War II and the study of Chinese ceramics in the Ryukyus has been undertaken for a long time. The historical particulars of the prosperity of the Ryukyu Kingdom based on relaying trade have been confirmed by actual artifacts from an early date and are continuing. Central to studies of porcelain in the Ryukyus for the purpose of building chronologies are studies of paste, type of vessel, and shapes (Kin 1989, 1990). The circulation of ceramics in the Ryukyus can be divided

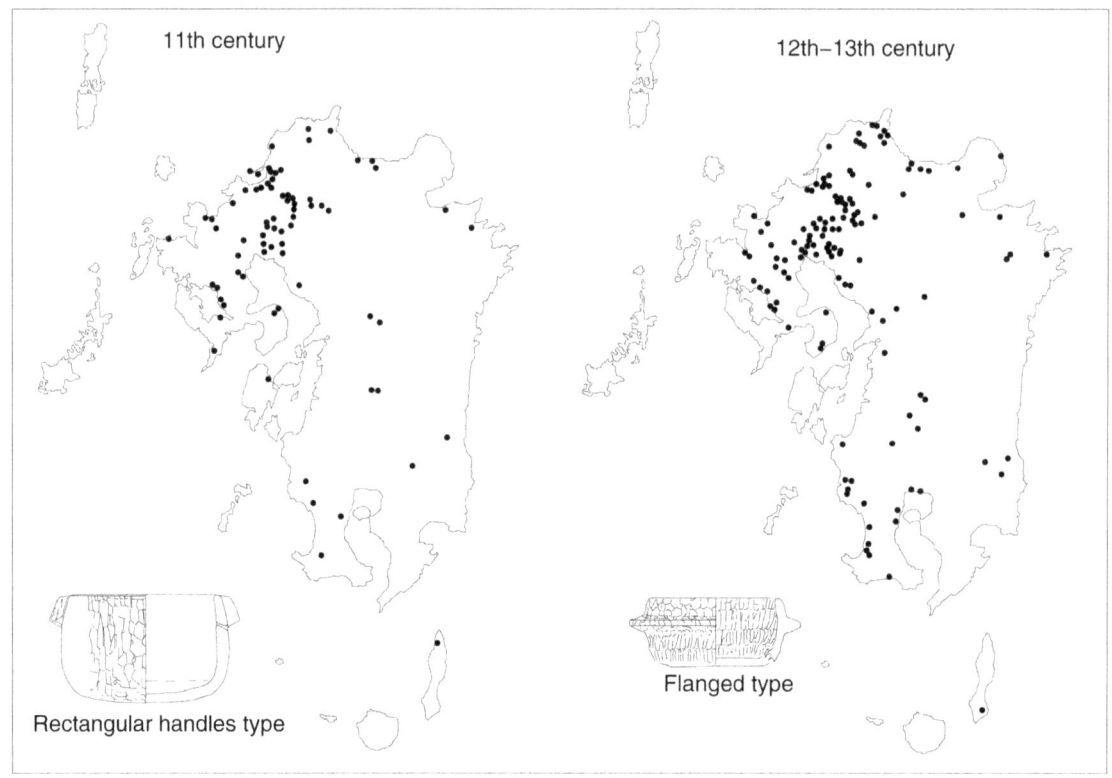

Figure 13. Distribution of soapstone cauldrons in Kyushu.

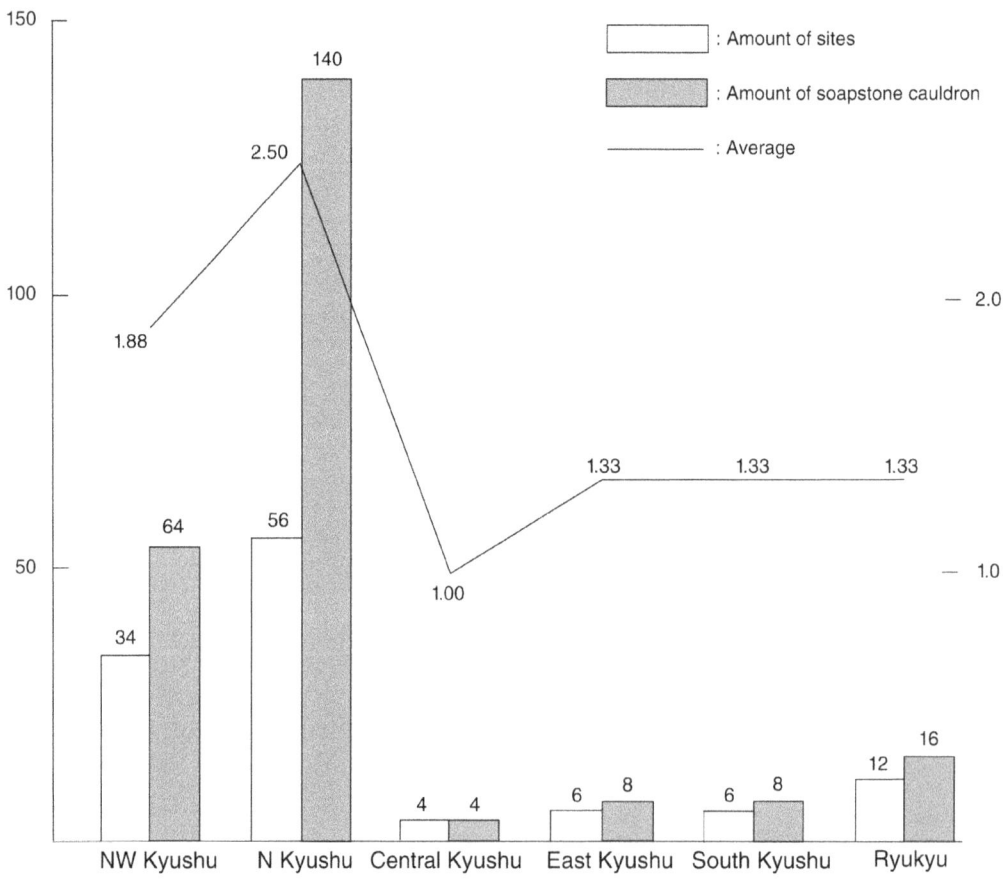

Figure 14. Distribution of soapstone cauldrons with rectangular handles in Kyushu and the Ryukyu Islands.

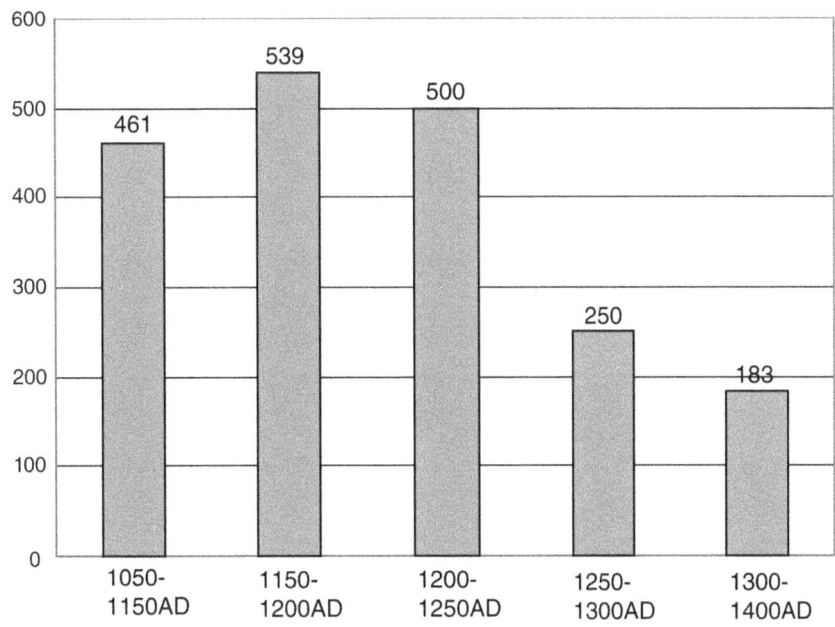

Figure 15. Number of sites with Chinese ceramics in Kyushu and the Ryukyu Islands.

into Period I (Initial Activity) late 11th and the first half or the 12th century, Period II (Early Gusuku Period), late 12th to 13th century), Period III (Gusuku Period) 14th to early 15th century. Kin (1998) proposed that certain types associated with the fortified centers increased with their development.

From the latter half of the 11th century to the 13th century there are no major differences in the Chinese trade ceramic assemblages found in Kyushu and the Ryukyus (Ryukyu Daigaku 2003; Tanaka and Morimoto 2004), Later, from the latter half of the 13th century ceramics which are rare in Kyushu are found in the Ryukyus. The Birosuku type of whiteware is an example. It has been dated to the end of the 13th century and the 14th century (Kin 1988). There is a strong probability that it comes from the kilns in the Min River region of Fujian Province (Tanaka and Morimoto 2004:357).

From these studies there is a deep understanding of the occurrences of Chinese trade ceramics in the Ryukyus, and the similarities and differences between the Chinese ceramics found in the Japanese Islands and the Ryukyus has become clear. It is possible to grasp the patterns of consumption in Kyushu and the Ryukyus and the general trends can be examined. The number of sites for each time period which have yielded Chinese ceramics in Kyushu and the Ryukyus are indicated in Figure 15. In Kyushu and Okinawa, consumption of Chinese ceramics increases from the latter half of the 11th century to the early half of the 12th century. The greatest number of sites occurs from the middle of the 12th century to the latter half, and the consumption rate remains stable from the beginning of the 13th century through the first half. However from the mid-13th century to the beginning of the 14th century, the number of sites suddenly drops to half. The lowest frequencies are from the beginning of the 14th century to the first half of the 15th century.

The number of sites yielding Chinese ceramics can be broken down by sub area—Fukuoka Prefecture/Northern Kyushu, Saga, Nagasaki Prefecture/Northern Kagoshima Prefecture, Kumamoto Prefecture/Central Kyushu, Oita, and Miyazaki Prefecture/Eastern Kyushu. The different areas of Kyushu share the same pattern, the peak occurring in the latter half of the 12th century and the first half of the 13th century and from the latter half of the 14th century the numbers decline (Figure 16). The overall trend shows a decline from the latter half of the 13th century. This trend is particularly striking in northern Kyushu (Yokota and Morita 1978). In other areas there is a similar trend, showing that throughout Kyushu the consumption of Chinese ceramics declines.

A different picture can be seen in the Ryukyus. While in Kyushu there is a decline in the number of sites from the latter half of the 13th century, in the Ryukyus the number increases. In Figure 17, I have divided the data for the consumption of ceramics into three periods—from the latter half of the 11th century to the first half of the 12th century, the mid-12th century to the first half of the 14th century, and the mid-13th century to the 14th century. This shows that in every part of Kyushu, the peak occurred from the latter half of the 12th century to the first half of the 13th century with a decline from the latter half of the 13th century. In contrast to this the Ryukyu peak is in the latter half of the 13th century. In this period the trend in the Ryukyus diverges from the trend in Kyushu.

Figure 16. Number of sites with Chinese ceramics in different regions of Kyushu.

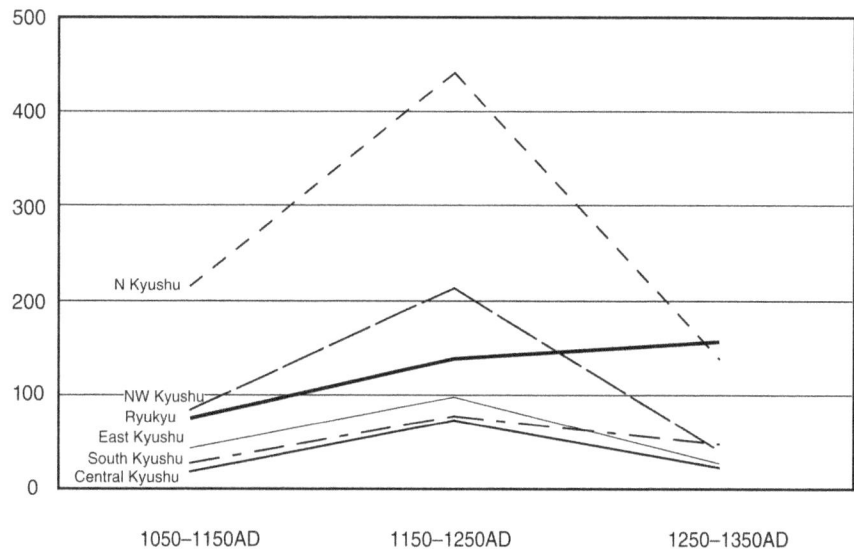

Figure 17. Changes in number of sites with Chinese ceramics from 1050 AD to 1350 AD.

ECONOMIC RELATIONS BEFORE THE ESTABLISHMENT OF THE RYUKYU KINGDOM, AS SEEN FROM FOOD VESSELS.

I would like to consider the interrelationships among production, circulation, and consumption of *kamuiyaki*, soapstone cauldrons, from Kyushu, which were used with it, and Chinese ceramics. The soapstone cauldrons of the latter half of the 11th century occur mostly in the port of Hakata; from an examination of consumption patterns of these, I believe that the soapstone cauldrons were distributed to the Ryukyus through Hakata. Chinese ceramics from the latter half of the 11th century to the first half of the 13th century show similar patterns of distribution in Kyushu and the Ryukyus indicating that the circulation patterns were related. *Kamuiyaki* Group A is distributed in Kyushu indicating that this is a period of strong economic relations between Kyushu and the Ryukyus. The circulation of *kamuiyaki*, soapstone cauldrons, and Chinese ceramics was related to Kyushu, particularly the central city of Hakata. This circumstance is not unrelated to the fact that *kamuiyaki* resembles Koryo ceramics. Koryo ceramics, which are abundant in Hakata, have been found in small quantities in the Ryukyus (Shinzato 2003b). There is a strong possibility that ceramic techniques were transmitted to Tokunoshima via Hakata. At that time, the port city of Hakata was the gateway for trade between Japan and Song China and for developing trade between Japan and Koryo Korea. If we consider carefully this idea which may seem too enthusiastic, *kamuiyaki* and associated Chinese ceramics used for food may be seen as a product of foreign trade in the East China Sea area, and the establishment of the Kamuiyaki Kilns in Tokunoshima may be seen as part of the long distance relations.

Kamuiyaki Group B was produced from the latter half of the 13th century to the 14th century. This is a period when the number of Kyushu sites yielding Chinese ceramics was declining and trade in Chinese ceramics to the Ryukyus was increasing, Also soapstone cauldrons were decreasing and from the distribution of *kamuiyaki* in Kyushu, the economic relations between Kyushu and Ryukyu were weakening. Also, the Birosuku Type of whiteware, rarely seen in the Japanese main islands, is frequently found in the Ryukyus. It is thought that direct economic relations between the Ryukyus and China were forming in the latter half of the 13th century. At this time the production of bowls in the Kamuiyaki Kilns decreased dramatically and the assemblage diversified. As a means of strengthening economic relations with China, the circulation of Chinese ceramics increased, and *kamuiyaki* production was reformed, affecting economic trends of the East China Sea Region.

Kamuiyaki Group B is abundant in the Okinawa Islands. At this time, in Okinawa and Sakishima fortified castles (*gusuku*) were being constructed and the changes leading to the formation of the Ryukyu Kingdom were occurring. The center of concentration of *kamuiyaki* was in the Okinawa Islands indicating that Okinawa had assumed predominance over Amami Oshima, and that from the latter half of the 13th century relations were becoming stronger. At this time the economic stage immediately prior to the formation of the Ryukyu Kingdom had been reached. It was in these economic conditions that *kamuiyaki* production changed.

CONCLUSION

Problems concerning *kamuiyaki* are not limited to production and circulation. Why were almost 200 kilns built in the middle of the Ryukyu Islands and what happened to the communities involved in production after the end of *kamuiyaki*? These questions are part of a huge number to be resolved in the future. On February 6, 2007, the Kamuiyaki Kiln sites were registered as a National Historic Site. They have great value in the study of Ryukyu Islands production and exchange, a field in which historical sources are very rare.

Translated by Richard Pearson

REFERENCES CITED

AKASHI, YOSHIHIKO
1999 Tokunoshima Kamuiyaki koyoseki saishu no nanto toshitsu doki ni tsuite [Concerning the southern islands stoneware collected at the Kamuiyaki old kiln site]. *Kyushu Rekishi Shiryokan Kenkyu Ronshu* 24:49–60.

ASATO, SUSUMU
1975 Gusuku jidai kaishiki no jakkan no mondai ni tsuite; Kumejima Yajiyaagama iseki no chosa kara [Several problems of the beginning period of the Gusuku Period, from the investigation of the Yajiyaagama Site, Kumejima]. *Okinawa Kenritsu Hakubutsukan Kiyo* 1:36–54.

1988 Ryukyu – Okinawa no kokogaku teki jidai kubun o meguru shomondai [Ryukyu: some problems concerning the temporal divisions in Okinawan archaeology] (1). *Kokogaku Kenkyu* 34 (4): 50–67.

1990 *Kokogaku Kara Mita Ryukyu Shi* [Ryukyu History Seen From Archaeology]. Naha: Hirugi Sha.

1991 Okinawa no hirozoko doki, kameyakikei doki no hennen ni tsuite [Concerning the chronology of Okinawan flat bottomed pottery and kamui type pottery]. *Koryu no Kokogaku* 6:579–593.

GI, NORIKAZU AND NOBUHIRO YOTSUMOTO
1984 Kamuiyaki Koyo [The Old Kilns of Kamuiyaki]. *Kagoshima Kokogaku* 18:145–149.

HIGASHI, TAKAYUKI
2003 Kassekisei ishinabe seisakusho ni tsuite [Concerning the production sites of stone cauldrons]. *Seikai Koko* 5:21–42.

IKEDA, YOSHIFUMI
2003a Zoho: Ruisueki shutsudo chimeihyo [Supplement: table of find locations of grey stoneware (ruisueki)]. *Ryukyu Daigaku Hobungakubu Ningen Kagaku Ka Kiyo; Ningen Kagaku* 12:212–242.

2003b Senko o yusuru kasseki nabe hahen ni tsuite [Concerning perforated fragments of stone cauldrons]. In *Amami Oshima Nase Shi Kominato Ufuganeku Iseki Gun Iseki Han'i Kakunin Hakkutsu Chosa Hokoku* [Report of Excavations to Determine the Extent of the Kominato Fuwaganeku Site Group, Nase City, Amami Oshima]: 82–85, ed. Nase Shi Kyoiku Iinkai. Nase: Nase Shi Kyoiku Iinkai, Nase.

2005 Nanto Shutsudo Ruisueki no Shutsuji to Bunpu ni Kansuru Kenkyu [Study Concerning the Descent and Distribution of Grey Stoneware

Found in the Southern Islands (Ryukyus)]. *Heisei 14-16 nendo Kagaku Kenkyuhi Hojokin Kihan Kenkyu B-12 Kenkyu Kekka Hokokusho [Report of Results of Research Supported by Science Research Funds in 2002-2004, B-2]*. Ryukyu Daigaku, Okinawa.

ISEN CHO KYOIKU IINKAI

1985a *Kamuiyaki Koyogun I: Showa 59 Nendo Juyo Iseki Kakunin Chosa [The Kamuiyaki Old Kiln Group; the Confirming Excavations of an Important Site in 1985]*. Isen Cho: Isen Cho Kyoiku Iinkai.

1985b *Kamuiyaki Koyoseki Gun II [The Kamuiyaki Old Kiln Site Group, Volume II]*. Isen Cho: Isen Cho Kyoiku Iinkai.

2001 *Kamuiyaki Koyoseki Gun III [The Kamuiyaki Old Kiln Site Group, Volume III]*. Isen Cho: Isen Cho Kyoiku Iinkai.

2005 *Kamuiyaki Koyoseki Gun IV [The Kamuiyaki Old Kiln Site Group, Volume IV]*. Isen Cho: Isen Cho Kyoiku Iinkai.

KIDO MASATOSHI

1982 Kusado Sengen iseki shutsudo no ishinabe [Stone cauldrons from the Kusado Sengen site]. *Kusado Sengen* 112.

1993 Ishinabe no seisan to ryutsu ni tsuite [Concerning the production and distribution of stone cauldrons]. *Chukinsei Doki no Kisoteki Kenkyu* IX.

KIN, SEIKI

1988 Birosuku type hakuji wan ni tsuite [Concerning Birosuku Type white ware]. *Boeki Toji Kenkyu* 8:148–158.

1989 Okinawa ni okeru 12,13 seiki ni chugoku tojiki [Chinese porcelain of the 12th and 13th centuries found in Okinawa]. *Okinawa Kenritsu Hakubutsukan Kiyo* 15:1–22.

1990 Okinawa no Chugoku tojiki [Chinese ceramics of Okinawa]. *Kokogaku Janaru* 320.

1998 Okinawa ni okeru boeki toji [Trade ceramics from Okinawa]. *Nihon Kokogaku Kyokai 1998 Nendo Okinawa Taikai Shiryoshu [Abstracts and Notes, 1998 Annual Meeting, Japanese Archaeological Association, Okinawa]*:147–158. Naha: Nihon Kokogaku Kyokai.

MISTUJI TOSHIKAZU

2001 Tokunoshima kamuiyaki yogun shutsudo sueki no keiko X sen bunseki [X ray fluorescence analysis of grey stoneware from the Kamuiyaki Site Group of Tokunoshima]. In *Kamuiyaki Koyo Gun*. Isen Cho: Isen Cho Kyoiku Iinkai.

MORITA, TSUTOMU

1983 Kassekisei yoki—toku ni ishinabe o chushin toshite [Soapstone containers—with special reference to soapstone cauldrons]. *Bukkyo Geijutsu* 148.

NISHITANI, TADASHI

1981 Korai, Chosen ryo ocho to Ryukyu no koryu—sono kokogakuteki kenkyu josetsu (The two kingdoms of Koryo and Choson and exchange with Ryukyu—An introduction to their archaeological study). *Kyushu Bunka Shi Kenkyusho Kiyo* 26:75–100.

OGINO, SHIGEHARU

1993 Chusei nishi Nihon ni okeru chozo yoki no seisan [The production of container vessels in mediaeval Western Japan] *Kokogaku Zasshi* 78 (3): 31–73.

ONISHI, TOMOKAZU

1996 Nanto Sueki no Mondai Ten [Some problematical points concerning grey stoneware of the southern islands]. *Minami Nihon Bunka* 29:19–35.

OSETO CHO KYOIKU IINKAI

1980 Oseto Cho Ishinabe Seisakusho Iseki [The Oseto Cho Stone Cauldron Making Sites]. *Oseto Cho Bunkazai Chosa Hokokusho* 1. Oseto Cho: Oseto Cho Kyoiku Iinkai.

RYUKYU DAIGAKU KOKOGAKU KENKYUSHITSU

2003 Ryukyu Retto Shutsudo no Boeki Toji no Kisoteki Kenkyu [Basic Study of Trade Ceramics Found in the Ryukyu Islands]. *Ryukyu Daigaku Kokogaku Kenkyu Shuroku No. 4*. Nishihara: Ryukyu Daigaku Hobungakubu Kokogaku Kenkyushitsu.

SATO, SHINJI

1975 Nanto no sueki [The sueki of the southern islands]. *Toyo Bunka* 48/49:169–204.

SHINZATO, AKITO

2002 Kasseki sei ishinabe no kisoteki kenkyu [Basic

study of soapstone cauldrons]. In *Senshi Ryukyu no Seigyo to Koeki [Subsistence and Exchange in the Prehistoric Ryukyus]*: 163–190, ed. Kinoshita Naoko. Kumamoto: University of Kumamoto.

2003a   Ryukyu Retto ni okeru yogyo seisan no seiritsu to tenkai. [Pottery production in the Ryukyu Islands]. *Kokogaku Kenkyu* 49 (4): 75–96.

2003b   Tokunoshima kamuiyaki koyosan seihin no ryutsu to sono tokushitsu [The products of the Kamuiyaki old kiln sites: their circulation and special features]. *Senshigaku, Kokogaku Ronkyu* IV:387–413.

2004   Kamuiyaki koyo no gijutsu keifu to seiritsu haikei [The genealogy of the techniques used in the old kilns of kamuiyaki and the background of their development]. In *Gusuku Bunka o Kangaeru [Considering Gusuku Culture]*: 325–352, ed. Nakijin Son Kyoiku Iinkai. Tokyo: Shin Jimbutsu Oraisha.

SHIRAKIHARA, KAZUMI

1999   Nansei Shoto no senshi jidai [The prehistoric period of the southern islands], *Ryuta Kokogaku*: 109–120.

SUMIDA, NAOTOSHI AND TAKUJI NOZAKI

2007   Kikaigashima Gusuku Iseki gun no chosa [Investigation of the Gusuku Site Group, Kikaigashima]. *Higashi Ajia no Kodai Bunka* 130:46–52.

SUZUKI, YASUYUKI (ED.)

1998   Kusado Sengen Cho Iseki no kasseki sei ishinabe [The soapstone cauldrons of the Kusado Sengen site]. In *Kusado Sengen Cho Iseki Chosa Kenkyu Hokoku [Study Report of the Kusado Sengen Cho Site Investigations]*. Hiroshima: Hiroshima Kenritsu Hakubutsukan.

SUZUKI, YASUYUKI

2006   Kassekisei ishinabe no ryutsu to shohi [Distribution and consumption of soapstone cauldrons]. In *Kamakura Jidai no Kokogaku [Archaeology of the Kamakura Period]*: 173–188, ed. Ono Masatoshi and Mitsuo Hagihara. Tokyo: Koshin Shoin.

2007   Kasseki sei ishinabe no tadotta michi [The road followed by the soapstone cauldrons]. In *Higashi Ajia no Kodai Bunka* 130:46–52.

TANAKA, KATSUKO AND ASAKO MORIMOTO

2004   Okinawa shutsudo no boeki toji no mondai ten—Chugoku sosei hakuji to Betunamu shoki boeki toji [Some problems concerning the trade ceramics found in Okinawa—Chinese coarse white ware and early Vietnamese trade ware]. In *Gusuku Bunka o Kangaeru [Considering Gusuku Culture]*: 353–370, ed. Nakijin Son Kyoiku Iinkai. Tokyo: Shin Jimbutsu Oraisha.

TAWADA, SHINJUN

1956   Ryukyu retto no kaizuka bunpu to hennen no gainen [A summary of shell midden distribution and chronology in the Ryukyus]. *Bunkazai Yoran* 1956:12–13.

YOKOTA, KENJIRO AND TSUTOMU MORITA

1978   Dazaifu shutsudo no yunyu chugoku toji ni tsuite—keishiki bunrui to hennen o chushin ni shite [Concerning imported Chinese ceramics from Dazaifu—with particular reference to typology and chronology]. *Kyushu Rekishi Shiryokan Kenkyu Ronshu* 4:1–26.

YOSHIOKA, YASUNOBU

1994   *Chusei Sueki no Kenkyu [The Study of Mediaeval Grey Stoneware]*. Tokyo: Yoshikawa Kobunkan.

2002   Nanto no chusei sueki: chusei shoki no kan higashi Ajia kaiiki no togei koryu [The mediaeval Sue ware from the southern islands: exchange of ceramics within the East Asian maritime region]. *Kokuritsu Rekishi Minzoku Hakubutsukan Kenkyu Kiyo* 94:409–439.

The Emergence of Ryukyu Royal Authority and Urasoe

Susumu ASATO
Okinawa Prefectural University of the Arts

Introduction

Urasoe was the capital of the Ryukyu or Chuzan Kingdom in its initial period, during the reigns of Kings Eiso and Satto. According to the gazetteer *Ryukyu Koku Yuraiki*, (lit. *Ryukyu Country Records of Origins*) published in 1713 (Iha, Higaonna, and Yokoyama 1940), King Eiso built the royal mausoleum, Urasoe Yodore, in the Song Dynasty Xianchun reign (1265–1274). Excavations have clarified that, as indicated in legend, the Yodore Royal Mausoleum was built in the latter half of the 13th century and was used by the First Sho Dynasty until the first half of the 15th century. In it we can see the international nature of the Ryukyu royal family in its earliest period. We can bring their character and religious outlook into relief. In this paper, based on archaeological research, I will discuss the development of royal power at Urasoe in the 13th century and Urasoe's relation with the East Asian world. In discussing the rise of royal power at Urasoe, I am referring to the rise of Ryukyu royal power and not necessarily to the process of state formation.

According to the *Chuzan Seikan* (1650) (edition of Iha, Higaonna, and Yokoyama 1941), Kings Shunten, Eiso, Satto, and the First and Second Sho lines came to power one after the other. Among these, the founder of the Ryukyu Kingdom, Shunten, and the son of the Sun God King Eiso, played an important role in the development of royal power. Also at the end of the Eiso family line, in the 14th century, Chuzan split into three regions of Chuzan, Sannan, and Sanhoku, but these were reunified in the 15th century.

In present studies, the royal line of Shunten is thought to be legendary, and a royal line can only be verified from the time of King Satto, who sent tribute to the Ming in 1372. In regard to King Eiso, there is divided opinion as to whether he actually existed as a king. There are no contemporary historical sources confirming his existence. The latter half of the 13th century, the time of Eiso, was a time of local lords who built fortified *gusuku* to defend local power. However, it is not clear whether state organization had evolved by that time.

According to general opinion, the formation of the Ryukyu Kingdom is interpreted in the following way. Up to about the 12th century a kind of primitive society (*genshi shakai*) continued to exist in the Ryukyus. In the 12th and 13th centuries, local lords emerged in every locality, built fortified *gusuku* and formed confederacies. In the 14th century these coalesced into the three kingdoms of Chuzan, Sanhoku, and Sannan. In the 15th century, the First Sho line captured control of the Chuzan Kingdom and defeated Sannan and Sanhoku, and unified the Ryukyu Kingdom. However it has not been clear whether the person Eiso existed or was anything more than a local leader.

Results of Urasoe Yodore Excavations

Urasoe Gusuku is a fortified castle 4 km to the north of Shuri. Below the castle is the Urasoe Yodore Mausoleum. The old name of Urasoe is Uraosoi, meaning the land governing the villages, and Yodore means tomb or paradise. The tomb is surrounded by a double or triple stone wall which was completely destroyed in World War II. After the war the Ryukyu government repaired the burial chamber but not the walls. From 1997 to 2005 the Urasoe City Board of Education repaired the walls to their present state and published four volumes of archaeological reports (Urasoe 2001, 2005*a*, 2005*b*, 2007), and I wrote a summary volume, *Ryukyu Oken to Gusuku (Ryukyu Royal Power and Gusuku)* (Asato 2006). This paper is a summary based on these recent reports and publication.

Urasoe Yodore underwent a major renovation in 1620. As a result of excavations (Figure 1), its construction and renovation can be divided into three periods prior to 1620 (Plate 6). Period I (Initial Urasoe Yodore)—first construction to the first renovation, latter half of 13th century to first half of 15th century (Figures 2 and 3). Period II—first renovation to second renovation, first half of 15th century to 1620. Period III—second renovation to 1620 (Figure 4 and Plate 7).

Figure 1. The excavation of Urasoe Yodore.

Figure 2. Reconstruction of Urasoe Yodore.

In Period I, (Initial Yodore) two large caves were dug into the cliff face and they contained several structures with tiled roofs and stone pillar bases. These were like wooden burial chambers. Inside these chambers bones were deposited in lacquered wooden coffins (Figure 5). Dating of these bones is thought to be 1273, based on the evidence summarized below.

The lacquered old type of wooden casket has diamond shaped metal fittings of the same type as the gilt bronze fittings on the palace shaped receptacle in the Saidaiji Temple (Nara), which is dated to the 13th century (Kubo 2003). The Urasoe structures which housed the caskets had stone pillar bases and roofs were tiled with Koryo-type tiles (Figure 6). The motif on the end of the circular tile ends is a lotus flower (Type 1B) such as those on the Koryo tiles found on Chindo, Korea, at the Yongjang Castle (Eight Petal Lotus Flower B). Yongjang Castle was a palace used for a short period, between 1270 and 1273 (Mokpo 1990) (Figure 7). The Urasoe Yodore Lotus Flower Type 1B tiles are found together as part of a set with flat tiles with the stamped inscription, *Mizunoto Tori Doshi Koraigasho Tsukuru* (*Koryo Tile Made in the Year "Mizunoto Tori"*). There are various interpretations of which 60-year cycle is correct. Considering the date of the Yongjang Castle, there is a high probability that it must be 1273. Radiocarbon determinations also support the date of 1273. The year 1273 is the ninth year of the Southern Song Xianchun reign stated in the *Ryukyu Koku Yuraiki*; therefore all of the dating information matches closely.

Figure 3. Enclosure No. 1, Urasoe Yodore.

The first renovation of the Yodore Mausoleum occurred in the first half of the 15th century. The stone wall construction method is termed *nunozumi* in which the spaces between the stones in each horizontal row line up above and below each other, creating a continuous line down the wall, like a vertical warp in cloth. According to Shi'ichi Toma (1988), the use of this method dates from the 14th century to the early 15th century. The first renovation can thus be dated to the first half of the 15th century. A large quantity of ceramics dating to the first half of the 15th century was found, and the radiocarbon dates also cluster around the early 15th century.

Figure 4. The east chamber of Urasoe Yodore.

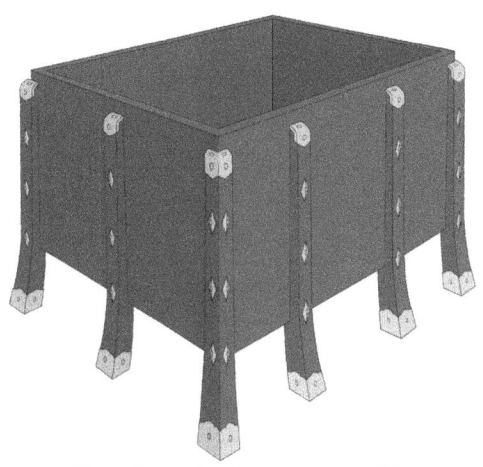

Figure 5. Postulated reconstruction of the lacquered wooden sarcophagus.

Figure 6. The Koryo-type roof tile with inscription of Mizunoto Tori Doshi, The Year, Mizunoto Tori, in the 60 year cycle, most likely 1273.

THE EMERGENCE OF RYUKYU ROYAL POWER

In the Initial Period of Urasoe Yodore, there were two manmade burial chambers, east and west, cut into the cliff face. The ceiling of the west chamber was 3.65 m high and the floor area was 123 m². The east chamber was the same size. The digging of the two chambers required the removal of 1000 m³ of rock. To excavate these caves required a large quantity of iron tools and a large labor input. The structures inside the caves had tile roofs as mentioned above; analysis of the tiles shows that they were made in the Ryukyus. The lacquer used to paint the caskets and the gilded metal fittings show the use of particular Ryukyu techniques (Kubo 2003; Yotsuyanagi 2006) Also the metal tools and gilded objects required for the project were made locally, judging from archaeological features which show manufacturing on site.

In the construction of the burial facilities various craftsmen were mobilized: carpenters, roof tilemakers, fine woodworkers, and specialists in lacquering, metalcasting, forging, metalworking, and gilding. These craftsmen would have been required for the construction of the castle. In order to sustain royal power, craftsmen would also have been required for the maintenance of the castle and mausoleum. Yodore surpassed the tombs of other local chiefs in scale, content, construction, labor, and craft organization required, and the quantity of iron tools. All of these support the existence of Eiso's royal power. Ryukyu royal power existed in Urasoe and extended at least to the

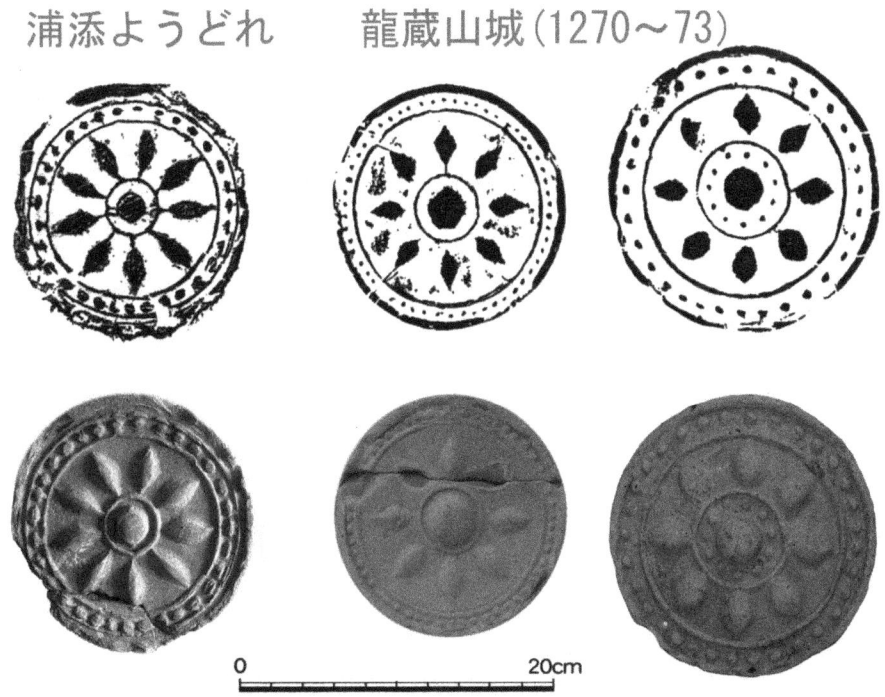

Figure 7. The Koryo-type roof tile found in the Urasoe Yodore (left) and the roof tiles found in Chindo, Korea (middle and right).

middle zone of Okinawa Island, but more likely extended to all of Okinawa Island and its satellites. Up to now, in Eiso's time, it is thought that local rulers and their large castles were grouped into local, competing confederacies but now it seems likely that in the late 13th century there was already royal power.

I defined large castles (*ogata gusuku*) as those having a *seiden* (palace) and an *una* (plaza), which are the nuclear facilities, as well as being of large size and complex structure. Examples are Shuri, Katsuren, and Zakimi. In Shuri, the *seiden* projects royal authority. Along with the plaza (*una*), it has a political function. The palace and plaza are not limited to Shuri; these are shared by large castles in all areas. They appear all over the Okinawan Islands in the 13th century. Up to now I thought that large *gusuku* indicate the emergence of local authority but there are some problems with this interpretation. Although it is a special feature of local lords to build large castles, why did they take the specific shape of the palace and plaza? If the large *gusuku* in each area indicated local confederacies then there should be variety in the style of the facilities.

There is the possibility of a new interpretation of the royal *gusuku*. In the 15th century Shuri, the royal capital of the First Sho Dynasty, was about 40,000 m² in area and was the center of a kingdom in south-central Okinawa Island, which would later become the Chuzan Kingdom. On the periphery were temples, mansions of the royal family retainers' houses, a large pond (*Ryutan*), and the mausoleum. Although there were other large *gusuku* such as Nakijin and Ozato, only Urasoe and Shuri were surrounded by facilities of royal capitals.

From recent excavations, it has been clear that from the latter half of the 13th century Urasoe was the largest castle of its time with an area of tens of thousands of square meters. From inside the castle a large quantity of Koryo-type roof tiles have been found, and it is thought that the palace had a tiled roof. The palace seems to have been built around 1273 judging from the date on the roof tiles. On its periphery there was the Gokurakuji, the Yodore Mausoleum, residences of the nobility (*gozoku yashiki*) such as the Toyama Agaribaru Site, mansions such as the Nakama Kushibaru Site, and villages such as Urasoebaru. There was also a large pond (Iyugumui) and other facilities. Urasoe shares several place names with Shuri. The Gokurakuji and the large pond, built in the 13th and 14th centuries, are subjects for future excavation. In sum, rather than appearing in the 15th century, the royal palace developed in Urasoe.

From the late 13th century to the 14th century, centering on Urasoe, which had a main palace building with a roof of Koryo-type tiles, large *gusuku* with core facilities of palace and plaza were distributed all over the Okinawa Islands. These large *gusuku* were politically subordinate to the Ryukyu royal authority or were in alliances, and

Figure 8. No.1 Sarcophagus.

the similarity of their palace layouts with palace and plaza shows that they were linked together, to the power of Urasoe. The distribution of the same style of palace therefore indicates the spatial extent of royal power, which at least covered all of Okinawa Island and probably extended to its satellites within the Okinawa Islands.

THE EMERGENCE OF ROYAL AUTHORITY AND EAST ASIA

I have concluded that Eiso's royal authority existed in the latter half of the 13th century. How did his royal power emerge? This emergence of power is discussed within the limits of Japan and Okinawa, but the power of the royal family buried in Urasoe Yodore arose from its international nature.

The bones in the large stone sarcophagi, Nos 1 (Figure 8) and 4, installed in the first renovation of Yodore, belong to the Initial Period, while the individuals buried in Nos 2 and 3 belong to the First Sho Dynasty. According to Professor Ken'ichi Shinoda of the National Museum of Science, who conducted analysis of mitochondrial DNA on the skeletons from No. 4, both have Haplotype F (Shinoda 2005), common in South China and Southeast Asia. At this time Ryukyu overseas trade with Southeast Asia had not yet occurred. Thus the mtDNA appears to be related to South China and the center of Quanzhou. Since mtDNA is transmitted through the mother, the most likely explanation is that one of the wives of King Eiso must have been overseas Chinese, from Quanzhou.

The clay analysis of the roof tiles from Urasoe Yodore showed that both the Koryo and Yamato types were produced in Okinawa (Urasoe 2005a), indicating that the manufacturing techniques were brought to Okinawa. Professor Naomi Doi of the University of the Ryukyus found that a male cranium from Sarcophagus No. 2 was typical of the Japanese medieval population (Figure 9). The average height of skeletons from Yodore was 157 to 163 cm for males and 146 to 148 cm for females (Doi 2005), while the averages for individuals from the of Shuri Tama Udun Mausoleum of the Second Sho Dynasty of the 16th to 19th centuries was 155.6 cm (males) and 144.8 cm (females) (Doi 2005), some 4 to 5 cm shorter than the average of the former population.

We can also see the international nature of religious concepts from the abundant evidence of both bone washing and cremation. The Amida Triad motif on the sarcophagus has been interpreted to mean that the royal family embraced the Jodo Shinshu Pure Land Buddhism, while the bird motifs indicate local Chinese religion (China 2005). The form of the sarcophagus base shares features with Islamic and Christian tombstone bases from Quanzhou. In addition the location and structure of the Yodore tomb shows belief in local Okinawan concepts of the other world of Nirai Kanai.

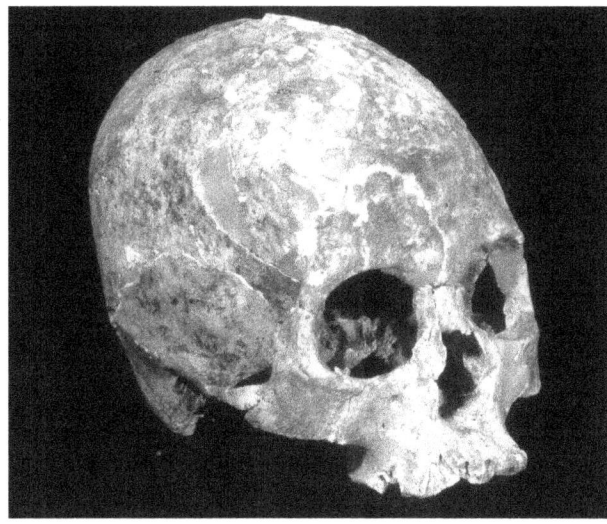

Figure 9. The skull of a medieval Japanese person found in Sarcophagus 2.

The people buried in Yodore, from their physical morphology and DNA, as well as their religious beliefs, had deep relations with the people of South China, Japan, and Koryo. The emergence of Ryukyu royal authority was based not only on Okinawan internal social development but also on foreign interaction including intermarriage. Judging from the Koryo-type roof tiles and mtDNA, the Mongol invasions of East Asia emerge as an important factor. The Yodore roof tiles are the same type as those found at the Yongjang Fortified Site, dated to some time around 1270, on Jin Island (Chindo). It was a palace of the state of Sambyeolcho, a polity derived from the military of Koryo, which briefly became independent in a rebellion against Koryo. In 1273 Sambyeolcho was pushed from Jin Island to Jeju Island (Chejudo) where its forces were defeated by Koryo and Mongol forces. There is a strong possibility that not only techniques such as roof tile making went to Okinawa but that some of the people of Sambyeolcho also went to Okinawa and contributed to the rise of the royal power of Eiso. The appearance of Haplotype F mtDNA in Okinawa indicates intermarriage between the Ryukyu royal family and overseas Chinese from Quanzhou at the time of Initial Yodore and predates the arrival of the "Thirty-six Families" from South China at the time of King Satto at the end of the 14th century. It is thought that the reason for the arrival of the South Chinese was to promote smooth trade relations, but the fall of Quanzhou in 1277 and the end of the Song Dynasty in 1279 must have been important factors as well.

At the time of the appearance of Eiso the Mongols invaded East Asia and claimed the allegiance of Koryo, the Southern Song had collapsed and even Japan experienced turbulence. It would be difficult to believe that only the Ryukyus did not feel the effect of these events.

CONCLUSION

I have discussed the emergence of royal authority of King Eiso at Urasoe in the second half of the 13th century based on the results of excavation. Also I believe that Urasoe provided the model for the Royal Castle of Shuri in the 15th century. Also, the royal power at Urasoe over the large castles was expressed through the uniformity of the palace and plaza. The large castles were linked by vassalage or confederacy. If these interpretations are true, then Urasoe controlled either all of Okinawa Island or all of the Okinawa group of islands through the large castles. The description in the *Chuzan Seikan* (Iha, Higaonna, and Yokoyama 1941) and legends of the Ryukyu Kingdom have been examined using archaeological data and traditional Ryukyu history. The emergence of royal authority was based not only on internal social development, but we must also consider international relations including intermarriage, with South China (centering on Quanzhou), the Koryo Kingdom of Sambyeolcho, and medieval Japan. Also, the upheavals caused by the Mongol invasions played an important role.

In this paper I have discussed provisional hypotheses which are very different from generally accepted interpretations. While we must try to draw a picture based on the analysis of historical facts, one by one, it is also necessary to place the investigation in a broad historical perspective. Following general opinion, Okinawan society was what we can term "primitive" (*genshi shakai*) up to about the 12th century. After that, within 100 years, a kingdom sprang up with surprising speed. In regard to this problem, on the contrary, we need to examine the presupposition that up to the 12th century society was primitive. I believe that while there was royal authority in the 13th century, the fully organized state organization of the Ryukyu Kingdom did not emerge until the latter half of the 14th to 15th centuries.

Translated by Richard Pearson

REFERENCES CITED

ASATO, SUSUMU

2006   *Ryukyu Oken to Gusuku [Ryukyu Royal Authority and Castles [Gusuku]]*. Nihon Shi Ribretto [Japanese History Libretto] *42*. Tokyo: Yamakawa Shuppansha.

CHINA, TEIKAN

2005   Urasoe Yodore no ishizushi to butsuzo chokoku [The stone sarcophagi and Buddhist carvings from Urasoe Yodore]. In *Urasoe Yodore no Sekizushi to Ikotsu Chosa no Chukan Hokoku [Preliminary Report of the Investigation of The Stone Sarcophagi and Human Bones from Urasoe Yodore]*: 28–51, ed. Urasoe Shi Kyoiku Iinkai. Urasoe: Urasoe Shi Kyoiku Iinkai.

DOI, NAOMI

2005   Urasoe Yodore shutsudo jinkotsu no jinruigakuteki chosa [A physical anthropological investigation of the human bones from Urasoe Yodore]. In *Urasoe Yodore no Ishizushi to Ikotsu Chosa no Chukan Hokoku [Preliminary Report of the Investigation of The Stone Sarcophagi and Human Bones from Urasoe Yodore]*: 18–21, ed. Urasoe Shi Kyoiku Iinkai. Urasoe: Urasoe Shi Kyoiku Iinkai.

IHA, FUYU, KANJUN HIGAONNA, AND SHIGERU YOKOYAMA (EDS.)

1940   *Ryukyu Koku Yuraiki: Ryukyu Shiryo Sosho 1, 2 [Ryukyu Country Records of Origins: Ryukyu Historical Materials Series 1, 2]*. Tokyo: Natori Shoten.

1941   *Chuzan Seikan; Ryukyu Shiryo Sosho 4 [Mirror of the Ages of Chuzan; Ryukyu Historical Materials Series 4]*. Tokyo: Natori Shoten.

KUBO, TOMOYASU

2003   Ryukyu, Ezo chi no kazari [Ornaments of the Ryukyu and Ezo Areas]. In *Tokubetsu Tenrankai, Kin'iro Kogei ni Miru Nihon Bi [Special Exhibition, Kazari in Gold; Japanese Aesthetics Through Metal Works]*: 240–263, ed. Kyoto Kokuritsu Hakubutsukan. Kyoto: Kyoto Kokuritsu Hakubutsukan.

MOKPO TAEHAKKYO PANMULGWAN

1990   *Cholla Namdo Jindo Gun 1990 Yongjiangsong [The Yongjiangsong, Jindo 1990, South Cholla]*. Mokpo: Mokpo University Museum.

SHINODA, KEN'ICHI

2005   Urasoe Yodore shutsudo jinkotsu to DNA bunseki [The human bones from Urasoe Yodore and analysis of DNA]. In *Urasoe Yodore no Ishizushi to Ikotsu Chosa no Chukan Hokoku [Preliminary Report of the Investigation of The Stone Sarcophagi and Human Bones from Urasoe]*: 22–23, ed. Urasoe Shi Kyoiku Iinkai. Urasoe: Urasoe Shi Kyoiku Iinkai.

TOMA, SHI'ICHI

1988   Gusuku no ishi zumi ni tsuite, jo [Regarding castle stone wall building I]. *[Okinawa Ken] Bunka Ka Kiyo* 5:18–37.

URASOE SHI KYOIKU IINKAI

2001   *Urasoe Yodore I. Ishi Zumi Iko Hen [Urasoe Yodore I Built Stone Features]*. Urasoe: Urasoe Shi Kyoiku Iinkai.

2005a *Urasoe Yodore II. Kawara Damari Iko Hen [Urasoe Yodore II. The Accumulation of Roof Tiles]*. Urasoe: Urasoe Shi Kyoiku Iinkai.

2005b *Urasoe Yodore no Ishizushi to Ikotsu Chosa no Chukan Hokoku [Preliminary Report of the Investigation of The Stone Sarcophagi and Human Bones from Urasoe Yodore]*. Urasoe: Urasoe Shi Kyoiku Iinkai.

2007   *Urasoe Yodore III. Kinzoku Koboato Hen [Urasoe: the Metal Workshop]*. Urasoe: Urasoe Shi Kyoiku Iinkai.

YOTSUYANAGI, KASHO

2006   *Urushi [Lacquer] I, II*. Tokyo: Hosei Daigaku Shuppankai.

The Significance of Chinese Trade Ceramics from Ryukyu: Focusing on Yuan Dynasty Blue and White Porcelain

MEITOKU KAMEI
SENSHU UNIVERSITY, TOKYO

INTRODUCTION

It is a well-known fact that trade ceramics have been discovered in "Old Ryukyu" (Ko Ryukyu), a term used to designate the period of polities that existed within today's Okinawa Prefecture from the 13th century up to the invasion by Satsuma in 1609. These trade ceramics have been excavated in considerable numbers chiefly from *gusuku* (castle) sites, and they are discovered in smaller settlements as well. They were brought into this region from the late 12th century, continuing throughout the Old Ryukyu Period. However the greatest quantity is discovered in the so-called Gusuku Period, which lasted for about 200 years, from the mid-14th century through to the mid 16th century.

The producer kilns for the trade ceramics excavated in Okinawa prefecture include the Lonquan kilns from Zhejiang Province, the Jingdezhen kilns from Jiangxi Province, and white ware kilns in Fujian Province. A lesser number of items from Korea and Thailand have also been unearthed. The Chinese ceramics were assembled in Fuzhou, a port frequented by missions from Old Ryukyu, and shipped to the port of Naha, where they were in demand by *gusuku* of every region. Furthermore, these ceramics were transported on Ryukyu merchant ships to various parts of Southeast Asia, Japan, and Korea during the Old Ryukyu Period.

YUAN DYNASTY BLUE AND WHITE WARES EXCAVATED FROM OLD RYUKYU

Among the ceramics excavated from Old Ryukyu Period sites, attention is frequently paid to the fact that there are many specimens of Yuan Dynasty blue and white ware. In this paper, I concentrate on this type. It is already known that a vast amount of Yuan Dynasty blue and white has been found in this region, but a precise accounting of the numbers and vessel types has not been reported. In 2005, the Senshu University Asian Archeology Team published *A Compendium of Yuan Type Ceramics Found in China* (Kamei 2005), bringing together detailed material on Yuan Dynasty blue and white wares from archaeological excavations in China. In 2007, we turned to the project *Collected Materials of Yuan Blue and White Wares Excavated in Japan*, measuring specimens and making measured drawings of all specimens excavated in this country (Kamei 2008). Based on the archaeological data, I want to focus on two aspects. First, I would like to compare quantitatively the Yuan Dynasty blue and white ware in Old Ryukyu with finds from the Japanese archipelago from Kyushu northward and those from China. Second, in view of the Ryukyu materials, I want to point out modifications to the traditional theories about the role of Yuan Dynasty blue and white wares as trade ceramics.

To begin, looking at the number of sites in which Yuan Dynasty blue and white wares have been excavated (Figure 1), sites from Kyushu northward do not exceed one quarter of the total, with the rest located in the Ryukyus. More precisely, the data on Yuan Dynasty blue and white ware excavated from Kyushu northward comprise 19 sites, 38 pieces, and 119 sherds. In the northern areas, sites extend up to Tohoku, and the Japan Sea area has many sites; in the case of North Kyushu, since the frequency of excavations in the Hakata Site Complex has been high, the number of sites yielding Yuan Dynasty blue and white ware specimens

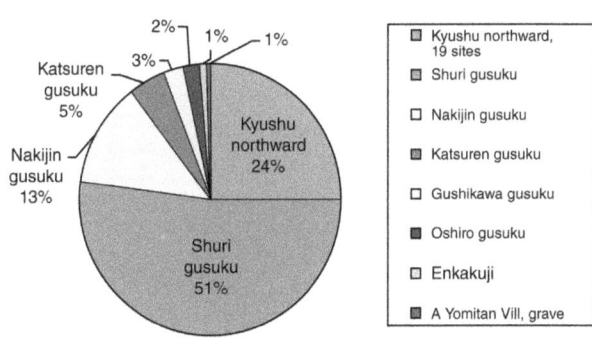

Figure 1. Yuan type blue and white wares excavated in Japan.

Table. 1 Sites on Okinawa and Kume Islands Yielding Yuan Blue-and-White Wares

	Site	The Location	Vessel Type
1	NAKIJIN *gusuku*	Nakijin Village Imadomari	jar 7, jar lid 1, large dish 5, bowl 1, cup 1, *meiping* 1, long-necked vase 1, incense burner 1, small jar, abbreviate brushwork small jar 2
2	KATSUREN *gusuku*	Uruma City, Katsuren,	jar 2, large dish 3, large bowl 1, long-necked vase 1
3	Yomitan Village grave	Yomitan Village, Sobe,	jar 1 (complete)
4	ENKAKUJI (Temple)	Naha City, Shuri Tonokura	large dish 1
5	SHURI *gusuku*	Naha City, Shuri Tonokura	jar 12, large dish 27, *meiping* 6, long-necked vase 7, dish 1, bowl-cup 19. stem cup 3, incense burner 1, pouring bowl 1, stand 1, covered box 1
6	OSHIRO *gusuku*	Nanjo City, Ozato	jar 1
7	GUSHIKAWA *gusuku*	Kumejima town Nakandakari	jar 2, jar lid 1, long-necked vase 2

(data from the following sources: 1. Kin et al 1983, Nakijin Son 1993, 2007. 2. Kamei and Chinen 1983, 3. Kamei 1994 5. Okinawa Ken 1998, 2005 7. Kumejima Cho 2005.

is relatively large. Looking at the vessel shapes, while there is not a remarkable large repertory, long-necked vases occur in slightly high numbers, and in the category of large wares, excavations have uncovered jars, *meiping*, and large dishes (*ban*)—among them, small sherds decorated with geometric patterns that merit attention. Additionally, the *meiping* excavated from the Kezôin Chapel at Toyohara Buddhist Temple (Kanemoto 1982: 8–29) and a *meiping* said to be excavated from the Shitokuji site (Tsurumaki 2003: 96–98, Fig. 65-820) are superb specimens of the "Zhizheng" archetype. Moreover, a stand excavated from the Kasai site (Sasaki 1983:191–192) with strings of relief beading is a fine example of this type of Yuan Dynasty blue and white ware.

Next, the data on Yuan Dynasty blue and white excavated from Okinawa Prefecture is tabulated below (Table 1). These are almost entirely individual sherds and later when I make a comparison with South and West Asia, it is not the sherd (*hahen*) count from Ryukyu excavations but rather the piece (*kotai*) count that one must attend to. Our method for determining a "piece" entails an inspection of each individual sherd by naked eye for its shape, location, motif, manufacturing technique, clay body, glaze, etc. When sherds with shared characteristics number more than one they are collectively counted as a "piece"; however, they are counted as only one in the sherd count. There are fragments where the surface is transformed by secondary fire or other disasters, or with missing parts such as rims or bases, that can be speculated as representations of single vessels, and in such an instance, the sherd count begins to approximate the piece count. Accordingly, we can say that, in terms of sheer numbers of fragments, more has been excavated than what is suggested by the "piece count" tabulated here (Figure 2).

I would like to point out the special characteristics of Yuan Dynasty blue and white ware excavated from Okinawa. The number of excavation sites, within an area that is narrow in comparison to Kyushu northward, numbers 7, with a total excavated piece count of 109 (839 sherds). Compared to Kyushu northward, the number of sites is only one-fourth, but the piece count is 2.8 times as much (the sherd count is seven times as much); a very large number. Among the total of 109 pieces of Yuan Dynasty blue and white excavated from the Ryukyus, Shuri Gusuku accounted for 79 pieces and 72% of the total, which puts it ahead of four other *gusuku*, and demonstrates a near monopoly in the possession of this type of ceramic. Among the vessel types excavated from Shuri Gusuku, large wares such as jars, large dishes, and *meiping* accounted for 58% of the total, and it is noteworthy that the large dish accounted for the largest percentage. The large dish, which is almost never found in consumption sites in China, was present in a total of 36 pieces from Ryukyu. Examples of jars with lugs in the shape of mythical beasts excavated from old tombs are conspicuous, possibly indicating ritual use. The long-necked vase is present in roughly the same piece count as Kyushu northward, but the amount of stem cups is not very high. The small jars in what is called the "abbreviated brushwork" type appear in only one instance at Nakijin Gusuku; at Shuri Gusuku, which yielded such a huge number of sherds, not a single piece of this type was found.

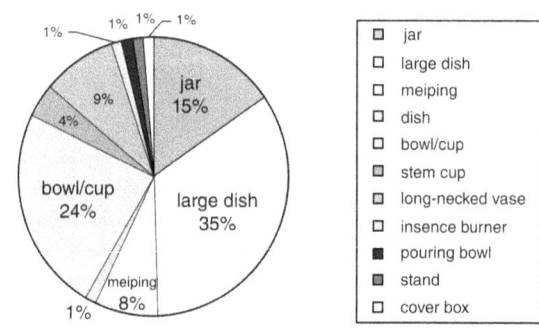

Figure 2. Vessel types of Yuan type blue and white wares excavated from Shuri Castle.

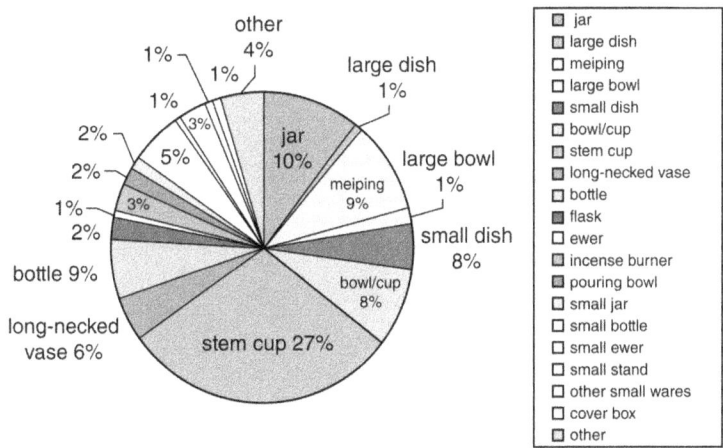

Figure 3. Vessel types of Yuan type blue and white wares excavated in China, excluding kiln sites.

YUAN-DYNASTY BLUE AND WHITE WARES EXCAVATED IN CHINA AND THEIR COMPARATIVE ASPECTS

Yuan Dynasty blue and white ware discovered in archaeological excavations of consumption sites in all of China (including underglaze copper red wares) as of June of 2005 numbered 195 pieces from 66 sites. What this number indicates is that in comparison with other Yuan varieties such as celadons and white wares, blue and white wares are clearly found in lesser numbers, and their diffusion is very limited. This can only reflect a very low level of production.

A breakdown of the vessel types is illustrated in Figure 3. I would like to point out the following patterns. Large wares such as jars, *meiping*, bowls, and bottles represent ¼ of the total discoveries, disproving the traditional theory that large wares were all made for export. Forty-one pieces of stem cups were found, accounting for over ¼ of the total. We can see that this vessel type, used for wine or in offertory ritual, was incorporated into the blue and white repertoire in quantity. Among excavated specimens of large dishes with a diameter exceeding 20 cm, only a single piece found in Hebei Province. The Hutian kilns at Jingdezhen manufactured quantities of these large dishes, so in this case we have support for the traditional theory that among the large wares, dishes were produced for the export market. Among excavated specimens of bowls with a diameter exceeding 18 cm, only two examples are known from China. Thus, the big difference between the results from Chinese excavations and specimens excavated from the Tughlaq Palace site in Delhi (Smart 1977), and items preserved in the Ardebil Shrine (Pope 1956) and the Topkapi Saray Museum (Krahl and Ayers 1986) is the absence or presence of these two vessel types, the large bowl and dish. The large dish and bowl shapes were used in China as tableware, but rather than blue and white, celadons from Longquan were used, thus reflecting a preference for certain kiln products rather than a difference in dining customs as is sometimes believed. As proof of this, in the Gao'an City deposit site from Jiangxi Province, among the 256 pieces of excavated ceramics, 20 pieces of blue and white wares were recovered, 7.9% of the total piece count, but the large dishes and bowls were Longquan wares, not blue and white wares. In archaeological excavations of the Hutian kiln site at Jingdezhen, the number of blue and white wares only occupied 0.45% of the total kiln waster count; the production quantity was extremely low but 70% of the total consisted of large dishes.

YUAN DYNASTY BLUE AND WHITE WARES AS TRADE CERAMICS

In the above paragraphs, I have used those data to provide a picture of Yuan Dynasty blue and white ware excavated from Japan, Ryukyu, and China. Based on that data, I would like to consider some points regarding the export of Yuan Dynasty blue and white ware.

Most scholars are in agreement with the long-held theory about Yuan Dynasty blue and white ware, namely that it developed with the importation of cobalt pigment for underglaze painting in tandem with demand from Islamic nations to the west. Evidence is found in the large jars, dishes, bowls, and *meiping* that are almost entirely represented in collections at the Topkapi Saray Palace and the Ardebil Shrine, or excavated from the Tughlaq Palace in Delhi (Medley 1974: 31–62, Hasegawa 1995: 101–102)).

However, in opposition to this theory, I would like to present Table 2. Looking at the large wares such as jars, dishes, bowls, and *meiping*, among the total of 277 pieces, the 160 pieces from South and West Asia occupy 60% of the total, and thus it is clear that large wares were exported mainly to those regions. However, the fact remaining is that 40% were excavated from China, Japan, and the Ryukyus; in particular the amount of *meiping* excavated from China was greater than from other regions, reflecting a sizable domestic demand.

TABLE. 2 YUAN-DYNASTY BLUE AND WHITE WARES FROM CHINA, JAPAN, OLD RYUKYU, SOUTH AND WEST ASIA

	Jar	Large Dish	Large Bowl	Meiping	Bottle	Long-Necked Vase	Flask	Bowl/Cup	Stem Cup	Ewer	Dish	Incense Burner	Pouring Bowl	Stand	Cover Box	Abbreviate Brushwork	Total
China	14	1	2	13	6	8	3	11	39	1	6	4	2	4	1	15	130
Japan	7	8	0	3		12	0	2	0	0	1	0	3	3	0	1	40
Old Ryukyu	25	36	1	7		11	0	20	3	0	1	0	1	1	1	2	109
South and West Asia	10	105	35	10	4	1	4	8	0	0	1	0	0	0	0	1	179
Total	56	150	38	33	10	32	7	41	42	1	9	4	6	8	2	19	458

Turning our focus to the large dishes and bowls, they have almost never been found in China; 70% of them are preserved in South and West Asia, showing a dominant share. However, regarding the large dish, the remaining portion, 30%, was excavated in Ryukyu and Japan, and the same thing can be said about the jar. Therefore jars and *meiping* were items of domestic demand in China, and large dishes, bowls and jars were produced for the purpose of export, with large dishes and bowls destined chiefly for South and West Asia. Over 40% of the dishes and jars were exported to the Ryukyus.

That is to say, while it has been recognized for some time that a significant number of Yuan Dynasty blue and white ware sherds has been excavated from Old Ryukyu, I believe that our research, which has clarified the amounts and types of excavated vessels, calls for a correction of the idea that the export routes of large wares proceeded along a "single track" to South and West Asia. This point may be reinforced by consulting notes about the number of trade missions sent to Southeast Asia in the diplomatic record of Old Ryukyu entitled *Rekidai Hoan* (Okinawa Kenritsu 1992): a total of 104 shipments took place between 1419 and 1570, with 65 shipments designated as having ceramic cargo (Kamei 1993). If we speculate that some 70,000 pieces of ceramics were carried in a single ship, it is natural to assume that Yuan Dynasty blue and white wares were included. Archaeological excavations in Southeast Asia have not yet made much headway in this area, but I believe that by looking at examples such as the Trowulan site in Indonesia where large wares have been discovered, the scale of activity in the Ryukyus in exporting a huge amount of Yuan Dynasty blue and white ware can be imagined. The number exported from Ryukyu far exceeds the amount of pieces preserved in South and West Asia.

Archaeological discoveries from Ryukyu clearly demonstrate that the share of Yuan Dynasty blue and white ware exported to that region was relatively high and therefore significant. As I have illustrated in Figure 4, the time has come to revise the assumption, shared by scholars worldwide, that Yuan Dynasty blue and white ware was made principally for export to South and West Asia. In particular, the new discoveries from Gushikawa Castle, Kumejima (Plate 8) and Shuri Castle (Figures 5 to 9) provide a rich resource for the study of porcelain trade during the Yuan Dynasty and the important role of the Ryukyus in East and Southeast Asian networks.

Translated by Richard L. Wilson, International Christian University.

REFERENCES CITED

HASEGAWA, SHOTOKU

1995   *Gen-Min no Seika [Yuan and Ming Blue and White Porcelain]*. Tokyo: Heibonsha.

KAMEI, MEITOKU

1993   Nansei Shoto ni okeru boeki tojiki no ryutsu keiro [The changing circumstances of the flow of trade ceramics in the Southwest Islands]. *Jochi Ajiagaku* 11:11–45.

2004   Yomitan kobo seika tsubo o megutte [Concerning the blue and white jar found in an old tomb in Yomitan]. *Urasoe Shi Bijutsukan Kiyo* 3:7–12.

KAMEI, MEITOKU (ED.)

2005   *Ashu Kotoji Kenkyu: Chugoku Shutsudo Gen Keishiki Seikaji Shiryo Shusei [Study of Asian Ceramics: Collected Materials of Yuan Type Ceramics from Archaeological Sites in China]*. Tokyo: Asian Ceramics Society.

2008   *Ashu Kotoji Kenkyu: Nihon Shutsudo Gen Keishiki Seikaji Shiryo Shusei [Study of Asian Ceramics: Collected Materials of Yuan Type Ceramics from Archaeological Sites in Japan]*. Tokyo: Asian Ceramics Society.

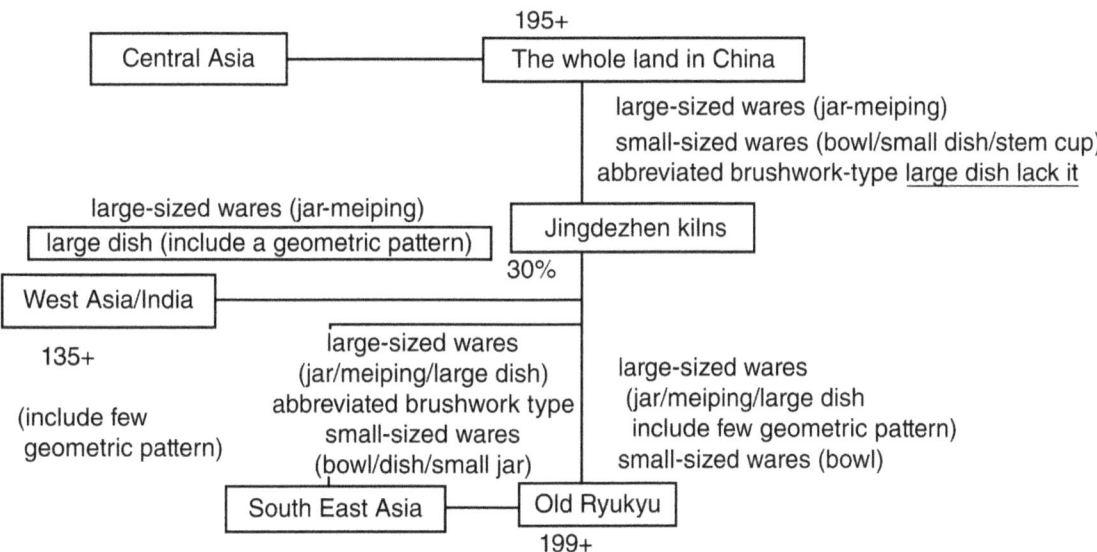

Figure 4. Conceptual diagram of Yuan type blue and white production, trade, and consumption (Totals are estimations).

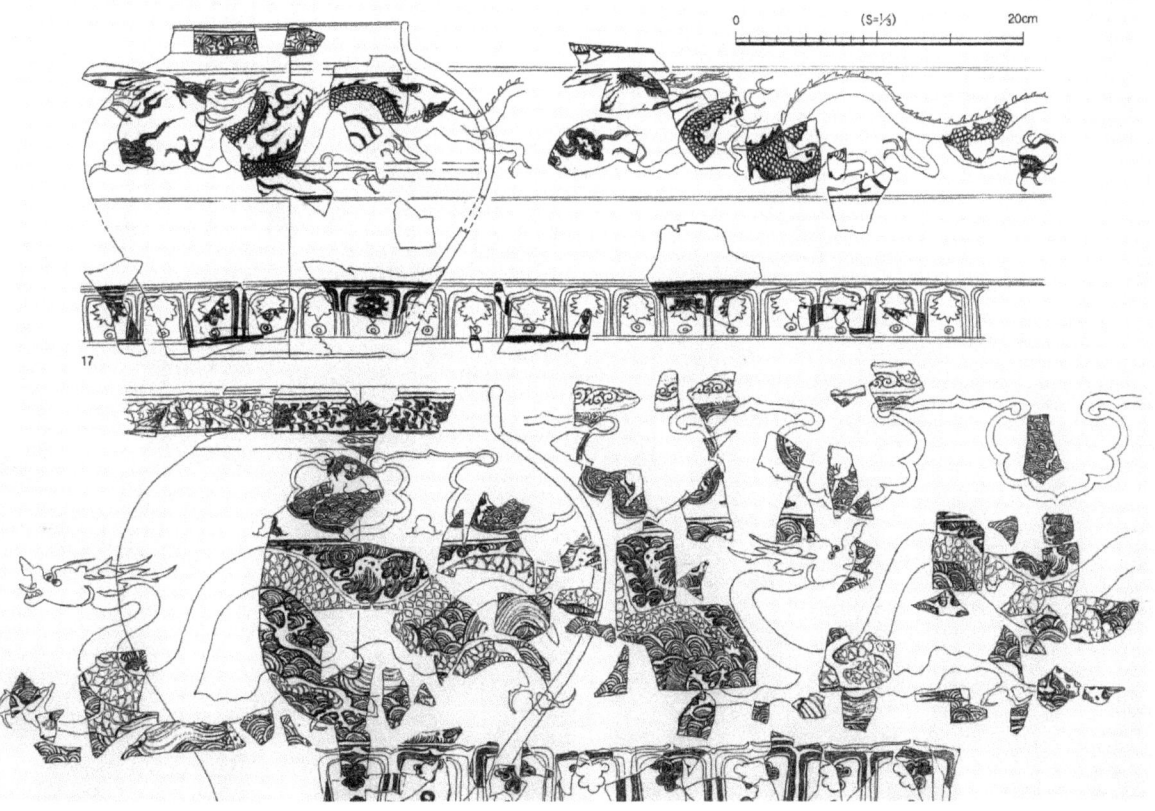

Figure 5. Blue and white jars from Nakijin Castle. (Courtesy Nakijin Son Kyoiku Iinkai)

Figure 6. Blue and white long necked bottle from Shuri Castle (Courtesy Okinawa Kenritsu Maizo Bunkazai Senta).

Figure 7. Blue and white large dish from Shuri Castle (Courtesy Okinawa Kenritsu Maizo Bunkazai Senta).

Figure 8. Blue and white large dish from Shuri Castle (Courtesy Okinawa Kenritsu Maizo Bunkazai Senta).

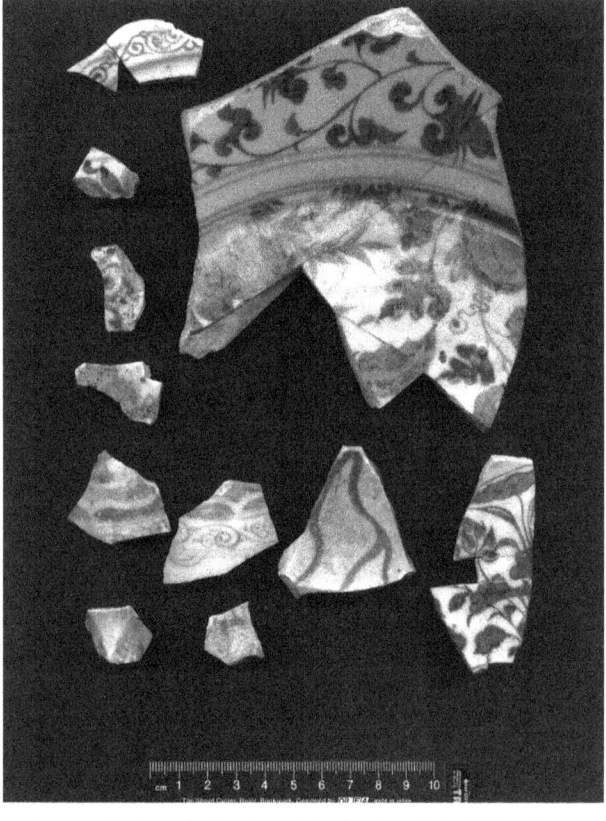

Figure 9. Blue and white large dish from Shuri Castle (Courtesy Okinawa Kenritsu Maizo Bunkazai Senta)

KAMEI, MEITOKU AND ISAMU CHINEN
1983   Katsuren joseki shutsudo no Gen Seika 1983. *Boeki Toji Kenkyu* 3:41–44.

KANEMOTO, KENJI
1982   *Toyohara dera II: Kezoin Iseki Dainiji Hakkutsu Chosa Gaiho* [Toyohara Temple II: Summary Report of the Second Excavation of the Kezoin Site]. Fukui Ken Maruoka Cho: Maroka Cho Kyoiku Iinkai.

KIN, SEIKI, TOMO MATSUDA, AND SUEHIRO MIYAZATO
1983   Nakijin joseki shutsudo Gen yoshiki seika to kyohan tojiki [Yuan type blue and white and associated ceramics from the Nakijin castle site]. *Toji Boeki Kenkyu* 3:32–40.

KRAHL, REGINA AND JOHN AYERS
1986   *Chinese Ceramics in the Topkapi Saray Museum*. London: Sotheby's Publications.

KUMEJIMA CHO KYOIKU IINKAI
2005   *Gushikawa Joseki Hakkutsu Chosa Hokokusho I [Report of the Excavation of the Gushikawa Castle Site]*. Kumejima: Okinawa Ken Kumejima Cho Kyoiku Iinkai.

MEDLEY, MARGARET
1974   *Yuan Porcelain and Stoneware*. London: Faber and Faber.

NAKIJIN SON KYOIKU IINKAI
1983   *Nakijin Joseki Hakkutsu Chosa Hokokusho [Report of the Excavation of the Nakijin Castle Site]*. Nakijin: Nakijin Son Kyoiku Iinkai.

2007   *Nakijin Joseki Shuhen Iseki [Sites Surrounding Nakijin Castle]*. Nakijin: Nakijin Son Kyoiku Iinkai.

OKINAWA KEN KYOIKU IINKAI
1998   *Shuri Joseki Kyonouchi Hakkutsu Chosa Hokokusho [Report of Excavations of the Kyonouchi, Shuri Castle Site]*. Naha: Okinawa Ken Kyoiku Iinkai.

2005   *Shuri Joseki Nikaiden Chiku Hakkutsu Chosa Hokokusho [Report of Excavations in the Nikaiden Area of Shuri Castle]*. Naha: Okinawa Ken Kyoiku Iinkai.

OKINAWA KENRITSU TOSHOKAN SHIRYO HENSHUSHITSU
1992   *Rekidai Hoan [Valuable Records of Successive Generations]*. Naha: Okinawa Ken Kyoiku Iinkai.

POPE, JOHN
1956   *Chinese Porcelain from the Ardebil Shrine*. Washington: Smithsonian Institute, Freer Gallery of Art.

SASAKI, TATSUO
1983   *Kasaijo: Kasai Joshi Hakkutsu Chosa Hokokusho [Kasai Castle: Report of the Excavation of the Site of Kasai Castle]*. Tokyo: Kasai Joshi Chosakai.

SMART, ELLEN S.
1977   Fourteenth Century Chinese Porcelain from a Tughlaq Palace in Delhi. *Transactions of the Oriental Ceramic Society* 1976–77:198–230.

TSURUMAKI, YASUSHI (ED.)
2003   *Joetsu Shi Sosho [Collected Writings of Joetsu Shi History]*. Joetsu Shi: Joetsu Shi.

The Architectural Landscape of the Kingdom of Ko Ryukyu

Takashi UEZATO
Institute for the Study of Okinawan Culture, Hosei University

Introduction

Once upon a time an independent state, the Ryukyu Kingdom, developed beyond the borders of Japan. In the study of Ryukyu history, there is a separate period which corresponds to the Japanese medieval period from around the 12th century to 1609 known as the Ko (Old) Ryukyu Period. From the 14th century the Ryukyu Kingdom participated in the Ming tributary system and became prosperous through relaying trade throughout the East Asian maritime world during the Ming trade prohibition. In this paper I wish to discuss several problems in the architecture of the Ko Ryukyu Period, from the point of view of written history.

Special Historical Features of the Ryukyu Kingdom in the Ko Ryukyu Period.

I would like to summarize as a premise to my discussion, the development of Ko Ryukyu and special features of the Ryukyu Kingdom from recent studies. One of the special features of the Ryukyu Kingdom is that it is difficult to separate the internal historical world from developments in the external world and one cannot grasp the situation by studying the history of a single state. Trade was not limited to state trade and involved the relationship of private trade including the Wako pirates, and Ryukyu was organically linked to the surrounding area. State development in the Ryukyus accelerated in the latter half of the 14th century. In 1372, The King of Chuzan, Satto, began a tributary relationship with Ming China, along with the northern and southern Ryukyu kingdoms of Sanhoku and Sannan. It appears that the Ryukyuans modified the trade route used by Japan and Yuan China. With the internal disturbances at the end of Yuan, the activities of the Wako pirates, and the deterioration of stability in the region, the main sea route changed from Hakata-Ningbo, the so called Taiyo Route, to the Higo Takase-Fujian Route (Nanto Route) (Enokimoto 2002; Hashimoto 2005). This was the reason for Ryukyu becoming the port of call for itinerant traders between Yuan and Japan. The vigorous use of the southern route from the 14th century has been substantiated by the distribution of trade ceramics (Kamei 1993).

Naha was a kind of "floating island" with a natural harbor, used by traders as a port of call. Its importance as a port grew with the rise of local Ryukyu power. It is also natural that it should develop through external trade on the Southern Route used at the end of the Yuan Dynasty (Uezato 2006). It is also proposed that Naha grew from the migration and commercial activity of the overseas Fujianese community of south coastal China, who founded the community of Kume Mura (Maehira 1992). The existence of the Chinese community before 1372 is also confirmed. The local power of the *aji* and the rulers of the three kingdoms used Naha to play an important role in the pattern of development of the state, since Naha was the location and center of private trade and provided important port facilities. Naha functioned as a receiver for the powers of private trade including the Wako pirates. It was also important in the tributary trade and benefited from various preferential treatments, and was also related to China through the Ming prohibition and the Ming security measures and the rearrangement of commercial relations which these generated (Okamoto 1999).

Based on the trading activities carried out by the Ming Period maritime traders living in the trading port town, Naha waited for the opportunity to have a relationship with royal power and the Kume Mura community. The people of Naha played a role as intermediaries between Ming and Ryukyu kings since previously this relationship did not have a firm foundation (Takahashi 1994). The Chinese settlement in Naha had power independent of the king. It played a role in the authorization of the tributary relationship including the provision of large ships and the establishment of the so-called Thirty-Six Families from Fujian. In addition to the foreign trading activities, the Chinese in Kume Mura had a special relationship to

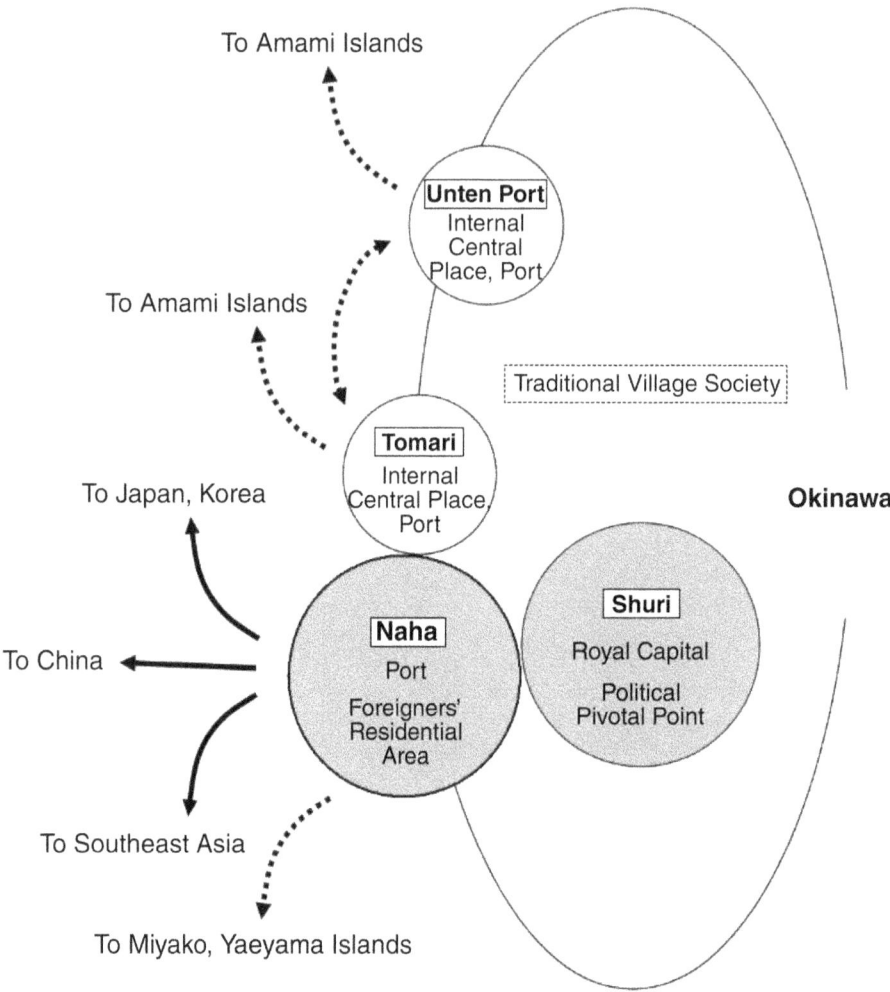

Figure 1. Diagram of Ko Ryukyu society.

the First Sho Dynasty of Chuzan. The Chinese copied the dynastic system of the Ming Dynasty, and several persons emerged who played the role of creating an affinity with the Ming system. They provided a model for state organization in the Chuzan Kingdom (Tomiyama 2004).

If we consider these points, Naha was a place with a totally different nature from the local society which developed in the Ryukyus up to the latter half of the 14th century. At the time that Ryukyu was entering into the tributary system, the local powers in Ryukyu used external powers to carry out political and economic activities. In the early 15th century we need to think of the relationship of Naha to the shift of the political center from Urasoe to Shuri.

In the society of Ko Ryukyu the palace of Shuri was linked to the port of Naha within one zone, as one part of a dual structured society of village and capital (Irumada and Tomiyama 2002) within the Ryukyu state (Takara 1989). A map of this dual structure of Okinawa might look like Figure 1. Of course it cannot be said that there was no location for external exchange other than Naha throughout the Ryukyus. The society of Ko Ryukyu was not completely egalitarian; however, Shuri and Naha exerted strong influence and were the political, cultural and economic base.

Aspects of the Port Town of Naha

In this section I would like to outline some of the aspects of the port town of Naha. The 15th century map, *Ryukyu Koku Zu (Map of the Country of Ryukyu)* gives the distribution in each area of *gusuku*, temples, shrines, as well as aspects of Naha port (Asato 2004; Uezato, Fukase, and Watanabe 2005). In a portion of the floating island of Naha, Kume Mura (also called Kumenri) contained houses of South Chinese, and there was also a Japanese residential area. From the map it is clear that the Japanese community was an old, developed residential community similar to that of the Chinese. The Japanese community was not surrounded by the earth walls surrounding the Chinese community as described by the 15th century Korean people who drifted to Okinawa. According to this map, Naha at the time of the First Sho Dynasty had a visible role as port, and the Japanese and Chinese communities are well confirmed.

Figure 2 presents a panoramic view of Naha (Uezato 2005), Naha was a separate island, termed a floating island. A 1 km causeway called the Chokotei connected it to the mainland, and led to the Shuri capital. In the Ko Ryukyu Period, Naha consisted of the Chinese community, Kume Mura, and the more narrowly defined Naha, which was divided into the districts of Higashi, Nishi, Wakasa Machi, Izumizaki, and Tomari. In Naha, which functioned as the port and center, there were the royal trading facilities of the Oyamise and the Tenshikan, which were the center of tributary trade activities with China. On a small island in the harbor there was the warehouse for foreign trade, Omono Gusuku. There was also the Tenpi Gu or Masobyo dedicated to Maso (Chinese Matsu), the Chinese female deity of maritime activity, and shrines and temples. It was the location of many religious institutions. It contained the facilities of foreign religions brought to Okinawa. On the floating island were the Chinese community of Kume Mura surrounded by earth walls and also the Japanese community, which included local Ryukyu people, living together. The Japanese community consisted of maritime traders, Zen priests, scholars, artisans, and Wako pirate captives. One group of Japanese was recruited by the kingdom for the administration of foreign trade.

SEVERAL PROBLEMS REGARDING THE ARCHITECTURE OF KO RYUKYU AND GUSUKU

Keeping in mind the above discussion, I would like to discuss several problems concerning the architecture of the Shuri Naha area, with particular attention to *gusuku*.

Some Problems Concerning Temples and Shrines

As noted above, religious institutions such as Buddhist temples, Shinto shrines, and the Matsu Shrine (Masobyo) all came to Ryukyu from foreign countries (Tables 1 and 2). The various religious facilities built in Okinawa created a concentrated religious atmosphere in one social stratum (Murai 1996). The foreign religious institutions were particularly concentrated in Shuri and Naha. They were traditionally for the people in the port who participated in the world outside of the Ryukyus. Most of the Shinto shrines concentrated in Naha were of the Kumano Gongen Sect (Figure 3) which had connections to overseas activities.

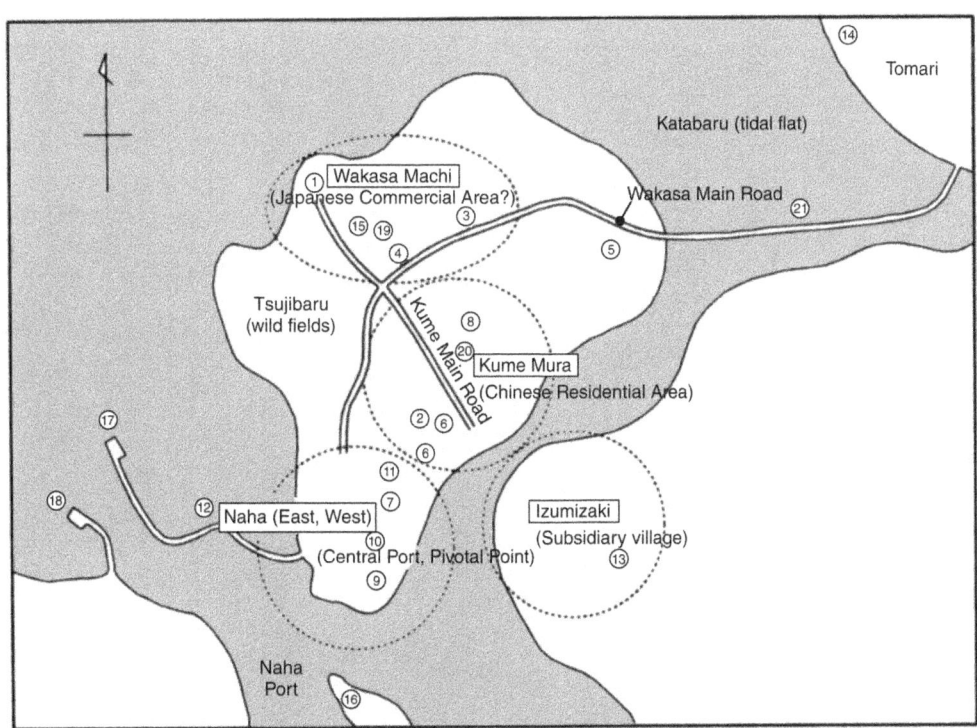

1. Naminoue Kumano Gongen, Gokokuji. 2. Tenmangu, Chorakuji. 3. Wakasa Machi Ebisu Den.
4. Wakasa Machi Jizodo. 5. Ukishima Jinja Chojuji. 6. Tenpi Gu. 7. Oyamisei. 8. Keirinji. 9. Naha Jizodo
10. Ebisu Den. 11. Tenshikan. 12. Oki Gu, Rinkaiji. 13. Wakuta Jizodo. 14. Ameku Gu, Seigenji
15. Tenson Byo. 16. Omono (Mimono) Gusuku. 17. Mie Gusuku. 18. Yarazamori Gusuku
19. Koganji. 20. Tozenji. 21. Chokotei

Figure 2. Conceptual map of Naha in the Ko Ryukyu Period.

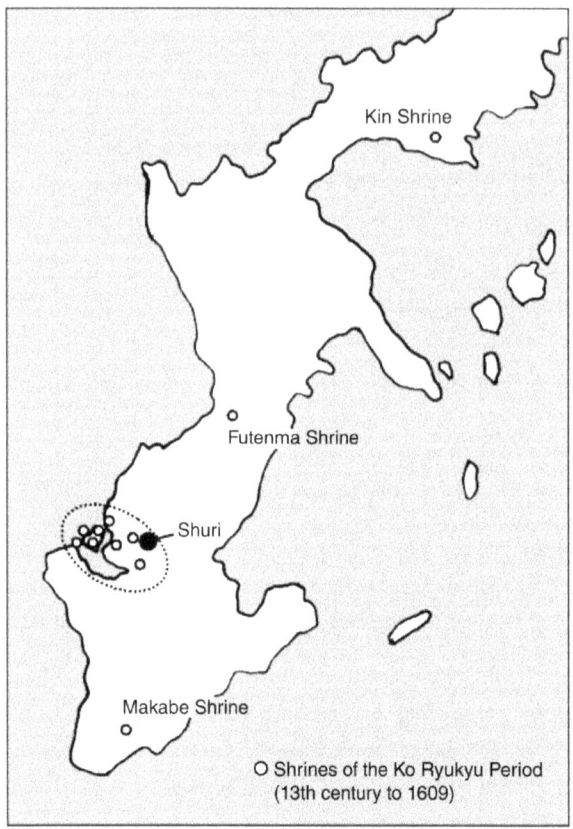

Figure 3. Distribution of Shinto shrines on Okinawa Island in the Ko Ryukyu Period.

In medieval Japan, Kumano was deeply connected to maritime activity and Kumano shrines occur at every point along maritime communication routes (Shinjo 1982). It is thought that this activity also extended from Kyushu to the Ryukyus. Shinto shrines were concentrated in Naha port because this is where Japanese lived.

At the time of Ko Ryukyu, the shrines and temples were concentrated in the central places of Naha and Shuri and the Ryufukuji was below the old capital of Urasoe (according to one opinion the Gokokuji Temple was also located there)(Tables 1 and 2). They were not found in other locations. The many temples clustered in Shuri and Naha were supervised by Zen priests and believers who were traveling back and forth to the Ryukyus, indicating the interaction between Ryukyu and Japan.

In regard to Buddhism in Ryukyu, there is a tradition that priests started to travel to the Ryukyus in the 13th century but it is only from the beginning of the 15th century that they actually lived in Ryukyu. At the beginning of the First Sho Dynasty, the Ho'onji, Gokurakuji, and Dai'an Zen Temple began as part of the system of temples called the *Zen Jissetsu* (the ten Rinzai temples below the rank of the Gozan main temples of Kyoto) (China 2002). In the *Ryukyu Koku Zu (Map of the Country of Ryukyu)*, centering on Shuri and Naha, several temples can be determined: Kokuseiji (Zen Temple), Keizenji, Ho'onji and Gokokuji. Buddhism prospered in the latter half of the 15th century at the time of Sho Taikyu when there was a spate of temple building. Many Japanese Zen priests who traveled outside of Japan were involved in the Ryukyus. The priest Kai'in Joko from the Kyoto Gozan Temples, who became Chief Abbot of the Ryukyu Enkakuji, and the Abbot of the Tennoji, Dankei Zenso, of Satsuma, these persons served as envoys to the Muromachi Bakufu. It is thought that the Enkakuji, built in 1492, held the function of office for foreign relations (Murai 1995). Also, Zen priests were deeply involved in the rituals of Ryukyu royal power and held the role of Protectors of the State (Irumada and Tomiyama 2002). Thus at the time of Ko Ryukyu, Buddhism did not have only a religious aspect but was related to the politics, external relations and culture of Ko Ryukyu.

It should be noted that at the time of Ko Ryukyu, Buddhist architecture exerted influence on the architecture of *gusuku*. According to Yamamoto's analysis of stone pillar bases and stone foundation platforms, one can see in 14th century *gusuku* buildings the change to free standing single

TABLE 1: SHINTO SHRINES OF THE KO RYUKYU PERIOD (FROM THE *RYUKYU SHINTO KI*)(YOKOYAMA 1970)

NAME IN THE *RYUKYU SHINTO KI*	LOCATION	TEMPLE NAME	CONSTRUCTION DATE	SECT
Naminoue Gongen	Naha	Gokokuji	Hong Wu Period (1368-1398)?	Kumano Gongen
Oki no Gongen	Naha	Rinkaiji		"
Shikina Gongen	Shuri	Shin'oji		"
Ameku Gongen	Naha	Seigenji	Zheng Hua Period (1465-1487)?	"
Sueyoshi Gongen	Shuri	Manjuji	Jing Tai Period (1450-1457)	"
Futenma Gongen	Nakagusuku	Jinguji		"
Hachiman Bosatsu	Naha	Jintokuji	Zheng Hua 2 (1462)	Yahata Dai Bosatsu
Ise Taijin	Naha	Chojuji	Jing Tai 3 (1452)	Tensho Taishin
Tenman Gu	Naha	Chorakuji	Jia Jing Period (1522-1566)	Tenjin

TABLE 2. TEMPLES IN THE NAHA AREA DURING THE KO RYUKYU
PERIOD (FROM THE *RYUKYU SHINTO KI* (YOKOYAMA 1970) AND THE
RYUKYU KOKU YURAIKI (HOKAMA AND HATERUMA 1997))

AREA	TEMPLE NAME
Naha (East, West)	Tokoji, Ryushoji, Daitokuji, Ryogaji, Saishoji, Seifukuji
Wakasa Machi	Koganji
Izumizaki	Cho'onji
Kume Mura	Tozenji, Zenkoji, Keirinji, Seitaiji

pillar bases, and raised foundation platforms (*kidan*) and in the early 15th century First Sho Dynasty to numerous pillar bases and stone platforms. This is the time when *gusuku* were changing from *shiro* (fortified castle) to *seifu, kyokan* (center of administration and residence). This was the result of the influence of Buddhist halls and pagodas according to Yamamoto (2000).

Yamamoto's hypotheses about the influence of Buddhist architecture on castle architecture can be seen from another aspect. At the time of Sho Taikyu, along with the building of temples, 23 bells were also made. One of these bells made in 1458, which stood in front of the Seiden, called the *Bankoku Shinryo* (the bridge of all countries) and the bell made in 1457, the *Gikojo*, these two bells were originally in Shuri Castle and Goeku Castle respectively. Another object made in 1458 is the Ozato Castle *Unban* (gong). It is a type of iron or bronze cloud-shaped gong (Figure 4). The finding of these objects in *gusuku* seems to be a clear indication of similarities in construction between castles and temples.

Originally in Zen temples the residence of the priests was called *kuri*—which had the meaning of kitchen. The same term was used in Ko Ryukyu to refer to the central government (Takara 1987). In the Kinsei (early modern) Period, the Shuri Seiden was called the Ufugui (Japanese Oguri) and the Shichiya Ufugui (Japanese Shimo oguri) and was divided into two levels, upper and lower. Within Shuri Castle there were two offices, *soshikuri* and *kinkuri*. Since *gusuku* and temples had the same aspects, the same term were used for internal spaces. Terms for the kitchen and living areas of the temple were used for the living quarters of the castle.

The rush of temple building in the mid-15th century under Sho Taikyu was noted above. The makers of the bells were two Japanese, Fujiwara Kuniyoshi and Fujiwara Kunimitsu. Their bell casting activities covered a wide area in the main Japanese Islands (Maehira 1991) and is thought to have extended to Okinawa. It is clear that one part of temple construction in Ryukyu employed Japanese techniques. The form of the Ryukyu bells shows special characteristics of bells from Buzen Kokura and Chikuzen (Northern Kyushu) (Tsuboi 1970). The distribution of bells covers the same areas as those covered by the activities of the Hakata traders, which extended to Tsushima, and from Korea to Ryukyu.

Figure 4. (1) Bankoku Shinryo bell. (2) Ozato Unban (Buddhist gong).

From these points concerning the mid-15th century development of Buddhism as the protector of the Ryukyu government, the foreign community in Naha, and the building of temples in Shuri and Naha, we can postulate the role of temple architecture in the development of castle building. The presence of stone pillar bases and stone foundation platforms seem to confirm this.

The upper structures of *gusuku* no longer remain; however in the time of Sho Taikyu in 1456, according to the Korean castaways' account in the *Choson Sejong Shillok* (*Record of King Sejong, Choson Dynasty*) (Ikeya, Uchida, and Takase 2005: 101–183) the royal castle was surrounded by triple-walled enclosures, inside of which there was a palace with two external stories and three internal stories, all lacquered red, and the roof was made of wooden boards (*itabuki*) covered with metallic paint (Takara 1996). In the first half of the 16th century the royal mausoleum and the stone gate of the Sonohiyan Utaki had wooden slat roofs (Figure 5). This building gives us a glimpse of the architecture of Ko Ryukyu. The construction of roofs of wooden boards (*itabuki*) was widespread in Japan in

Figure 5. (Left) Stone Gate of the Sonohyan Utaki. (Right) Tama Udun Mausoleum.

the medieval period, and there is a possibility that this technique was brought in with Zen temples. At the time of Ko Ryukyu, there were also buildings with Koryo-type and Yamato-type roof tiles, which have been found in large quantities at only the following four sites: Urasoe, Shuri, Katsuren, and Sakiyama (S. Uehara 2000).

What was the nature of the relationship between Buddhist priests and *gusuku*? In Ko Ryukyu, the royal rituals which took place in Shuri Castle were a mixture of Chinese rituals and Ryukyu indigenous sun worship, based on Japan *Onmyo* (*Ying-yang*) concepts, with influence from Japanese medieval Zen and Pure Land Buddhism (Tomiyama 2004). In the Okinawa rituals which came from the Chinese Imperial Palace, the king, dressed in Chinese robes, sat opposite from the Zen priests according to the *Chosen Min Jitsuroku* (The Choson Annals of the Ming Dynasty). Since Buddhism came from outside, and penetrated deeply into the royal power of Ryukyu, it can be hypothesized that the adoption of temple architecture beginning in the 15th century did not have only a simple functional explanation.

Some Problems Concerning the Gusuku of the Royal Capital

In the 16th century, in the centralization of power by Sho Shin, the *aji* (chiefs or nobles) were gathered into the royal capital of Shuri. As a result of this, the historical role of the *gusuku* as residence and stronghold came to an end. With the exception of a few castles such as Nakijin, most of them were deserted. From the time of Sho Shin, from the later part of the Ko Ryukyu Period, *gusuku* are hardly mentioned. Only the castle at the top of the *gusuku* hierarchy retained its religious and administrative function. From the 16th century, the early part of the Second Sho Dynasty to the Satsuma Invasion of 1609, the *gusuku* had a military function I would like to consider. Sho Shin did not put an end to the military aspects of castles; rather, the strategic locations of Shuri and Naha were strengthened. With the concentration of the *aji* in the capital and their relinquishing of weapons, Ryukyu was disarmed, according to the usual accounts (Iha 1922). However regional *aji* still maintained

power to defend the country (Uezato 2002). In the *Omoro Soshi* songs, the royal military (*Shiyori Oyaikusa*) (Shuri militia) are referred to. These militia served in the invasion of Yaeyama in 1500. In the 16th century unification of the islands from Amami to Yonaguni, the largest extent of the Ryukyu Kingdom, there was a new stage of development of castles for military defense.

From the 16th century residential, military, and defensive functions of the *gusuku* were maintained only in the cases of Shuri, Nakijin, and Urasoe, as far as can be determined. Shuri Castle was the residence of the king, Nakijin Castle had political, military, and religious functions as the residence of the Sanhoku Governor, and Urasoe was the residence of the first son of Sho Shin, Sho Iko and his family. Tomi Gusuku, Yarazamori Gusuku, and Mie Gusuku maintained their defensive role.

It is important to note that castles with forms which did not previously exist appeared for the first time. Yarazamori Gusuku (built in 1554) and Mie Gusuku, built around the 16th century, were small single enclosure fortifications for Naha port. Takara (1980) classified them as special cases.

In the Late Ko Ryukyu Period, the consideration of *gusuku* forms requires different terms of reference. Once the stage of centralization and strengthening of the country had been realized, *gusuku* cannot be seen as free-standing points, but need to be seen as points in a region. The castles remaining in Shuri and Naha became more complex and new defensive types made their appearance. The currents in the development of the defensive aspects of Shuri and Naha from the 16th century, can be considered.

In the Sho Shin Period, on the north side of Shuri Castle, the Kankai Mon and the Kyukei Mon gates and an outer enclosure were added. In 1522, a military road was built from Shuri Castle to the south side of Naha port and it is possible that at this time Tomi Gusuku was quickly developed as a military garrison. In 1554, Yarazamori Gusuku was built at the entrance to Naha Port, adding to the defensive system of Shuri and Naha. In 1546 an enclosure and gate, the Keisei Mon, were added to strengthen the defenses of Shuri. By the 16th century when Mie Gusuku was built on the north shore of Naha Port, the defensive system of Shuri and Naha were complete.

Figure 6 shows *gusuku* which formed a defensive system in Shuri and Naha from around the 16th century. Shuri Castle which served as the royal residence had defenses in the inner and outer enclosures, and the Shuri commercial area, surrounding places like Torazu mountain (Torazuyama) was enclosed, and the Shuri Iriguchi leading to Urasoe, near the Taihei Bridge had a natural fortification like the road cuts of Kamakura. From Shuri to Naha, a road extended to the north shore of Naha Harbor, the Chokotei, and on the south side the Madama Road extended to the Madanbashi Bridge. On the south side was the fortification of Tomi Gusuku and on the north side Yuo Gusuku. The port was defended on both sides by Yarazamori Gusuku and Mie Gusuku, and it is likely that there was an iron chain defending the entrance of the port and cannons on both sides. In the event of an emergency there were defensive forces which could be dispatched to the fortresses and with local soldiers they could provide protection.

In this way the 16th century stage of development of the central places of Shuri and Naha had a structure of defense, and Shuri and Naha can be regarded as a cluster of *gusuku* forming the royal capital, with facilities serving the political and port functions of a trading state. Large scale wood and stone construction projects were based on the coordination of labor from the whole kingdom. This system functioned at the time of the Satsuma invasion in 1609. The cluster of *gusuku* constituting the royal capital which began with the emergence of the *aji* around the 12th century, developed military functions in its final form.

Next, I would like to consider one part of the royal capital *gusuku* group, Yarazamori Gusuku and Mie Gusuku. These two *gusuku* have particular elements that do not seem to come from the internal development of Ryukyu *gusuku*, but come from military fortifications. Yarazamori has a single, regular rectangular enclosure, with openings at 16 places on the seaward and landward side for cannons. It appears to have served for maritime defense. Mie Gusuku has the same structure (Uezato 2000). These two castles have a particular military function which diverges from the original development pattern of *gusuku*. What was the nature of the assumed threat to the capital *gusuku* group built in the 16th century? At this time the Ryukyu royal power had no internal coercive power. They had some external defense in the *gusuku* in the Naha port area; however Shuri and Naha had no surrounding moat or palisade so the defensive system was only meant for attacks from the sea. The primary factor in the construction of the defensive system can be seen in the state of affairs in 16th century maritime Asia. In 1553, the Ming took decisive action to control private trade by attacking the center for private trade, the Tanshan Islands. Events on the China coast and maritime Asian world incited the Ming to take action. This is the rise of the Great Wako of the Jia Jing Period. In order to counteract the development of Wako activity, the fortifications Yarazamori and Mie Gusuku were constructed at the entrance to Naha Harbor, and it is thought that Naha and Shuri were fortified. It seems very likely that Ryukyu relied on China for the know-how for building fortifications against the Wako. Ming China fortified coastal commercial areas government buildings, and other places with guns and weapons. For instance in Shandong, the entrance of the Penglai maritime fortifications was fortified with platforms for cannons similar to those of Yarazamori Gusuku. It is necessary to compare the Ryukyu fortifications against the Wako with those of China.

It is also necessary to look at the fortification system in the center of Ryukyu, Kume Mura, in the center of the floating island of Naha. The Chinese community of Kume Mura has a strong image of "Chinatown." In Ko Ryukyu it was surrounded by an earth wall, described in the *Choson Sejong Shillok* (*The Records of King Sejong of Choson*). Kume Mura was referred to as the *Toei* or *Eichu*, which has the meaning of enclosed area or military depot or inside the depot. Kume Mura was the community of the "Hundred Families," a kind of a miniature Chinese-walled city.

Whether Kume Mura was actually fortified cannot be confirmed in the following account. In 1606, the leader of the Chinese tributary delegation, Xia Tzu Yang recorded in the *Shi Liuchiu Lu* (Account of a Mission to the Ryukyus) (Xia and Harada 2001) that Kume Mura was considered a safe place in an emergency. There is also an account of Ryukyu soldiers using the Kume Mura fortress at the time of the Satsuma invasion of 1609 in the *Ryukyu Iri no Ki* (*Account of the Entry to Ryukyu*) (Kagoshima Ken 1984: 252–262).

The earth wall of Ko Ryukyu is not mentioned in accounts of the Kinsei (Early Modern) Period. There has not yet been a specific excavation project to locate the fortifications but nothing has been found from written sources. The fortifications of Kume Mura should be re-examined. They will be of a different origin or ancestry than the Ryukyu *gusuku* (including the gusuku constructed of earth). As mentioned above Naha was a different space from the rest of Ryukyu. From the beginning it had a strongly distinctive character, and it was a kind of intermediate space between Japan and China, and it developed as a kind of separate living space constructed from outside of Ryukyu society.

It is necessary to study other Chinese communities that developed overseas. For instance at the beginning of the 15th century, for instance, the relay point for the voyages of Zheng He to the Arab and African world, according to Chinese accounts of the original site, had four gates and a palisade, and a watch tower and fortifications (*Ma Huan, Ying Ya Sheng Lan* (*Excellent Guide of Remote Water Paradise*)) (Ma 1969).

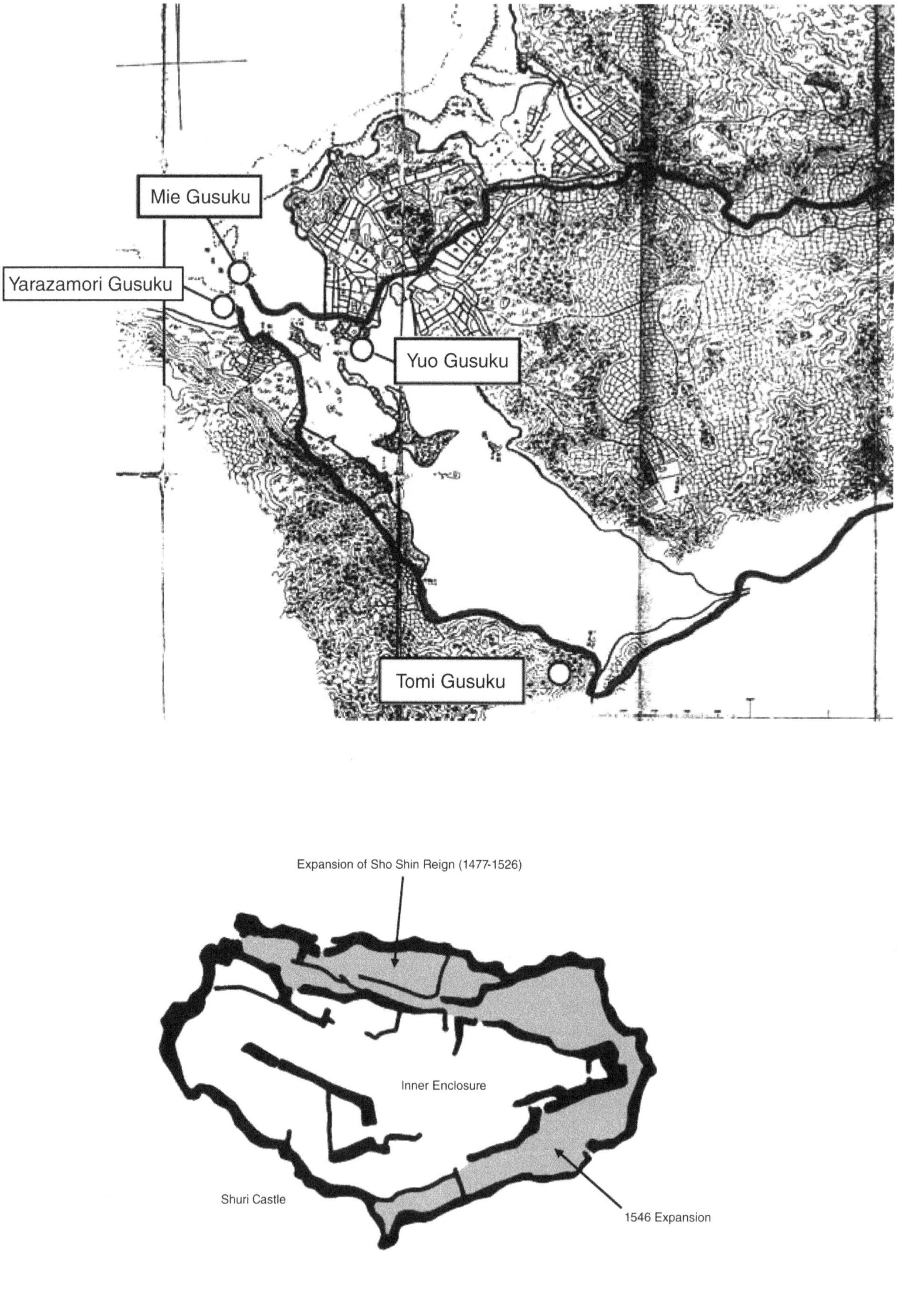

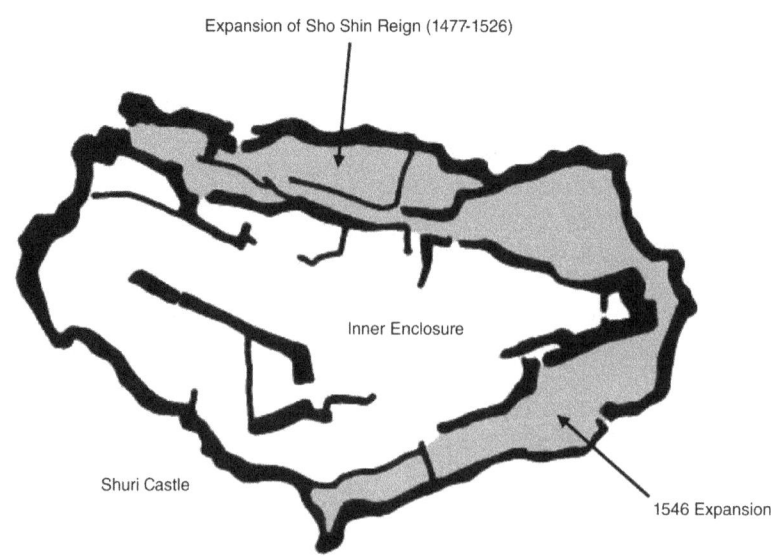

Figure 6. Map of the Gusuku of the Royal capital of the 16th century.

Conclusions

I have discussed some problems of the architecture of Shuri and Naha, the center of the Ryukyu Kingdom, with particular reference to *gusuku*. Emphasis has been placed on the development of unified power in Shuri and Naha. This structure basically did not change in the Kinsei (Early Modern) Period. Shuri and Naha were the urban areas and everything else was countryside (*inaka*). The social organization had an extremely centralized structure. I anticipate that future studies of Ko Ryukyu will take note of urban spaces.

Translated by Richard Pearson

References Cited

Asato, Susumu
2004   Dazaifu Jinja kyuzo [*Ryukyu Koku Zu*] ni miru 15 seiki no Ryukyu Okoku [The Ryukyu Kingdom as seen in the [*Map of the Country of Ryukyu*] belonging from ancient times to the Dazaifu Shrine]. *Ajiagaku* 11:11–45.

China, Teikan
2002   Sho Hashi shibun to Ko Ryukyu Bukkyo [An investigation of Sho Hashi and Ryukyu Buddhism] *Okinawa Bunka* 93:1–17.

Enokimoto, Wataru
2002   Genmatsu nairan no Nichigen kotsu [Interaction between Yuan and Japan at the time of the disturbances at the end of Yuan]. *Toyogakuho* 84:1:1–31.

Hashimoto, Yu
2005   *Chusei Nihon no Kokusai Kankei [Foreign Relations of Mediaeval Japan]*. Tokyo: Yoshikawa Kobunkan.

Hokama, Shuzen and Eikichi Hateruma (eds.)
1997   *Teihon: Ryukyu Koku Yuraiki [Standard Edition: Ryukyu Country Records of Origins]*. Tokyo: Kadokawa Shoten.

Iha, Fuyu
1922   *Ko Ryukyu no Seiji [The Politics of Ko Ryukyu]*. Tokyo: Kyodo Kenkyusha.

Ikeya, Machiko, Akiko Uchida, and Kyoko Takase (eds. and trans.)
2005   *Chosen Ocho Jitsuroku Ryukyu Shi Shiryo Sei: Yakuchu Hen [Ryukyu Materials in the Annals of the Choson Kingdom, translated and annotated]*. Okinawa: Gajumaru Shorin.

Irumada, Nobuo and Kazuyuki Tomiyama
2002   *Nihon no Chusei 5. Kita no Hiraizumi, Minami no Ryukyu [Mediaeval Period of Japan 5. Hiraizumi of the North, Ryukyu of the South]*. Tokyo: Chuo Koron Shinsha.

Kagoshima Ken (ed.)
1984   *Kyuki Zatsuroku Kohen [Latter Volume of Miscellaneous Documents]*. Kagoshima: Kagoshima Ken.

Kamei, Meitoku
1993   Nansei Shoto ni okeru boeki tojiki no ryutsu keiro [The changing circumstances of the flow of trade ceramics in the Southwest Islands]. *Jochi Ajiagaku* 11:11–45.

Ma, Huan (author) and Hiroshi Ogawa (trans.)
1969   *Eigai Shoran: Teiwa Seisei Kenbunroku [Excellent Guide of Remote Water Paradise]*. Tokyo: Yoshikawa Kobunkan.

Maehira, Fusa'aki
1991   Ryukyu no keisei to higashi Ajia [The formation of Ryukyu and East Asia]. In *Shinpan Kodai no Nihon [New Publication, Ancient Period of Japan]* 3: 463–484, eds. Tsuboi, Kiyotari, and Kunio Hirano. Kyushu, Okinawa. Tokyo: Kadokawa Shoten.

1992   Taigai kankei ni okeru kakyo to kokka: Ryukyu to Minjin Sanjurokusei o megutte [Overseas Chinese and the state in relation to overseas relations: concerning the Thirty Six Families of Min people and Ryukyu]. In *Ajia no naka no Nihon Shi: Kaijo no Michi [Japanese History within Asia: the Maritime Trade Route]*: 245–264, eds. Arano, Yasunori, Shosuke Murai, and Masatoshi Ishii. Tokyo: Tokyo Daigaku Shuppankai.

Murai, Shosuke
1995   *Higashi Ajia Okan—Kanshi to Gaiko [Highways of East Asia—Chinese Han Dynasty Poetry and Foreign Trade]*. Tokyo: Asahi Shinbunsha.

1996   Minato machi meguri: Setonaikai kara Baruto kai, Hokkai e [Around the port towns: from the Inland Sea to the Baltic and the North Sea]. Chusei Toshi Kenkyukai (ed) *Tsu, Tomari, Shuku, Chusei Toshi Kenkyu* 3:56–82.

OKAMOTO HIROMICHI

1999 Mincho ni okeru choko koku Ryukyu no ichizuke to sono henka [The position of the tributary state of Ryukyu in Ming, and its changes]. *Toyoshi Kenkyu* 57: 4:1–35.

SHINJO, TSUNEZO

1982 *Shinko Shaji Sankei no Shakai Keizaishiteki Kenkyu [Study of the History of Society and Economics of Pilgrimage to the Shrines and Temples: New Manuscript].* Tokyo: Hanawa Shobo.

TAKAHASHI, KOMEI

1994 Ryukyu Okoku [The Ryukyu Kingdom]. *Iwanami Koza Nihon Tsushi* 10:303–317.

TAKARA, KURAYOSHI

1980 *Okinawa Rekishi Josetsu [Disputed Themes in Ryukyu History].* Tokyo: San'ichi Shobo.

1987 *Ryukyu Okoku no Kozo [The Structure of the Ryukyu Kingdom].* Tokyo: Yoshikawa Kobunkan.

1989 *Ryukyu Okoku Shi no Kadai [Problems in the History of the Ryukyu Kingdom].* Naha: Hirugi Sha.

1996 Ryukyu okoku seiritsuki no shiryo ni kansuru oboegaki [A note relating to Shuri castle at the time of the development of the Ryukyu Kingdom]. In *Zenkindai ni Okeru Nansei Shoto to Kyushu; sono Kankeishi Kenkyu [The history of Relationships between the Southwest Islands and Kyushu in the Premodern Period]*: 109–129, ed. Maruyama Yosei. Tokyo: Taga Shuppan.

TOMIYAMA, KAZUYUKI

2004 *Ryukyu Okoku no Gaiko to Oken [Foreign Trade and Royal Authority of the Ryukyu Kingdom].* Tokyo: Yoshikawa Kobunkan.

TSUBOI, RYOHEI

1970 *Nihon no Bonsho [Japanese Temple Bells].* Tokyo: Kadokawa Shoten.

UEHARA, SHIZUKA

2000 Kogawara kara mita Ryukyu Retto no koryushi [A history of trade in the Ryukyu Islands seen from roof tiles]. *Kodai Bunka* 52:3:167–171.

UEZATO, TAKASHI

2000 Ryukyu no kaki ni tsuite [Concerning Ryukyu fire arms]. *Okinawa Bunka* 91:73–92.

2002 Ko Ryukyu no guntai to sono rekishiteki tenkai [The army of Ko Ryukyu and its historical development]. *Ryukyu Ajia Shakai Bunka Kenkyu* 5:105–128.

2005 Ko Ryukyu, Naha no Wajin kyoyuchi to kan Shina Kai sekai [The Japanese settlement in Naha at the time of Ko Ryukyu and the world around the China Sea]. *Shigaku Zasshi* 114:7:1–33.

2006 Ryukyu Naha no minato machi to [Wajin] Kyoryuchi [The port town of Naha, Ryukyu and the Japanese community]. In *Kokogaku to Chusei Kenkyu 3: Chusei no Taigai Koryu [Archaeology and Medieval Studies 3: Medieval Overseas Trade]*: 81–109, eds. Ono, Masatoshi, Fumihiko Gomi, and Mitsuo Hagihara. Tokyo: Koshi Shoin.

UEZATO, TAKASHI, KOICHIRO FUKASE, AND MIKI WATANABE

2005 Okinawa Kenritsu Hakubutsukan Shozo [*Ryukyu Koku Zu*] sono shiryoteki kachi to [*Kaito Shokokki*] to sono kanrensei ni tsuite [*the Map of the Country of Ryukyu*], its value as historical material and the map [*Several Countries of the Eastern Sea*] and their relationship. *Komonjo Kenkyu* 60: 24–45.

XIA, TZU YANG (AUTHOR), NOBUO HARADA (ED. AND TRANS.)

2001 *Shi Ryukyu Roku [Account of a Mission to Ryukyu].* Okinawa: Gajumaru Shorin.

YAMAMOTO, MASA'AKI

2000 14, 15 seiki no soseki, kidan ko [Thinking about the 14th and 15th century pillar base stones and stone foundation platforms]. In *Takamiya Hiroe Sensei Koki Kinen Ronshu: Ryukyu, Higashi Ajia no Hito to Bunka: Vol. 1*: 343–360, ed. Takamiya Hiroe Sensei Koki Kinen Ronshu Kankokai. Urasoe: Shoseido.

YOKOYAMA, SHIGERU (ED.)

1970 *Ryukyu Shinto Ki. Benrensha Taichu Shu [Account of the Ways of the Gods in Ryukyu. Collection of Benrensha].* Tokyo: Kadokawa Shoten.

The Kingdom of Ryukyu: Culture, Politics, Mentality

ARNE RØKKUM
DEPARTMENT OF ETHNOGRAPHY
MUSEUM OF CULTURAL HISTORY, UNIVERSITY OF OSLO

INTRODUCTION[1]

One question to begin with: Would it be justified to say that a *Kingdom* of the Ryukyus (*Ryûkyû ôkoku*) carried the implication of a *Nation* of Ryukyu (*Ryûkyû koku*)? We know that nationhoods wane with the waning of state sovereignty. On the other hand, if we maintain that the term "nationhood" is not congruent with the term "statehood," would it not be justifiable to assume that a Ryukyuan nationality may have prevailed even after the fall of the kingdom in 1879? In a broader, comparative view, the following may be the normal case.

Nationhood has a beginning; it is firmly embedded in historical memory. Japan and its emperorship might even be seen as the exceptional case. The historical depth of its dynasty invites a collective memory colored by the certainty of myth rather than the contingency of history. But let me add the following provision. Meiji Japan was actually an epoch of nation-making. One should consult Fujitani (1996) about the creation of ceremonies. Inspiration was drawn also from Europe, the *tennô* began to resemble a worldly oriented European sovereign, yet without renouncing on spiritual leadership (Bolitho 1985). A survey of African ethnographies of kingship by de Heusch prompts the following assessment (de Heusch 1997:231), "Sacred kingship is a symbolic device, an illusory mechanism of production with the capacity to drive economic development."

In a comparative perspective, the Ryukyuan example may turn out to be much more commonplace. Nationhood did not grow from a shared sense of oneness, of a perception as a people. Nor were its origins exceptional. The *Ryûkyû koku* did not come into being with an identity writ large. Nationhood might have been the totalized outcome of governance itself in a given historical and geopolitical situation.

Bringing unity to the disparate island territories can be seen as the corollary of bureaucratic centralization. By the 14th century, a shift of power was under way—from chiefship to kingship. From within the territory of the island of Okinawa itself, a tripartite chiefship configuration merged into a single political entity. From the outside, an opportunity opened up for partnerships in tribute trade under the aegis of Imperial China. A retrospective account may indeed reveal the play of power politics peculiar to the age and region. It might also reveal a more longitudinal cultural style compatible with tribute trade but also with person-to-person reciprocities of a more modest social scale. A civility underlying the *Pax Sinica* allowed exchanges to flourish along Asian seaways in the wake of the Chinese withdrawal from large-scale maritime activity. Kingship evolved, then, as an overlay for such centralized power, made necessary perhaps by a need to communicate effectively within a regional sphere of Chinese dominance. The formation of the kingdom of Ryukyu carried an economic rationale as well. Pearson (2001:35) writes, "Okinawan state development appears to have been based on what is termed wealth finance rather than staple finance." And according to Sakamaki (1964:388), "The tremendous profits that were realized went primarily into the royal coffers, strengthening the king's government as against the former regional lords of the islands." Wada (2006:54-55) comments on the link between unification and overseas trade.

An embryonic central authority may have ceded its jurisdiction to feudal Japan as the latter saw a role for itself in the wider East Asia maritime region. This leads me to ask yet another question. Is it possible that the communicative aspect pervading the formation of the kingdom, its dramaturgy, might have gone into history as a force of its own, as one or more cultural styles recognizable in the archipelago? And wouldn't this become the unique characteristic of Ryukyuan kingship itself, subduing local,

---

[1] The ethnographic content of this essay comes from serial fieldwork in the Southern Ryukyu Islands since 1976. Many ways of hospitality, understanding, and patience on part of my hosts fill this retrospect. Let me also thank Jean Claude Galey for inviting me to give a talk on kingship in the Ryukyus for a seminar at the École des Hautes Études en Sciences Sociales in Paris in 2004.

territorially bound, interest in society to make way for a code of bureaucratic administration and festival decorum? The pursuit of tribute trade and diplomacy would very likely have amounted to an encodement of power with an amount of legitimacy not easily matched by territorial chiefs.

So my intention here is to explore the implications for indigenous society of a nation status once bequeathed by a Chinese emperor in recognition of exemplary submission. Could this be a lasting paradox for people in this chain of islands spanning the East China Sea from Japan to Taiwan—an autonomy granted by forms of exchange, the forms, if not their content, surviving to this day as a very active signification?

A KINGDOM AND ITS UNDERLYING RECIPROCITIES

The suzerainty of the Chûzan, Middle Mountain, in 1429 followed the acquisition of a code, not of self-assertion, but of deference. Tribute state status was recognized by the Chinese Ming Emperor in 1430. The tribute gift and the kowtow merged with island-wide ritual address evoked for negotiating with awe-inspiring others. The name Shô was recognized as the name of a royal house and of a lineage (see Kishaba 2000:29). The title to the royal function reads as follows—The Middle Mountain King of the Ryukyuan Nation (*Ryûkyû koku Chûzan ô* in Japanese). The tribute relation was encoded by norms of virtue from Confucian ethics.

Nor should we forget the geopolitical situation which allowed exchange patterns to flourish with partners across the sea. Ethnographies from Oceania have shown this to be a viable possibility without much centralizing power. The objects circulating in *kula* exchanges in the Trobriands may in fact be perceived by the Melanesians as the material manifestation of civility circulating as *personal* tribute (Mauss 1954). Unlike cargoes of barter, these objects also serve as tokens of peaceful intention. But now, here in 14th century Asia, peaceful intention was brought about, not by discrete chains of dyadic partnerships themselves, but by the hegemonic, if relatively unobtrusive, presence of a great power requiring only the observation of a certain etiquette, such as the acceptance of credentials from minions in the outlying areas. Credentials for tribute trade were accepted by the Chinese Emperor, but the network itself was not governed by China. As phrased by Robinson (2000:122), "Ming China was not the center around which governments organized maritime diplomacy and the Ming tribute system was not the only framing of hierarchical diplomatic relationships in maritime East Asia." I estimate that it was such prevalence of forms, or even a rule *through* forms, which facilitated the right of existence for such minor power centers as the one on the Middle Mountain on Okinawa Island.

A side view on the Austronesian speaking aborigines of Taiwan may illustrate the contrast between kinship, which may thrive with acephalous networks of exchange, and chiefship/kingship. The Yami and the Bunun, among whom I have carried out fieldwork (Røkkum 1991 and 2002*a*), may even have a somewhat more tangible sense of themselves as one or the other—a people—than the Ryukyuans as the Uchina. The idea that a people come together as an entity by way of a common extraction serves as a conduit for communication when strangers meet. Even people in far-off places are one's kin in an extended sense. To take the example of the Bunun, amalgamation of power ends at the upper echelon of segmentation along a gradient from lineage to moiety, tribal group and tribe. A single individual can claim identity at junctures along this gradient, from the particular to the more inclusive, as the situation demands.

Whereas kinship for the Taiwanese aborigines has the potential of merging identities as a map conjoins places, for the Ryukyuans kinship has the potential of incorporation as a de facto people, but only if attention is paid to a defined material quantity, some definable wealth, which includes ancestral tablets. By tilting toward the concrete more than the abstract, kinship in the Ryukyus differs from that of the Malayo-Polynesian speaking Taiwanese suggested above. Its focus lies on succession to a given status—a title and its material referent, one that also conflates an inherited past.

A royal center can prevail where power is consolidated, transformed, and replicated. In the Ryukyu Islands, power was not vested in a single individual to begin with. Power was shared—between brother, the King and (ideally) his sister, the Chief Priestess. The role of the Chief Priestess (*kikoe ôgimi*) was one of translating governance as a worship matter throughout the archipelago to allow for a functional division between Great Mothers (*ôamu*) in the shrine hierarchies and Great Mothers in the secular hierarchies, populated largely by male officials. So, in the historical instance of the emerging Ryukyu Kingdom, the role of women in management functions extended to the public realm. The word designating their incumbencies is *nyokan*, Female Official(s). *A Notandum for Female Officials* (*Nyokan Osôshi*) from the years 1706-1713 details their functions. According to this manuscript, an all-male secular council of state assisting the king was made up of three members (*sanshikan*). This council, however, was matched by an all-female body also with three members (*ôsetobe*). Another all-female council of state assisted the Chief priestess: the *mihira ôamushirare,* and in the rank level below, the *utchiamu* and *sajiamu*. (For further detail on the court hierarchies see Røkkum 1998.)

Gender became the key to balanced reciprocity within the field of governance. A female-dominated religious bureaucracy was able to operate along with another, male-dominated secular bureaucracy for surveying, record keeping, supervision of collective works, and tax collection. When speaking of a "kingdom," it almost goes without saying that it must have been a *monarchy*. Yet the dual rule to which I am referring here should more properly be termed a *diarchy* (see also Røkkum 1998 and 2006.) This is also the term used by Valeri (1990). He depicts Hawaiian kingship in the way of an alternation between active and passive aspects held either by one person or, alternatively, by two persons in conjunction as man to woman.

As is widely acknowledged in the literature on the Ryukyus, a special relationship obtains between brother and sister. Kagiya (2002) enlarges the comparative view on the issue of cross-sibling solidarity by adding material from Rai Jua Island in East Indonesia. Generally, in the tradition of the folklorist Kunio Yanagita, this is interpreted as a sentimental or even magical bond; the sister is the spiritual guardian of the brother. This, I want to suggest, is only part of the explanation, and I agree with a position taken by Kawahashi (2002). She perceives a risk of making the role of the sister in Ryukyuan contexts a case of male-female difference itself. Her word for such naturalization of spiritual guardianship is *essentialism*.

In my view, the magical bond view misses the very crucial aspect that the issue is not an assumed female/male differentiation of religious temperament, but a differentiation of rights with regard to the corporate kernel of society: the house. The female: custodian of historical relics of the house. The male: custodian of ancestral tablets. When the female rule of succession is one of sister to brother's eldest daughter and the male of father to eldest son, there will be a joint sister/brother custodianship of the house in every generation. This rule of house incorporation cuts across other, island-bound or territorial, differences that I would like to work out in some more detail further on in this essay. It has been documented by Sakima (1982 [1926*a*]) with regard to Okinawa Island and by myself with regard to Yonaguni Island (Røkkum 1998). Masao Higa (2002) describes the position of female officiants in agnatic tomb associations (*munchû*) in central Okinawa by stating that it is not altered by marrying and moving and transferring to another house. I noted a constant relevance of the brother/sister link in society matters very recently on Ishigaki Island.

The priestess (*tzukasa*)[2] of Tonoshiro (*tûnusuku*), a capital shrine in Ishigaki City, is an elder sister of the present head of the house of *amayâ*. She is married, and lives just a few minutes away from this natal house of hers. Marriage, as we know, grants relations of affinity, yet there is no emphasis as such on links between her house of residence and house of origin. *In spite of* marriage, and the great value accorded the father/eldest son link, she retains a title to the *amayâ* through her own agnatic extraction. The eldest son of her brother at *amayâ* has his own family, and resides there with his father, but in his own apartment. The eldest daughter of the head of the *amayâ* lives in Shizuoka on the main island of Japan. Her husband is from that prefecture. What lies ahead is the daughter's return to Ishigaki with her husband, to anticipate a future as a priestess of Tonoshiro. She will perform as such in tandem with her brother, who will be a head of the *amayâ*. A brother/sister relationship replicates throughout the generations, and so also for the sociological house—it perpetuates an agnatic extraction for sons *and* daughters from generation to generation. We may be justified in describing Ryukyuan society as a "house society."

Now let me once again extend the comparison to nearby Taiwan and an ethnography written by Lo Su-mei (2004). It would be a misrepresentation of the ethnography of Amis society in east Taiwan to portray the role of women, where the brother–sister dyad is highlighted, in terms of the differential role of the sexes as such, or of a public/private dichotomy. As in the southern Ryukyu Islands, a complementary role for male and female is a template for realizing the larger picture of social organization, including such important arrangements as the cycle of annual rituals and age-sets. Field research among the adjoining Puyuma by Cauquelin (2004) yields a similar result: bilocal residence patterns and optional male–female succession rules add to the picture of gender complementarity.

So as we begin with kinship, a Ryukyuan house society resembling the known instances of house societies in Southeast Asia (cf. e.g. Howell 2003, Røkkum 2003) may reveal that the success of nation formation may even depend, to some extent, on skills of incorporation not simply in the macro format of geopolitics, but in the micro format of local life where there is ample space for interests to be negotiated around the key issue of authentic succession.

It strikes me that lineage identity is fraught today with uncertainty and tension caused by the underlying implication of title to house, land, and ancestral tablets. Kinship in the South Ryukyus is thus a matter not simply of personal identity but of collective identity, as one of house incorporation. But as Lévi-Strauss (1982) realized when he proposed the term "house society," it is not kinship as such but a vocabulary *derived* from kinship which is the defining characteristic.

On the island of Yonaguni—or *dunaŋ* in the vernacular—in the extreme southwest, some houses have a specific role in this double leaning towards history and kinship. They are Origin Houses (*dâmutu*), with their own congregations of worshipers and their own priestesses (*bunai tidigaŋ*). The general notion in the island concerns the alignment of such founding houses line with places in the terrain, places that epitomize exceptional deeds such as voyages to far-off places. The sacred cargo, which forms the inherited wealth of these houses, is treated as the bounty from such

---

[2] A note on language: Indigenous Ryukyuan gloss is transcribed in the International Phonetic Alphabet, and may accompany in parentheses words written in standard Japanese.

excursions out of the island. In my experience, contact with the outside was never spoken of as mediated by the court at Shuri.

In the historical instance, therefore, kinship in Ryukyuan society is not just a term for harmony and continuity across the generations, a veneration, but a term for ongoing discourse. On Yonaguni Island, female shamans—entrusted as Knowers (*munuci*)—act as genealogists, probing into such issues of descent and property management to determine how house ancestors are wrongfully identified. A recurring theme is adversity in the family. Could mistaken kinship be caused by some irregularities in the way things were conducted in the past? The shaman inspects the family name and its extraction. She goes to the job very much in the fashion of an ethnographer, interviewing family members, inspecting the memorial tablets on the mortuary altar. Then she identifies the cause as one of misplaced ancestry. A particular ancestor—a family name is uttered—was posted on the island as an official under the royal court at Shuri. He had a concubine. The couple's children, then, were affiliated with the lineage of their mother. This translates in her vocabulary as a fully diagnosable condition. She inspects her patient. The sloppy posture and lackluster eyes are the tell-tale signs of an incurred curse (*ta'tai*). Thus a flaw in the history of a house bears upon the life chances of its present members. Destinies of houses link up with the destinies of bodies. The solution comes with some revamping of the house pedigree.

The afflicted family is advised to make a sacrificial offering. The shaman sees a need to trace the whereabouts of people long since dead. First, their bodily incarnation, by localizing the well where they fetched drinking water. But there can be no end to adversity unless obeisance is also paid at the house of the official's legitimate wife. The pedigree itself needs to be rewritten. Therefore, the final stop is at the town office where the family name is duly registered in the characters of a different family, with residence on Okinawa Island, one which retains the unbroken agnatic and therefore legitimate link of descent to a Shuri official once on duty in Yonaguni Island.

Kinship takes on a validity across islands and across many generations in a totally ad hoc fashion in response to a historical issue not of harmony but of contention. Obligations must be fulfilled as a way of paying homage to true ancestors. Ceremony, authenticity, and succession remain the key terms. But the person-to-person connectivity which is rekindled in this way does not come about with an easy heart. Form takes precedence, for only ceremony and refined language of rites honoring the dead can transmit one's innermost feelings (*umui*).

Somewhat paradoxically, 1 an institutional framework of nationhood such as that under a Ryukyuan dynasty, may have preserved social identities on the parochial, smaller scale while gravitating toward precincts of power. Enforced bureaucratic centralization, on the other hand, created channels of communication in virtue of a declared subject status.

The Yaeyamas in the southern end of the archipelago submitted to royal rule in the year 1500. A royal envoy took up residence on Yonaguni Island in 1510. Standing stones—known as *bidiri*—link people on Yonaguni to that past. Yet they are not memorials in the strict sense. They may point to former origin houses, although I find very little storytelling underpinning this. Many people shy away from the lithic remains, and I was sometimes asked if I experienced anything out of the ordinary when I ventured into these zones. But power in this Ryukyuan construction is even more plainly evident through the realization of the ranks and functions of another age.

A territory-bound attention stretches northward from the island, toward the former capital of the kingdom. It may even seem that the image of paying obeisance to the Ryukyu court has been frozen within the historical consciousness. 97 years after the fall of the kingdom I took part in a ritual at a site of an old watch hut, near the triangular stone layout of a sacred hearth that had been an observation post in the past. But the focal point of the site was a round sandstone, known as the *karahai*, into which the dial of a geomantic compass had been engraved. Female participants in the ritual were priestesses (*k'abu*) dressed in yellow hemp robes (Figure 2).

Yellow-robed priestesses perform a public, if not an official, function. They remain on duty even in between their officiating functions at calendrical rituals. They protect the island and the sea lanes to the capital, so are not expected to be away for any considerable span of time. During the dynastic age, and indeed to the present, the *k'abu* come to this spot at the top of a plateau overlooking the island's eastern cape to pray for safe passage for people and vessels traveling by sea between Yonaguni and the port city of Naha. The senior priestess (*ubuk'a*) has a male counterpart, the *dumuti*. The title refers to his function as chief councilor, a man responsible for overseeing two action groups in the island, the *dagusa*, with reference to rice fields, and *uganbusa* with reference to *k'abu* shrines. Another male participant in the ritual occupied the role of shrine custodian, a *tidibi*, and a third was the owner of a cargo ship on the route between Yonaguni and Naha.

In the southern Ryukyus, a subject under the kingdom meant primarily being subject to taxation. The Satsuma fiefdom of feudal Japan had installed a poll tax regime to meet the need for revenue. On Yonaguni Island, heavy taxation kept the population in poverty until well after the demise of the kingdom in 1879. The ritual at the eastern cape is a rehearsal of associated forms. A *tidibi* of *ndimura* village made this connection explicitly in a conversation about the worship of moon and stars. Under the taxation regime, the islanders were forced to work far into the night, so they took up a worship of celestial bodies as one way of ensuring protection of their own bodies.

As the title of this symposium indicates, the kingdom was an archipelagic state. Sea travel gravitated toward the capital on Okinawa Island. Even today, I find little cultural latitude for ad hoc island-to-island contact. There may be physical obstacles to take into account: the choppy open waters of the Black Current and the coral reefs capping the islands. I sometimes asked why there was no sightseeing on nearby islands. My neighbor to the west in *ndimura* village told me he would only visit the island of Kohama (which I used as an example) if urged to so on the occasion of some business, in which case he would return to the harbor as soon as possible. A neighborhood female shaman explained the bad state of affairs with a story of a Kohama man. On arriving at the almost depopulated Yonaguni Island, he killed a dog kept by a woman who lived alone as a sole survivor. The storyteller warned me: "Please remember not to sing the Kohama song (the *kohamabusi*) when at sea."

Even with the ease of travel today people on Ishigaki Island rarely visit the island of Yonaguni, although most know Tokyo well. Some who actually have made the trip speak of an experience similar to arriving at a point of entry in a foreign country, not least because they cannot grasp the spoken language. Yet when I tell them about things I have experienced myself on the island, people recollect practices that were also prevalent on Ishigaki Island one or two generations earlier. Now let me quote from the online edition of Yomiuri News a dispatch dated October 11, 2007, which more tellingly will underscore my point, "Three years ago, residents of Yonagunicho [Yonaguni Township—my insert] voted against a planned merger with the island municipalities of Ishigaki and Taketomicho, saying the islands are too different from each other." (http://www.yomiuri.co.jp/dy/national/20071011TDY03301.htm)

Within the island of Yonaguni, only 4 km separate the northern capital village, *tumaimura*, and the south-coast village where I lived, the *ndimura*. Yet there is a felt distance as well. It is often spoken of in respect of a small fishing population in the village of *kubura*, which is at the same distance in a westerly direction. Although the villagers have been there since the early 20th century, they are conventionally identified as an immigrant population from the township of Itoman on Okinawa Island, who remain faithful to ways of worship unlike those practiced by the indigenous people of Yonaguni. Relations between some settlements in the island are reportedly hostile, even war-like. Until five or six decades ago, a procession of the south village of Higawa heading for the feast of the First Fruit's, the *uganfututi*, in the northern village, was forced to take a roundabout route to avoid the ire of field owners in an area of the disbanded *nmanaga* settlement. I was told that it was the sight of the village banner in the procession that provoked the sense of animosity.

House enclosures with their standing stones can be discerned in dense patches of brushwood. Such defunct Origin House sites leave only a faint impression in the undergrowth itself, yet many people on the island keep an awareness of them in their apperception of the terrain, as *kandaga*, "spirit high," and they are visited by island priestesses and village functionaries on an annual occasion of prayer in the cold season. An order across the fields and brushwood is a lineament of partly real, partly evoked paths. A network of allied Houses and bush shrines of the past evokes heroic action. In one defunct house site on the central *nmanaga* perimeter, a woman incarnates a female chief named *saŋai isuba*. At *fuzan* in the eastern part of the island, the *dunaŋbara azi* incarnates another, a male chief.

Now, back again to the Taiwanese parallel. Whereas people on Taiwan are supported by the abstract indices of kinship matrices in matters of belonging, the Ryukyuans incorporate themselves, under a former nation, under a house regime centered upon ancestral tablets and old heirlooms, under a secret society regime centered upon festival masks, and under an island territory order with such vestiges of the past as fortifications and house sites or whatever may be their remains, such as standing stones, hearthstones, and wells. People situate themselves in a material world which traces a common ancestry back to the age of the kingdom. This being the case, I have tried to capture an image of life in the Ryukyus by collecting and exhibiting material identifiers such as wooden masks and banners with their heavily ornamented poles. These are emblems of initiation groups and territorial communities. They provide an opportunity to experience power and authority (some masks carry ornamented signs of kingship), and become objects of dispute if motifs are imitated. Let me describe here a replica recently on show at the Oslo University Museum of Cultural History (Figure 1; item no. 1 from the right).

The banner is attached to an ornate banner pole, actually, an object of offense when carried across the *nmanaga* terrain. The top of the pole of the Higawa banner (or *ndimura* in the local pronunciation) is a tool for safeguarding the harvest. It is a three-pronged weapon, actually, two Chinese halberds flanking a spear. The spear is also the tongue of a dragon. Patterns on the surface of the object, as well, are telltale signs of a dragon. The banner displays the two Chinese characters of the village name Higawa.

For almost 4 months in 1976 I accompanied a male shaman, born on Yonaguni. He was native to the island, but was now determined to loosen people's bonds to narrow territorial locales. He envisaged a past when the Origin Houses on scattered islands enjoyed contact with each other. As in the case of a House of Suna, a founding house of the village

Figure 1. Oslo Cultural History Museum Ryukyu banners (Photo credit: Ann Christine Eek / Museum of Cultural History, University of Oslo)

of Sonai, he urged contact with a village of the same name on the island of Iriomote. His reasoning was couched in a vocabulary kinship, and he perceived parallel lines of descent. But he was aware also of the limitations of kinship, and broadened the compass of his vision to global proportions. In fact, I became aware of his epistemological activity when, one day, market women recounted a rumor about a man walking around in the island trying to make people believe the sweet potato did not arrive from China, but from a land called Greece. To this Knower, the sweet potato was an index of the coming of something he did not actually pronounce as civilization, although he worked hard on the particulars, such as the origin of living in houses and burying the dead in tombs. His vocabulary differed insofar as it did not anchor religious experience in what can be grasped as the sacred remains of past stem houses. Rather, it seemed strongly motivated by a Taoist knowing of terrestrial and atmospheric conditions, first and foremost, of a possibility of both vapors and dusty remains of ancestral bones in stalactite caves. This was an awakening of some sort, but as he envisaged more connections across the archipelago than he could possibly trace in his pilgrimages, his influence began to fade. The female head of the House of Suna felt deserted. On each and every visit to the island, she asked me, "You haven't heard anything from him, have you?"

Still today, people on Yonaguni distrust itinerant shamans attempting to import practices characteristic of Okinawa Island to the territory. I noticed this during fieldwork. The most common objection concerned the limited chance of success of exchanges of any kind with the spirit world that required only a minimum of presentations from the human side: salt, rice brandy, seaweed, and some grains of raw rice. Mainland Japanese who followed their own custom of casting one-yen and five-yen coins onto sacred sites were seen as something even worse, an affront to the sanctity of the place. This was related to me by the female head of the house of Suna.

Cult groups in the South Ryukyus settle their interest on endogenous growth. Whatever lies beyond the horizon is intriguing only insofar that they can be conceived as the places of origin of the masked, material spirits of agricultural increase. These are also perceived as places to deposit, by acts of exorcism, samples of vermin that pose a threat to field crops. I found no actual records of exchanges with people from afar, or even with people in the near waters. But the separateness portrayed by the heavy wooden masks topped with fronds on some islands in the central area of the Yaeyamas may be precisely what induces the gifts of annual fruition: an occasion for welcoming such arrivals is the festival of the First Fruits, the *pûru*. An advent of the gods calls for the local territory itself to be placed under the control of a male initiation society. One such arrival can be watched as a procession headed by two members, one wearing a red mask, the other a white one, each bearing a banner pole. The parallel phalanxes of red group and white group depart from an islet off Komi on Iriomote Island. They reach land across a mangrove flat. I noticed intermittent stops with the lowering of banners. These were moments for paying respect. I visited the islet, and saw pottery sherds from previous ages protruding all around. This, one might wonder, might possibly grant the historicity of the arrivals. They might as well have been real.

Figure 2 Invoking the Umata ancestors

On the more remote island of Yonaguni, where women rather than men preserve the knowledge of strange arrivals from afar, a cataclysm of contact is staged as battle scenes in the compounds of present or past Origin Houses during the cold season (the *kanbunaga* or *maciri*) rites (Figures 2, 3, and 4).

South Ryukyuan local society resembles a Southeast Asian "house society" in the sense that local belonging is qualified by inherited ancestral wealth. People recognize relationships not just with each other but also with beads, masks, musical and percussion instruments, and banner pole tops. People invest certain objects with ideas; material objects become subjects in their own right. The matter at hand is the actual appropriation, or even physically touching these artifacts, conceived either as something to be wished for, such as a full harvest in the case of banner poles, or to be avoided for any one not so entitled, in the case of inherited festival wealth. Even the category of the house involves an idea that sacred items, obtained through inheritance, were appropriated from another land, somewhere on the Asian continent. In the Yaeyamas, the homeland of sacred objects is sometimes glossed as Annam, an area with entrepots in the tribute trade, just as Fujian farther north is an area of historical reference for people on Yonaguni. Thus, for example, in the backyard of the founder house of Umata on Yonaguni Island there is one half of a giant clam. (Figure 2). It was on the first day of my fieldwork in 1976 that the head of the house took me to the place. His quandary was how to make contact with the owner of the matching part of the shell. The only thing he knew was that he resided somewhere in the Fujian Province.

Sacred cargoes may have been received by the ancestors, or even stolen. Their keepers are keepers of a knowledge of how humans, cattle and vegetable species reproduce with ease. The gaze is set somewhere across the horizon and the motif of reaching out there, making contact, is captured in an annual event during the cold season of the year, the *kanbunaga* or *maciri*.

The festival celebrates life not burdened by outside regimes. So there may be an inertia of some sort to count on: the island with its ruins of chieftain strongholds or only the standing stones reminiscent of them. Actual or imaginary historical moments can be recaptured in ritual. Such occurrences can be a trip to the Ryukyuan capital or to the Fujian coast for instance. Out of an even deeper past comes an image of the islanders themselves emigrating from two islands in the south, the *ubudunaŋ* and the *haidunaŋ*—High Dunang and South Dunang.

This orientation in time and space defines a common structure for people within a single territory; it may not easily induce interisland movement. As I said earlier, the *k'abu* priestesses are not encouraged to travel. People living adjacent to Origin Houses that worship past arrivals from beyond the horizon are bound to life-long attendance at festivals, an attachment granted not by blood but by physical propinquity. Émigrés return to the islands to honor their ties to the soil. If they are not likely to return ever again, they take a sample of soil back with them as an object of worship. But the islanders loathe speaking about permanent absence. Even people who have lived on the main islands of Japan for decades are said to be "delayed on a trip." Foreign objects are "travel" objects. Bananas of a familiar shape found at the market are "travel bananas"

Figure 3 Invoking the Kucima ancestors

Figure 4 Invoking the Dunanbara ancestors

even when they come from the nearby island of Ishigaki. Outside men marrying local women are spoken of with a pejorative, attaching to them forever some frivolity of transitory status.

The whole mass of protuberant features of the terrain lends itself to a classification of centripetal force: hills, escarpments, promontories, and lagoon passage points. The connections are "spirit trails" (*kan-nu-miti*). Here, a cultural gravity upon the island itself projects somewhat of an inverse image of the Trobriand experience of *kula* in Melanesia. The freedom of physical and cultural navigation lies buried somewhere in the past; it is evoked only by myth and ritual, as in a now defunct test for induction into a sisterhood focused on the worship of freshwater springs. The test imitates a send-off for two ships (see Røkkum 2006).

Along with the historical origin of kingship as a social fact came the means of trade with people further afield than the geographical confines of the islands themselves, first in respect of China whose customs were emulated and with which maritime trade in tribute goods was pursued; second in respect of an island world, whose constant presence for itself was upheld by an officialdom of male and female officeholders, and third by defining domestic sea routes as routes for transporting taxation goods. Remaining houses of local influence in the southernmost part of the archipelago still subscribe to the idea of wealth-as-cargo, resulting from both overseas and domestic maritime activity, yet the social activity spurred by this orientation is not one of object circulation but of object possession on behalf of a house, a local group, or an age-set.

Royal partnerships

The integrity of the kingdom in the larger format of court and bureaucracy was sustained by codes of reciprocity originating from tribute trade and diplomacy. For a minor power, ways of balancing interest would have been vital. Akamine comments on the precarious dual dependence on China and Japan (2004:114). For a view on the contact between the Ryukyus and China, see Nishizato and Uezato (1991). The title of King of the Middle Mountain (Chûzan) was hereditary and succession handled locally, but admittance to the office depended on the Chinese Emperor's acceptance, bestowed at an investiture ceremony. Such emphasis on qualification for the royal function parallels the observation made by Galey (1990:130–31) regarding the Indian Princely State of Tehri-Garwhal.

Ryukyuan ritual preserves acts known from the past, such as acts of paying taxes, in money as well as in goods. This idea along with kinesthetics of rubbing one's hand in prayers (by women) and performing ninety-nine kowtows (by men) run through many kinds of ritual in the southern Ryukyus. On Yonaguni Island, the submission materializes as the arrangement of a set of commutable items upon a lacquer tray placed on the ground. Fragments of an iron pot go into the other world as ingots. Strips of white paper go as fabrics. Flax threads go as spinning yarn. A prayer vocabulary, which on Yonaguni Island is known as the *usutui*, enable the ritualist to quantify and praise the offerings. And then, in the end, the transaction itself: offerings go into a makeshift incense burner, either in the usage of a mound of coral sand or a kerosene can incinerator for simulated paper money. The invocation ends with the words, "Nothing can be left behind, no thoughts, no deeds." A transaction which might resemble a fiscal transaction is in fact one which balances a relationship. An otherworldly gatekeeper named *busuganaci* takes care of that. This stylized technique of making relationships negotiable may relieve some of strain of quotidian matters as well. As the woman in charge of the ritual makes a final clasping gesture with her hands, her voice fades into a monotonous murmur of the numbers and quantities that went into the transaction. Just as the officials in the past, she is also a keeper of records and someone who can tell how much is needed to clear the balances.

Rituals in the South Ryukyus today are concluded by multiplying an act of submission 99 times. The male initiation society which returns once a year to the depopulated island of Aragusuku, not only counts the number of kowtows, they are actually performed. The inexorable return underlying such tribute predicates hierarchy. Cf. Takara (1998 [1993]:78) who sees the subordination to a Ming Emperor as a key element in the diplomatic arrangements interlinking several countries. Forms expressing intent are rehearsed as oral, tonal, and plastic performances, as an exchange of courtesies, in the flaunting of woven garments, and in the presentation of alcoholic beverages and ceremonial dishes.

The kingdom of the Ryukyus replicated the house organization of traditional society by elevating the brother–sister relationship to a pivotal place, in the royal palace itself. The material reality of such houses was not produced by their architectural outlines, however, but by the heirlooms stored in their interiors. Although these were originally acquired sometime in the past by house ancestors, under no circumstance are they allowed to be taken away to be sold, bartered, or given away as gifts. Traditional Ryukyuan society carries a principle of "inalienable wealth" in Weiner's terms (1992), although in its most restrictive reading as what has been accumulated down the generations must be withheld from further circulation in the present.

Even the category of tribute itself invites of a restrictive reading. Whereas the debt incurred by the receiver of gifts is offset by the added status of the giver, the tribute validates the highness and lowness of parties to a partnership. In Chinese society, according to Yan (2002:68), there is ethnographic evidence of an "asymmetrical gift that flows up the ladder of society." So I think there is a historical and cultural continuum to think of in the light of our contemporary ethnography of the Ryukyus.

Exchange was codified also in power politics as Europeans made their way into a region dominated by the Chinese. In his book, the British commander Basil Hall (1818) describes his encounter with Ryukyuans. Mutual understanding was augmented by the exchange of niceties. But the British were not granted an audience with the King. The crews of Alceste and Lyra were given provisions necessary for their sustenance, but were not allowed to offer anything in return. And with no return gift there could be no obligation, no substance to relationships. The British commander set off for other destinations in the East China Sea, but not without a festive farewell. Etiquette was observed to the end, but the denial of a royal audience and opportunity to repay gifts from the British might reflect the geopolitics involved in the situation: agents from the southern Japanese fief of Satsuma were keeping an eye on the situation.

What interests me, taking the broader view, is how societies so-to-speak iconize certain material in graphical and interactive styles. From the Asian domain, there are, besides, the Javan principalities, "theatre-states" in Clifford Geertz's (1980) term, and the "empty" or "passive" centers noted by the ethnographies of writers such as Cunningham (1973) and Errington (1989). From Southeast Asia emerges a pattern of power as resting with a ruler who is passive— an empty center, a king in a power vacuum such that he takes on female characteristics. With particular reference to the Ayuthian kingdom, Tambiah (1976, 1985) describes mandala-like configurations of pivotal architecture as the material components of galactic societies. Quite apart from military power, a ceremonial artfulness with a force of its own seems to characterize these polities configured around a center and ruler.

A sacred duty of governance was not assumed by the Ryukyuan king himself, but by a sister or other female relative, and ultimately, by the priestesses around the archipelago. Increase rituals focused on the territory itself, as a source of wellbeing and perennial rejuvenation. It was a female responsibility under the diarchic extension of kingship. For a comment on kingship and control over natural resources, see Hicks (1996:620). Ryukyuan kings configured a presence for themselves that eschewed normal contact. Some aura of alterity might have been part of this. Nonetheless, when I speak with people today about the royal lineage, there is no indication of a lingering sense of awe. It follows that Ryukyuan kingship was more than the creation of a power constellation within the outer rim of East China tribute states. It was a creation of local interest. Feeley-Harnik (1985:299) makes this balance between outside and inside interests a specific point in a note on the role of women in central African versions of kingship. Royal cults are not simply the making of foreign influences, "Popular cults [are] taken over by royalty in the process of establishing their rule..."

But even if a Ryukyuan king may not have been a god-king, yet, as the British experience indicates, a certain distance to the mundane was upheld. He was carried in a sedan chair in a procession outside the castle grounds. Semantics may have played some role in separating the king from the ordinary. On Yonaguni Island, a stone altar in the eastern half of the cardinally aligned house compound connects the residents with the *tida'n ganaci*, Sun Lord (Røkkum 1998:59). The celestial referent is encountered also in written Japanese from the age of the Kingdom: *Shuri tenganachi*, Sun Lord of Shuri (the capital).

On Yonaguni Island in our time, the corpse taken to the tomb is a "king for a day", after resting on a *lit-de-parade* behind an arrangement of burning incense sticks. It is sent off ensconced in a vermillion sedan chair (see also Røkkum 2006). Soon after I settled down on Yonaguni island for fieldwork, my farmhouse courtyard was "requisitioned" because a new funerary sedan chair needed building. It was spoken of only as the *tagaraduGu*, the Precious Implement. The occasion of its eventual inauguration evoked in quite obvious terms parallel images of king and corpse: for its inauguration, the highest ranking man on the island was invited to take a key part in the ceremony. He would be held aloft in the procession to what would be the first deceased's final resting place in the cemetery. But the mayor refused. The bureaucrats refused. The schoolteachers refused. And in the end when the criteria for royal likeness loosened quite a bit, I followed the example of these predecessors and declined the offer.

Conclusion

If there is anything we can find in the Ryukyus today which evokes a past kingdom, it may not just be tradition itself. History is not transferred or deposited, it is negotiated. It *involves* the present, first of all, through the statuses and functions that actualize a morally grounded idea of good behavior, of courteousness. History is therefore present in styles of behavior, most tangible at ceremonial occasions. On Yonaguni Island in the outer fringes of the archipelago, I have been exploring the many ways in which people invoke history by social means. I see a material side to this, first and foremost, in activities contained in ritual life. Exceptional status is allocated to houses, lineages, functions in festival, and to an imagery of points and lines across the island territory. A final example will illustrate how such mediated experience of the past is still in the making.

During fieldwork I included the Aragabana promontory of Yonaguni Island in a map of spirit trails, as a sacred point, an important juncture of movement across the territory of the island (Røkkum 2006). Sometime later, a discovery was made of geological features on the seabed said in scholarly terms to be the remains of a colossal built structure. Just as an itinerant shaman turned to the past to find hidden sources of civilization, so also today, features of landscapes and seascapes are conceptualized in ways interpreters would prefer to call "civilization." No wonder, therefore, the place name Aragabana is now about to replaced by the name Iseki-saki, the Ruins Point.

REFERENCES CITED

AKAMINE, MAMORU
2004 *Ryûkyû Ôkoku [Kingdom of the Ryukyus]*. Tokyo: Kôdansha.

BOLITHO, HAROLD
1985 Japanese kingship. In *Patterns of Kingship and Authority in Traditional Asia:* 24–43, ed. Ian Mabett. London: Croom Helm.

CAUQUELIN, JOSIANE
2004 *The Aborigines Of Taiwan: The Puyuma From Headhunting To The Modern World*. London: Routledge-Curzon.

CUNNINGHAM, CLARK E.
1973 Order in the Atoni house. In *Rodney Needham: Right & Left*: 204–238, ed. Rodney Needham. Chicago: University of Chicago Press.

ERRINGTON, SHELLY
1989 *Meaning and Power in a Southeast Asian Realm*. Princeton: Princeton University Press.

FEELEY-HARNIK, GILLIAN
1985 Issues in divine kingship. *Annual Review of Anthropology* 14:273–313.

FUJITANI, TAKASHI
1996 *Splendid Monarchy: Power And Pageantry In Modern Japan*. Berkeley: California University Press.

GALEY, JEAN CLAUDE
1990 Reconsidering kingship in India: An ethnological perspective. In *Kingship and the Kings*: 123–187, ed. Jean-Claude Galey. Chur: Harwood Academic Publishers.

GEERTZ, CLIFFORD
1980 *Negara: The Theatre State in Nineteenth Century Bali*. Princeton: Princeton University Press.

HALL, BASIL
1818 *An account of a voyage of discovery to the West Coast of Corea and the Great Loo-Choo Island, with an appendix containing charts, and various hydrographical and scientific notes, and a vocabulary of the Loo-Choo* language by H. J. Clifford, Esq., London: John Murray

HEUSCH, LUC DE
1997 The symbolic mechanisms of sacred kingship: Rediscovering Frazer. *The Journal of the Royal Anthropological Institute*, 3:2:213–232.

HICKS, DAVID
1996 Making the king divine: A case study in ritual regicide from Timor. *Journal of the Royal Anthropological Institute* 2:4:611–624.

HIGA, MASAO
2002 Saikô: Ryûkyû rettô bunka kenkyû no shin shikaku [Research on the culture of the Ryûkyû Islands from a new angle: another writing]. In *Ryûkyû-Ajia No Minzoku To Rekishi: Kokuritsu Rekishi Minzoku Hakubutsukan Higa Masao Kyôju Taikan Kinnen Ronshû [Ethnology And History Of Ryukyu-Asia: A Collection Of Essays On The Occasion Of The Retirement By Professor Masao Higa From The National Museum Of Japanese History]*: 17–38, ed. Masao Higa. Ginowan: Gajûmaru Shorin.

HOWELL, SIGNE
2003 The house as an analytic concept: A theoretical overview. In *The House in Southeast Asia: A Changing Social, Economic and Political Domain:* 16–33, ed. Stephen Sparkes and Signe Howell. London: Routledge-Curzon.

KAGIYA, AKIKO
2002 Indoneshia no 'onari'gamishinkô': Okinawa to taihisasete [Sister goddess worship in Indonesia: A comparison with Okinawa]. In *Ryûkyû-Ajia No Minzoku To Rekishi: Kokuritsu Rekishi Minzokuhakubutsukan Higa Masao Kyôju Taikan Kinnen Ronshû [Ethnology And History Of Ryukyu-Asia: A Collection Of Essays On The Occasion Of The Retirement By Professor Masao Higa From The National Museum Of Japanese History]*: 355–387, ed. Masao Higa. Ginowan: Gajûmaru Shorin.

KAWAHASHI, NORIKO
2002 Kaminchû o hanaseru koto: Sûzan Seredo no 'josei reiteki yûetsu no datsuhonshitsuka' wa tadashii senryaku ka? [To speak about the

kaminchû: Is Susan Sered's 'de-essentialization of woman as spiritual superior' the right strategy?]. In *Ryûkyû-Ajia No Minzoku To Rekishi: Kokuritsu Rekishiminzoku Hakubutsukan Higa Masao Kyôju Taikan Kinnen Ronshû [Ethnology And History Of Ryukyu-Asia: A Collection Of Essays On The Occasion Of The Retirement By Professor Masao Higa From The National Museum Of Japanese History]*: 270–296, ed Masao Higa. Ginowan: Gajûmaru Shorin.

KISHABA, KAZUTAKA

2000   *Ryûkyû Shô-Shi No Subete [All About The Shôs]*. Tokyo: Shin Jinbutsu Oraisha.

LÉVI STRAUSS, CLAUDE

1982   *The Way of the Masks*, translated from the French by Sylvia Modelski. Seattle: University of Washington Press.

LO, SU-MEI

2004   *Distinction De Sexe Et Organisation Sociale Chez Les Amis De' Tolan (Taiwan Est): Les Relations Frere-Soeur Et Homme-Femme Dans Le Cycle Annuel (Doctoral Dissertation)[Sexual Distinctions and Social Organization of the Ami People of Tolan, East Taiwan: Relations of Brother-Sister and Man-Woman in the Annual Cycle]*. Paris: École des Hautes Études en Sciences Sociales.

MAUSS, MARCEL

1954 [1923–24] *The Gift: Forms And Functions Of Exchange In Archaic Societies*, translated by Ian Cunnison, London: Cohen & West. Originally published as Essay sur le don, in *Sociologie et Anthropologie*, Paris: Presses Universitaires de France.

NISHIZATO, KIKÔ AND KEN'ICHI UEZATO

1991   *Chûgoku-Ryûkyû Kôryû-Shi [History Of Intercourse Between China And Ryukyu]*. Naha: Hirugi-sha.

NYOKAN OSÔSHI [NOTANDUM FOR FEMALE OFFICIALS]

1706–13 The Nakahara *Zenchû Archives ms*, transcribed by Kojima Yoshiyuki. Shintô Taikei Jinja-hen [The Shinto Shrines Editing Program] 52: Okinawa. Tokyo: Zaidan Hôjin Shintô Taikei Hensankai, 1982.

PEARSON, RICHARD

2001   Archaeological perspectives on the rise of the Okinawan state. *Journal of Archaeological Research* 9:3:243–285.

ROBINSON, KENNETH R.

2000   Centering the king of Choson: aspects of Korean maritime diplomacy, 1392–1592. *The Journal of Asian Studies* 59:1:109–125.

RØKKUM, ARNE

1991   The pig and the flying-fish: performative aspects of Yami culinary categories. In *The Ecology Of Choice And Symbol: Essays In Honour Of Fredrik Barth*: 258–279, ed. R. Grønhaug et. al. Bergen: Alma Mater.

1998   *Goddesses, Priestesses, and Sisters: Mind, Gender and Power in the Monarchic Tradition of the Ryukyus*. Oslo: Scandinavian University Press.

2002a   Meat and marriage: An ethnography of aboriginal Taiwan. *Bulletin of the National Museum of Ethnology* [Osaka] 26: 4:707–737.

2003   Fixed spaces for fluxed sentiments: defense perimeters for life and death domains in the South Ryukyus. In *House in Southeast Asia: A Changing Social, Economic and Political Domain*: 219-239, ed. Signe Howell and Stephen Sparkes. London: Routledge-Curzon.

2006   *Nature, Ritual and Society in Japan's Ryukyu Islands*. London: Routledge.

SAKAMAKI, SHUNZO

1964   Ryukyu and Southeast Asia. *The Journal of Asian Studies* 23:3:383–389.

SAKIMA KÔEI

1982 [1926a]) *Nyonin Seiji-Kô: Rei No Shimajima* [Introducing Governance By Females: The Islands Of Souls]. Tokyo: Shinsensha.

TAKARA, KURAYOSHI

1998 [1993] *Ryûkyû Okoku [Kingdom of Ryukyu]*. Tokyo: Iwanami Shoten.

TAMBIAH, STANLEY J.

1976   World conqueror and world renouncer: A study in Buddhism and polity. In *Thailand Against A Historical Background*. Cambridge Studies in Social Anthropology, 15, ed. Jack Goody. Cambridge: Cambridge University Press.

1985 *Culture, Thought, and Social Action: An Anthropological Perspective.* Cambridge, Massachusetts: Harvard University Press.

VALERI, VALERIO
1990 Diarchy and history in Hawaii and Tonga. In *Culture and History in the Pacific*, ed. Jukka Siikala. The Finnish Anthropological Society Transactions No. 27.

WADA, HISANORI
2006 *Ryûkyû Ôkoku No Keisei: Sanzan Tôitsu No Zengo [The Shaping Of The Ryûkyû Kingdom: Before And After The Unification Of Sanzan].* Ginowan: Gajûmaru Shorin.

WEINER, ANNETTE B.
1992 *Inalienable Possessions: The Paradox Of Keeping-While-Giving.* Berkeley: University of California Press.

YAN, YUNXIANG
2002 Unbalanced reciprocity: asymmetrical gift giving and social hierarchy in rural China. In *The question of the gift: Essays across disciplines*: 67–84, ed. Mark Osteen. London: Routledge.

Appendix 1
Recent Discoveries on Kikai Island

RICHARD PEARSON
EMERITUS ANTHROPOLOGY UBC VANCOUVER, SAINSBURY INSTITUTE FOR THE STUDY OF
JAPANESE ARTS AND CULTURES, NORWICH UK

Intensive, wide area excavations on several sites of the Gusuku Site Group on Kikai Island in the past five years have transformed our comprehension of the Late Shellmound Period and the emergence of complex society in the Ryukyus. The remains of substantial buildings set on posts dug into the ground, cremation burials, and ceramics from Kyushu, indicate the existence of a Japanese government outpost involved in collecting and relaying local products to the Yamato government in Dazaifu, northern Kyushu.

Records of sporadic contacts between the central Yamato government and the Amami Islands and Okinawa in the period from 600 to 1000 have been discussed by historians, but archaeological verification in the Ryukyus has been vague. Records of tributary missions to the Yamato court in the 7th and 8th century, as well as some evidence that tribute ships to Tang China sometimes took a southern route through the Ryukyus, are well known (Yamazato 1999). However archaeological evidence of a strong relation between the northern Amami Islands and the Japanese main islands has not previously been confirmed.

The Gusuku Site Group consists of eight named localities totaling some 135,000 sq m in area, on the island of Kikaishima, on a raised terrace called the Yamada Daichi. It spans a period from the 8th to 12th centuries. Excavations have been conducted annually since 2003.

At the Yamada Handa Site there are two buildings with raised floor (set on very large posts) of 2 bays by 3 bays, with an area of 150 sq m and several more buildings of medium size. They are of Kamakura style. There are a central open area running east-west, an east-west road running from below the terrace, and surrounding clusters of buildings. The settlement plan resembles that of Japanese main island local administrative centers, which have administrative buildings, storehouses, and plaza area. A burial area contained cremations interred in earth pits and burials in wooden coffins without cremation. Suzuki (2007:28) concluded that the site was a central place (*kyoten*) and political and economic center, probably from the 10th century. Grave goods included *kamuiyaki* narrow neck jars (*tsubo*) and Chinese white ware. The burials are thought to belong to a migrant population from the main Japanese islands, who lived at the site (Suzuki 2007:27).

Two separate periods of occupation are indicated; the latter half of the 8th century to first half of the 10th century and the latter 11th century to first half of the 12th century. A diverse ceramic assemblage was recovered. *Hajiki* (red earthenware) with black inclusions of mica in the paste is of the type which circulated in Dazaifu and southern Kyushu. *Sueki* (grey stoneware) was likely produced in Dazaifu. It resembles examples from the trading entrepot of Mottaimatsu in southern Kyushu. Fabric impressed earthenware, used for evaporating salt water to produce salt, was also found. Local pottery is of the Kaneku Type, which has been divided into 5 sub types dating from the 6th to 11th centuries. Chinese trade ceramics include Yueh ware bowls of Dazaifu Types I and II and I (2) I (3). These are the types which come from temples and administrative sites in Kyushu (Nakajima 2007).

White wares with beaded rim, and South Chinese white wares were also found. Remains of iron working have been recovered, including tuyeres and slag, fragments of copper, and soapstone cauldrons. The substantial number of soapstone cauldron fragments suggests that Song traders, who are thought to have controlled the circulation of these cauldrons, lived at the site. Unlike sites on Amami such as Tsuchimori Matsunoto, Yomisaki, Nagahama Kaneku, and Kominato Fuwaganeku, there are no large quantities of *Turbo* shells at the Gusuku sites. However, these sites are located inland, whereas the others are located in sand dunes, in which shell is well preserved.

Sumida and Nozaki (2007: 50) reported that the early earth pit graves had graves goods consisting of small white ware boxes and bronze and iron artifacts while later ones had *sueki* and white wares.

Takanashi (2007:66) concluded that the Gusuku Site Group must have been the locus of political authority connected to Yamato. In layout, the site resembles contemporary government office sites (*kanga*) on the main islands of Japan. Finds of high quality Yueh ceramics of the 8th to 10th centuries at the Yamada Nakanishi and Yamada Handa sites are unique in the Ryukyus. The very large buildings with raised floors and excavated post construction, and the unusually large quantities of soapstone vessels suggest an official site. Takanashi has examined all of the known sites with Kaneku type local pottery, and has found three groups: (1) sites with Kaneku pottery and no other types, (2) sites with Kaneku pottery plus small quantities of *haji* and *sueki* (presumably made in Kyushu), and (3) sites with no local Kaneku pottery and exclusively *haji* and *sueki*. The sites with almost no local pottery are concentrated on Kikaishima. They appear to be trading sites where main island Japanese were part of the community. Judging from similarities in artifact types these sites had close relations with Dazaifu the Yamato government's administrative center in northern Kyushu and the gateway to continental Asia in the 8th to 11th centuries. Sites with Kaneku type local pottery and small quantities of *haji/sueki* have large quantities of *Turbo* shells and iron; they appear to be sites where local goods such as *Turbo* shells, used for mother of pearl decoration, were exchanged for goods such as iron implements. Sites with only Kaneku pottery appear to be local habitation sites. The early 7th century Fuwaganeku Site, Amami Island, may have received iron goods from the Gusuku Site Group. Iron was not available in the Okinawa Islands to the south until several centuries later.

Kamei (2006) describes two heirloom Yueh ware spouted vessels and a grey stoneware bottle, found in the village of Onotsu in northwestern Kikaishima. He states that with the Kikai finds, the southern limit of these Yueh wares in Japan has been extended from Tanegashima to Kikai, and that in the Japanese main islands they are found in administrative sites, temples and shrines, and elite residences and tombs. They confirm the importance of Kikai as a government outpost in the northern Ryukyus.

The Kikai discoveries have substantiated the unique role of the Kasari Peninsula of Amami and Kikai Island in the history of the Ryukyus (Ikeda 2005, Ikehata 2007, Pearson 2007). They have highlighted the importance of tributary relations with Yamato in the 7th and 8th centuries as an important chapter in the social history of the Amami Islands and the Ryukyus in general, and added weight to the consideration of the southern navigation route to Tang followed by some tribute missions of the 8th and 9th centuries. Heretofore the Late Shellmound Period has appeared as a kind of black box with rapid social change occurring only at its end, at the beginning of the Gusuku Period, in the 11th and 12th centuries. However this situation has changed with the discoveries from Amami and Kikai, which show increasing social complexity through several centuries. The special place of the Amami islands has become evident in the past decade; the finds from Kikaishima in the last 5 years have added a new dimension to our comprehension of the southern frontier of Yamato and the processes of secondary state formation of the Ryukyu Kingdom.

REFERENCES CITED

IKEDA, KOICHI
2005 Kokogaku kara mita Kikaigashima [Kikaigashima as seen from archaeology]. In *Kikaigashima Kenkyu Shimpojiumu: Kodai, Chusei no Kikaigashima, Shiryo Shu [Study Symposium on Kikaigashima: Kikaigashima in the Ancient and Medieval Periods, Symposium Materials]*: 35–39, ed. Kikai Cho Kyoiku Iinkai. Kikaigashima: Kikai Cho Kyoiku Iinkai.

IKEHATA, KOICHI
2007 Kodai, chusei no Kagoshima to Kikaishima [Kagoshima and Kikaishima in the Ancient, Mediaeval Periods]. *Higashi Ajia no Kodai Bunka* 130:109–117.

KAMEI, MEITOKU
2006 Nanto ni okeru Kikaishima no rekishiteki ichi [The historical position of Kikaishima in the southern islands [northern Ryukyu]]. *Higashi Ajia no Kodai Bunka* 129:85–109.

NAKAJIMA, KOJIRO
2007 Dazaifu kara mita Kikaishima [Kikaishima seen from Dazaifu]. *Higashi Ajia no Kodai Bunka* 130:89–95.

PEARSON, RICHARD
2007 Early mediaeval trade on Japan's southern frontier: grey stoneware of the East China Sea. *International Journal of Historical Archaeology* 11:2:122–151.

SUMIDA, NAOTOSHI AND TAKASHI NOZAKI
2007 Kikaishima Gusuku Iseki Gun no chosa [Investigation of the Gusuku site, Kikaishima]. *Higashi Ajia no Kodai Bunka* 130:46–52.

SUZKUI, YASUTAMI
2007 Kodai no Kikaishima no shakai to rekishiteki tenkai [Kikaishima in the Ancient Period: society and historical development]. *Higashi Ajia no Kodai Bunka* 130:20–45.

TAKANASHI, OSAMU
2007 [Nanto] no rekishiteki dankai: Kaneku shiki doki shutsudo no iseki no saikento [Historical stages of the [southern islands]; reexamination of sites yielding Kaneku Type pottery]. *Higashi Ajia no Kodai Bunka* 130:53–81.

YAMAZATO, JUN'ICHI
1999 *Kodai Nihon to Nanto no Koryu [Exchange Between Ancient Japan and the Southern Islands]*. Tokyo: Yoshikawa Kobunkan.

Appendix 2
Archaeology of Sakishima

RICHARD PEARSON
EMERITUS ANTHROPOLOGY UBC VANCOUVER, SAINSBURY INSTITUTE FOR THE STUDY OF JAPANESE ARTS AND CULTURES, NORWICH UK

The Sakishima Islands are composed of two cultural and geographic island subgroups, Miyako and Yaeyama. The Miyako Islands are about 270 km southwest of Okinawa, while the Yaeyama Islands are about 411 km from Okinawa in the same general direction. Taiwan lies 277 km to the west of the center of the Yaeyama Islands. Miyako and its off-lying islands, Irabu, Ikema, Korima, Tarama, and Minna, comprise an area of 227 sq km. They are comprised primarily of raised coral limestone, and have low undulating terrain and almost no forest resources. Although there are few rivers substantial water is available in limestone caves.

Within the Yaeyama Islands, surrounding the high, geologically complex islands of Ishigaki and Iriomote and Yonaguni, are the low islands of Taketomi, Kuroshima, Hateruma, Hatoma, and Aragusuku. The total area is 584 sq km.

The culture history of the Sakishima Islands diverges from those of the north and central Ryukyus. The chronology of the Yaeyama Islands is given in Table 1. The chronology of the Miyako Islands follows the same general pattern, although Periods 3 to 5 in the table are based solely on Yaeyama sites.

Although a land bridge connected the Sakishima Islands to Okinawa in the Late Pleistocene, and human remains have been found at Pinza Abu on Miyako Island, this land bridge collapsed some time around the end of the Pleistocene and rising sea levels expanded the distance of separation. Until the 12th century the historical development of the people living on these islands followed a different path from the other islands of the Ryukyus.

Holocene populations began to live in Sakishima around 4500 years ago, judging from recently recalibrated radiocarbon dates (Summerhayes and Anderson in press). Five archaeological periods are recognized (Table 1) Kin 1994, Ohama 1999). The sequence of 'ceramic to aceramic' in Periods 1 and 2 (Kin 1994) is peculiar to the Sakishima Islands. At present there is a hiatus of 800 years between

TABLE 1. SAKISHIMA SITE CHRONOLOGY

PERIOD	DATE	MAJOR CHARACTERISTICS
5. Panari Period	17th–19th centuries	Panari shell tempered pottery, shapes imitate Okinawan hard fired ceramics. Okinawan, Yaeyama, Japanese hard fired ceramics. Iron slag, tuyeres, bone tools. Cultivated rice, millet, no stone tools.
4. Nakamori Period	14th–17th centuries	Reddish earthenware, flaring mouth, lugs slightly lower on body than Shinzato Period. Some steatite tempered vessels. Yuan, Ming trade ceramics, walled settlements. Iron slag, tuyeres, bone tools, no stone tools. Cultivated rice, millet. Song to Ming coins (Ishigaki 2008*a*).
3. Shinzato Period	12th–13th centuries	Reddish earthenware, rectangular mouth, 4 external lugs, flat bottom, imitates imported soapstone cauldron. Southern Song (few Northern) ceramics, Stone tools, cultivation of rice, millet (Ishigaki 2008*a*).
2. Aceramic Period	(?) 500 BC–12th centuries	Diagnostic *Tridacna* and chipped, also semi-polished stone adzes. Remains of wild boar, shellfish. Tang coins, no cultivation, no pottery. Sites behind low coastal dunes near fresh water. Cooking using heated sandstone rocks.
1. Shimotabaru Period	2500–500 BC (?)	"Thumb nail impressed" coarse ceramics, low straight sided bowls, with some incision. Chipped, also semi-polished stone adzes, remains of wild boar, shellfish, no cultivation. Sites behind low coastal dunes near fresh water (Ishigaki 2008*b*).

Table 2. Yaeyama Sites and Features

Period 3

Birosuku, Ishigaki Island, Layer 2 (Ishigaki Shi 1983; Okinawa Ken 1994: 14; Takemoto and Asato 1993:253). 2 oval dwellings, marked by shallow depressions and post molds, the first, with no interior hearth, consists of 10 post molds, has a diameter of about 3 m. Second, also oval with a diameter of about 3 m had interior hearth about 1.2 m long and 20 cm deep. Also post molds of platform structure thought to have ritual use, 2 curved pendants (*magatama*) and 1 small glass bead found in association. Row of hearths about 1 m in diameter, found in another part of the site. No site plan provided in report.

Shinzatomura East, Taketomi Island (Takemoto and Asato 1993:255; Okinawa Ken 1994: 33–36). Site is divided into east and west components, dividing point being an ancient well. East section is dated to 12th to 13th centuries. Rectangular post mold arrangement 6.8 x 4.8 m was uncovered

Period 4

Shinzatomura West, Taketomi Island (Okinawa Ken 1994: 33–36). This component has house features with post molds, surrounded by stone walls. Openings about 70 cm wide between adjoining house compounds. No arterial internal road in settlement, only single gate to outside. Communal open plaza-like space. Seventeen houses were recorded and 4 were excavated. These were house compounds comprised of several buildings. Compound No. 1 had three houses, and one possible elevated storehouse; Compound No. 2, three houses and two possible elevated storehouses; Compound No. 3, one latrine: Compound No. 4, two house sites.

Birosuku, Ishigaki Island, Upper Layer (Ishigaki Shi 1983; Kin 1983). Rectangular structure with 7 post holes, dated to 14th century. Associated with a drainage ditch. Stepped feature 1.2 m x 1.6 m may be a latrine. Kin (1999:71) proposes that site was walled at this time.

Hanasuku, Taketomi Island (Okinawa Ken 1994: 29–32; Ono 1997; Nakamori 1999; Ono 1999: 37–54). Site lies on a ridge about 15 m above sea level, with defensive walls as high as 4 m. Village site about 500 m east-west, 200 m north-south, containing about 40 clustered dwelling sites in bilaterally symmetrical arrangement. In each half, Hanasuku and Kumara, there is a large house in a single enclosure 30 m x 30 m surrounded by 7 or 8 medium and small dwelling areas comprising a block 50 m x 60 m. Around these are more enclosed dwelling sites, and each of the major blocks has an ancestral shrine (*utaki*) attached to its corner.

Donanbaru, Yonaguni Island (Okinawa Ken 1988). Difficult to determine from the narrow trench excavation. Possible elevated dwellings or storehouses, some post molds had stones in them, as if they were pillar bases. Blacksmith area was located. Trade ceramics, particularly Chinese celadon. date from the beginning of the 14th century to the beginning of the 16th century.

Furusutobaru, Ishigaki Island (Ishigaki Shi 1977, 1984, 1991; Toma 1983; Takemoto and Asato 1993: 253–254; Okinawa Ken 1994: 8–13; Shimoji 1999). Situated on a limestone ridge overlooking Miyara Bay. Fifteen walled enclosures have been identified. Enclosures 1-4 are in a line with the seaward edge of the ridge while the others form a row further inland. Spaces of 190 m between Nos and 4 and 5, 40 m between 5 and 6, and 40 m between the two rows of enclosures may be the result of earlier damage to the site. Enclosures 1 and 2 have been excavated. No. 2 had walls up to 2 m thick with a single entry way and central hearth. The large hearth was 130 cm x 85 cm and 10 cm deep. In No. 2 there were 100 post molds, some containing stone wedges. No clear pattern could be interpreted. Enclosure 5 had an interior area of 600 sq m. The walls were 1.8 and 2.5 m thick. No. 15 enclosure was a rectangle with length and width of 23 m and 20 m respectively. Burials with 17th century, mostly 18th century Tsuboya or Chinese ceramics are later than the main site occupation. This site is known as the residence of the rebel leader Oyake Akahachi (see below).

Uemura, Iriomote Island (Okinawa Ken 1991; Takemoto and Asato 1993: 262)) Excavation of 500 sq m took place around an area known from tradition to be used for blacksmithing. It was divided into Area 1 dated to the late 15th to 16th centuries and Area 2, dated to mid 14th to mid 15th centuries. In Area 1 there was an accumulation of chunks of coral 1.7 m. x 3.1 m. Along its northern edge was an area of burned earth, sand and iron slag 20 to 25 cm in diameter, which appears to be a blacksmith's hearth.

Kerai Kedagusuku, Iriomote Island (Ishigaki Shi 1991). Traditional house site of the leader, Kedai Kedagusuku, on the Sonai peninsula above the modern site of Sonai. Area said to be traditional iron working area had a stone platform surrounded by pits containing slag, but no tuyeres recovered.

Ishigaki, Ishigaki Island (Ishigaki Shi 1993*a*). Eight single flexed burials, no grave goods.

Hirakawa, Ishigaki Island (Ishigaki Shi 1993*b*). Five single flexed burials, no grave goods.

---

carbon dated sites of Periods 1 and 2 (Ohama 1999), and the relationship between the people of Period 1 and people of Period 2 is unclear.

While the thick brown low fired pottery of the Shimotabaru culture does not resemble closely the prehistoric pottery from the east coast of Taiwan the chipped adzes without polishing, which must have been digging tools, are identical in both cultures. Therefore some archaeologists think that the first populations from Sakishima came from the east coast of Taiwan (Summerhayes and Anderson in press). Eastern Taiwan is considered by some scholars to be the homeland of the Austronesian people, who migrated through Southeast Asia to far away islands such as Polynesia and Madagascar. The postulated Austronesian migration is thought to have begun in the third millennium BC. Eastern Taiwan was also the center of a trading network in jade which extended far into the Philippines. It is now known that green jade, used to make adzes and ornaments found in the Philippine islands of Luzon and Palawan, comes from Fengtian in eastern Taiwan. Is it possible that Austronesian peoples also populated Sakishima?

While the low fired coarse paste of Shimotabaru pottery does not resemble the paste of Taiwan wares, external lugs are present on the pottery of both areas and unpolished chipped stone adzes, thought to be digging tools, are also common to both areas. *Tridacna* shell adzes found in Sakishima have been linked to those found in a burial in Duyong Cave, Palawan, Philippines. However their dating is incompatible, since the Duyong adzes have been dated to 3000 BC to 4300 BC (Bellwood 1985: 224), which is earlier than the arrival of people in Sakishima. Future finds of shell adzes in the Philippines may clarify the dating. Many items from Taiwan cultures are absent in the Shimotabaru Culture: these include bark cloth beaters, pottery spindle whorls, and earrings. We need to explain these absences.

Is it possible that the first people of Sakishima drifted north from the Philippines and belong to a pre-Austronesian culture from that area? There are still many questions regarding the original people of Sakishima, and to answer them will require co-operation with many different kinds of scholars of different backgrounds.

The Aceramic Period is thought to begin around 500 BC, judging from the dates of the shell adze site of Urasoko, Miyako Island. Abundant pieces of burned sandstone suggest that people cooked with heated rocks since there were no pottery containers. Sites such as Sakieda have yielded caches of Tang coins, which may indicate direct contact by Chinese traders. Period 3, the Shinzato Period, is represented by the Birosuku Site, Ishigaki Island, and Shinzato Mura East, Taketomi Island. Trade goods dating to the 12th to 13th centuries, *kamuiyaki* sherds, and reddish earthenware which imitates steatite cooking vessels are diagnostic (Zaidan 2003: 381-400). Traditional accounts indicate that some extended families migrated from Okinawa and other islands in the Ryukyus to islands such as Miyako and Taketomi.

In Period 4 the Sakishima Islands were absorbed into the Ryukyu Kingdom (Pearson 2003). A summary of the major sites of this period is provided in Table 2. The Takagoshi and Sumiya sites are located on Miyako island. Sumiya on Miyako Island and Furusutobaru on Ishigaki Island were residences of protohistoric chiefs in the 15th century and Sumiya continued to be occupied in later centuries (Pearson 2003).

REFERENCES CITED

BELLWOOD, PETER
1985   *Prehistory of the Indo Malaysian Archipelago*, 1st Edition. Honolulu, University of Hawaii Press.

ISHIGAKI SHI KYOIKU IINKAI
1977   *Furusutobaru Iseki [The Furusutobaru Site]*. Ishigaki: Ishigaki Shi Kyoiku Iinkai.

1983   *Birosuku Iseki [The Birosuku Site]*. Ishigaki: Ishigaki Shi Kyoiku Iinkai

1993a   *Ishigaki Kaizuka [The Ishigaki Shellmound]*. Ishigaki: Ishigaki Shi Kyoiku Iinkai.

1993b   *Hirakawa Kaizuka [The Hirakawa Shellmound]*. Ishigaki: Ishigaki Shi Kyoiku Iinkai.

ISHIGAKI SHI SOMUBU SHISHI HENSHUSHITSU (ED.)
1991   Kerai Kedagusuku Yuraiki [Historical Account of Kerai Kedagusuku], *Ishigaki Shi Shi Sosho I [The History of Ishigaki City I]*. Ishigaki: Ishigaki Shi Somubu Shi Shi Henshushitsu, 1–24.

ISHIGAKI SHI SOMUBU SHISHI HENSHUSHITSU
2007   *Kenkyu Shi–Yaeyama no Kokogaku no Ayumi [History of Research-History of Yaeyama Archaeology]*. Ishigaki Shi Kokogaku Visual Han 1 [Archaeology of Ishigaki City Visual Edition No. 1]. Ishigaki: Ishigaki Shi.

2008a   *Tojiki kara mita Koryu Shi (History of Trade as Seen from Ceramics)*. Ishigaki Shi Kokogaku Visual Han 5 [Archaeology of Ishigaki City Visual Edition No. 5]. Ishigaki: Ishigaki Shi.

2008b   *Shimotabaru Ki no Kurashi [Livelihood in the Shimotabaru Period]*. Ishigaki Shi Kokogaku Visual Han 2 [Archaeology of Ishigaki City Visual Edition No. 2]. Ishigaki: Ishigaki Shi.

KIN, SEIKI
1983   Birosuku Iseki [The Birosuku Site]. *Okinawa Dai Jiten [Encyclopedia of Okinawa]* 3:333.

1994   Doki-mudoki-doki: Yaeyama kokogaku hennen no shi'an [Ceramic-nonceramic-ceramic: A proposition on the archaeological chronology of the Yaeyama Islands]. *Nanto Koko* 14:83–92.

1999   Saihakken sareta Yaeyama no kosonraku [Re-examination of old villages in Yaeyama]. In *Mura ga Kataru Okinawa no Rekishi [Villages Tell the Story of Okinawan History]*: 69–76, ed. Rekishi Minzoku Hakubutsukan. Tokyo: Shin Jinbutsu Oraisha.

NAKAMORI, TON
1999   Hanasuku Mura Iseki Hakkutsu Chosa no Gaiyo [Brief Report on the Excavation of the Hanasuku Village Site]. In *Mura ga Kataru Okinawa no Rekishi (Villages Tell the Story of Okinawan History)*: 77–99, ed. Rekishi Minzoku Hakubutsukan. Tokyo: Shin Jinbutsu Oraisha.

OHAMA, EISEN

1999   *Yaeyama no Kokogaku [Archaeology of Yaeyama]*. Ishigaki: Sakishima Bunka Kenkyusho.

OKINAWA KEN YONAGUNI CHO KYOIKU IINKAI

1988   *Donanbaru Iseki [The Donanbaru Site]*. Naha: Okinawa Ken Yonaguni Cho Kyoiku Iinkai.

1994   *Gusuku: Gusuku Bunritsu Chosa Hokoku Sho III Yaeyama Shoto [Gusuku: Report on Survey of Gusuku Distribution, 3, Yaeyama Archipelago]*. Naha: Okinawa Ken Kyoiku Iinkai.

OKINAWA KEN KYOIKU IINKAI

1991   *Uemura Iseki: Juyo Iseki Kakunin Chosa Hokoku [The Uemura Site: Report of the Excavations Confirming the Existence of an Important Site]*. Naha: Okinawa Ken Kyoiku Iinkai.

ONO, MASATOSHI

1997   Mura ga kataru Yaeyama no Chusei [The Mediaeval Period of Yaeyama as told from villages]. *Osenkai* 14:80–86.

1999   Mitsurin ni kakureta Chusei Yaeyama no mura [Mediaeval villages hidden in the jungle]. In *Mura ga Kataru Okinawa no Rekishi (Villages Tell the Story of Okinawan History)*: 37-68, ed. Rekishi Minzoku Hakubutsukan. Tokyo: Shin Jinbutsu Oraisha.

PEARSON, RICHARD

2003   Excavations at Sumiya and other Sakishima sites: variation in Okinawan leadership around 1500 AD. *IPPA Bulletin* 23:95–111.

SHIMOJI, KETSU

1999   Hakkutsu sareta mura: Ishigakijima Furusutobaru Mura [An Excavated Village: Furusutobaru, Ishigaki Island]. In *Mura ga Kataru Okinawa no Rekishi (Villages Tell the Story of Okinawan History)*: 101–112, ed. Rekishi Minzoku Hakubutsukan. Tokyo: Shin Jinbutsu Oraisha, .

SUMMERHAYES, GLENN AND ATHOLL ANDERSON

in press   An Austronesian Presence in Southern Japan: Early Occupation in the Yaeyama Islands. *Asian Perspectives*.

TAKEMOTO, SEISHUN AND SHIJUN ASATO

1993   *Okinawa: Nihon no Kodai Iseki [Okinawa: Ancient Sites of Japan]* Vol. 47. Osaka: Hoikusha.

TOMA, SHI'ICHI

1983   Furusutobaru Iseki [The Furusutobaru Site]. *Okinawa Dai Jiten [Encyclopedia of Okinawa]* 3:397–398.

ZAIDAN HOJIN OKINAWA KEN BUNKA SHINKOKAI (ED.)

2003   *Okinawa Kenshi Kakuronhen Daini Kan: Koko [History of Okinawa Prefecture, Detailed Examination Volume 2: Archaeology]*. Okinawa (Haebaru): Okinawa Ken Kyoiku Iinkai.

Appendix 3
Useful Reference Materials for Ryukyu Archaeology

MIYAGI, EISHO AND HIROE TAKAMIYA (EDS.)

1983   *Okinawa Rekishi Chizu: Koko Hen [Historical Atlas of Okinawa: Archaeology].* Tokyo: Kashiwa Shobo.

OKINAWA TAIMSU SHA (ED.)

1983   *Okinawa Dai Hyakka Jiten [Okinawa Encyclopedia].* Naha: Okinawa Taimsu Sha.

SAKAMAKI, SHUNZO

1963   *Ryukyu: A Bibliographical Guide to Okinawan Studies.* Honolulu: University of Hawai'i Press.

SAKAMAKI, SHUNZO (ED.)

1964   *Ryukyuan Names: Monographs on and Lists of Personal and Place Names in the Ryukyus.* Honolulu: East-West Center Press.

TAKEMOTO, SEISHUN AND SHIJUN ASATO

1993   *Okinawa: Nihon Kodai Iseki [Okinawa: Ancient Sites of Japan Series]*, Vol. 47. Hoikusha: Osaka.

ZAIDAN HOJIN OKINAWA KEN BUNKA SHINKOKAI (ED.)

2003   *Okinawa Ken Shi Kakuronhen 2 Koko [History of Okinawa, Detailed Examination, 2, Archaeology].* Okinawa (Haebaru): Okinawa Ken Kyoiku Iinkai.

Appendix 4
The Successive Rulers of Chuzan (Ryukyu) *(from Sakamaki 1963:288)*

(In an alternate scheme, the First Sho Dynasty (1429–1469) was established by Sho Hashi in 1429 and the Second Sho Dynasty (1470–1879) was established by Sho En in 1470 [ed.])

THE SHUNTEN DYNASTY

Shunten (1187–1237) 舜天
Shunba Junki (1238–1248) 舜馬順熙
Gihon (1249–1259) 義本

THE EISO DYNASTY

Eiso (1260–1299) 英祖
Taisei (1300–1308) 大成
Eiji (1309–1313) 英慈
Tamagusuku (1314–1336) 玉城
Sei-I (1337–1349) 西威

THE SATTO DYNASTY

Satto (1350–1395) 察度
Bunei (1396–1405) 武寧

THE SHO SHISHO DYNASTY

Sho Shisho (1406–1421) 尚思紹
Sho Hashi (1422–1439) 尚巴志
Sho Chu (1440–1444) 尚忠
Sho Shitatsu (1445–1449) 尚志達
Sho Kinpuku (1450–1453) 尚金福
Sho Taikyu (1454–1460) 尚泰久
Sho Toku (1461–1469) 尚徳

THE SHO EN DYNASTY

Sho En (1470–1476) 尚圓
Sho Sen-I (1477) 尚宣威
Sho Shin (1477–1526) 尚真
Sho Sei (1527–1555) 尚清
Sho Gen (1556–1572) 尚元
Sho Ei (1573–1588) 尚永
Sho Nei (1589–1620) 尚寧
Sho Ho (1621–1640) 尚豐
Sho Ken (1641–1647) 尚賢
Sho Shitsu (1648–1668) 尚質
Sho Tei (1669–1709) 尚貞
Sho Eki (1710–1712) 尚益
Sho Kei (1713–1751) 尚敬
Sho Boku (1752–1794) 尚穆
Sho On (1795–1802) 尚温
Sho Sei (1803) 尚成
Sho Ko (1804–1828) 尚灝
Sho Iku (1829–1847) 尚育
Sho Tai (1848–1879) 尚泰

REFERENCES CITED

SAKAMAKI, SHUNZO

1963   *Ryukyu: A Bibliographic Guide to Okinawan Studies.* Honolulu: University of Hawai'i Press.

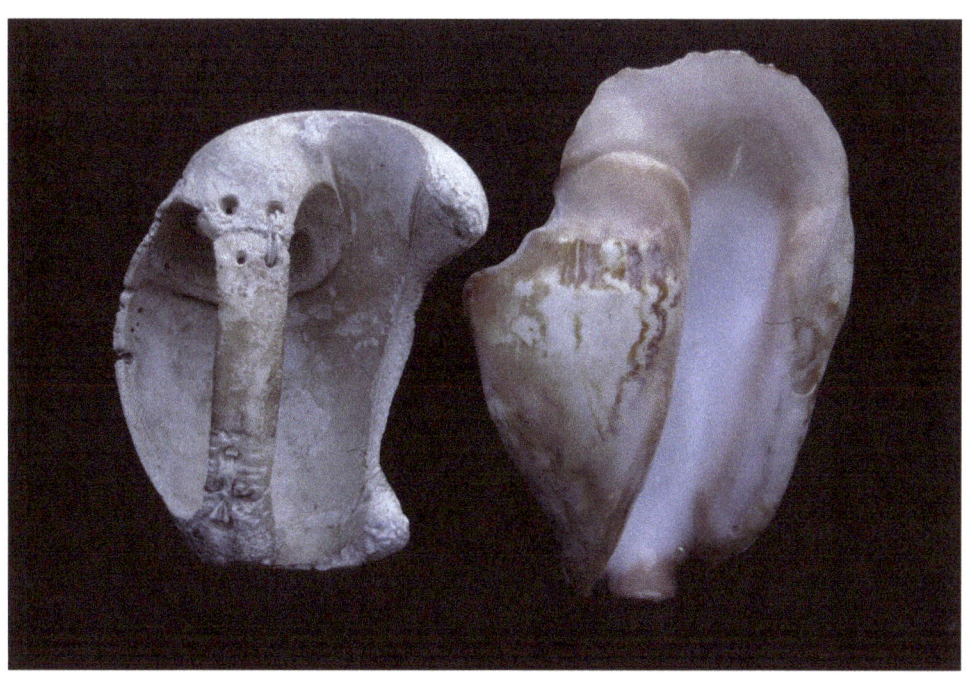

Plate 1. Bracelets of Broad Pacific Conch of agricultural people. Right: recent Broad Pacific Conch.
Left: bracelet of Broad Pacific Conch from Doigahama Site, Yamaguchi Prefecture (refer to Kinoshita p. 19).

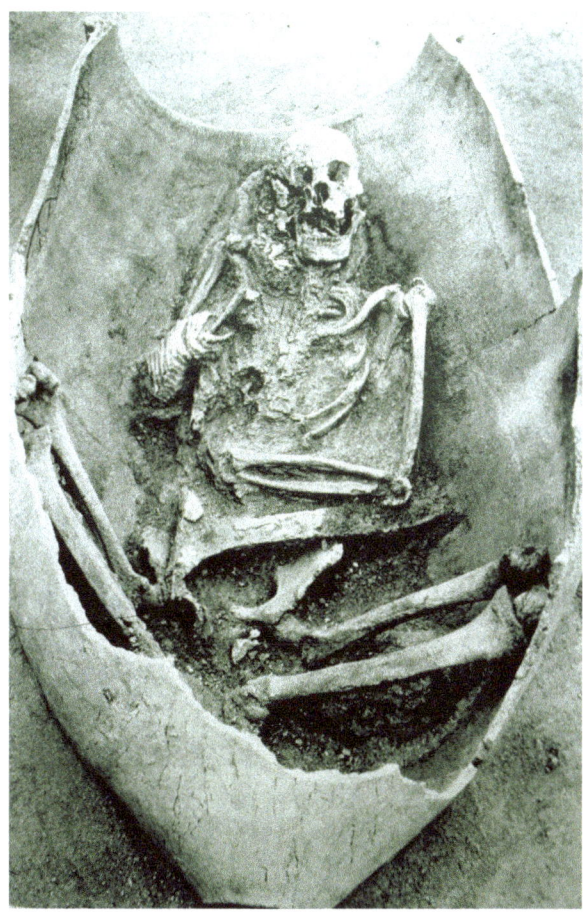

Plate 2. Bracelets of Broad Pacific Conch worn by male in Burial 34 of the Tateiwa Site Fukuoka Prefecture
(Tateiwa Iseki Chosa Iinkai 1977, Fig. 8) (refer to Kinoshita p. 24).

Plate 3. Momenbaru Site burial. Individuals showed physical characteristics of both Ryukyu islanders and Yayoi Kyushu coastal people (refer to Kinoshita p. 27).

Plate 4. Grave 8, Hirota Site, Tane Island, Kagoshima Prefecture (refer to Kinoshita p. 29).

Plate 5. *Kamuiyaki* vessels showing shapes and surface treatments (refer to Shinzato p. 41).

Plate 6. Evolution of Urasoe Yodore (refer to Susumu Asato p. 57).

Plate 7. The west chamber of Urasoe Yodore (refer to Susumu Asato p. 57).

Plate 8. Sherds of Yuan Dynasty blue and white jar from Gushikawa Castle, Kume Island.
(Courtesy Kumejima Cho Kyoiku Iinkai) (refer to Kamei p. 66).

www.ingramcontent.com/pod-product-compliance
Lightning Source LLC
Chambersburg PA
CBHW050941010526

44108CB00060B/2880